DILEMMAS OF INCLUSION

Dilemmas of Inclusion

Muslims in European Politics

Rafaela M. Dancygier

PRINCETON UNIVERSITY PRESS

PRINCETON AND OXFORD

Published by Princeton University Press,
41 William Street, Princeton, New Jersey 08540

In the United Kingdom: Princeton University Press,
6 Oxford Street, Woodstock, Oxfordshire OX20 1TR

press.princeton.edu

Cover images courtesy of Shutterstock

Library of Congress Cataloging-in-Publication Data

Names: Dancygier, Rafaela M., 1977–author.
Title: Dilemmas of inclusion : Muslims in European politics / Rafaela M. Dancygier.
Description: Princeton : Princeton University Press, [2017] | Includes bibliographical
references and index.
Identifiers: LCCN 2017007689| ISBN 9780691172590 (hardcover : alk. paper) |
     ISBN 9780691172606 (pbk. : alk. paper)
Subjects: LCSH: Muslims—Europe—Political activity. | Islam and politics—Europe. | Political
parties—Europe. | Representative government and representation—Europe. | Muslims—
Europe—Social conditions.
Classification: LCC D1056.2.M87 D35 2017 | DDC 324.088/297094—dc23 LC record available
at https://lccn.loc.gov/2017007689

British Library Cataloging-in-Publication Data is available

This book has been composed in Adobe Text Pro and Gotham

Printed on acid-free paper. ∞

Printed in the United States of America

10 9 8 7 6 5 4 3 2 1

To Jacob and Maya

CONTENTS

FIGURES AND TABLES

Figures

Tables

ACKNOWLEDGMENTS

This book began with the observation that ethnic politics is alive and well in European cities today. In immigrant enclaves, bonds of ethnicity, religion, and kinship that structure social relationships seamlessly spill over into the electoral arena. Whether or not a candidate hails from the same home village or belongs to the same kinship group can sway voter decisions and swing election outcomes from Birmingham to Brussels.

That such bonds can be activated during elections is of course nothing new; but that they are so powerful and decisive in advanced democracies with mature electoral institutions, well-functioning bureaucracies, high levels of economic development, and extensive welfare states is an important reminder that what some consider to be premodern ties remain relevant and useful even in highly modernized states.

This insight led to another observation: Political parties that campaign on modern, progressive platforms might also have to appeal to groups who are neither progressive nor popular among core voters. As I later highlight, this tension is also not a new one. It characterizes minority political inclusion across countries and goes back many decades. We know little, however, about how parties resolve these tensions in the contemporary European context, where the large-scale settlement of Muslim communities presents political parties with sharp inclusion dilemmas. Much of this book is therefore devoted to exploring how parties incorporate Muslim candidates and voters and to illuminating the consequences that emanate from this inclusion. To do so, I also propose more general arguments about how and when parties decide to bring in minority electorates.

In writing this book, I have benefited from the advice and support of many individuals. Big thanks go to Elizabeth Saunders who over the course of many phone calls not only helped me realize that my interest in European ethnic politics could easily sustain a book, but also offered numerous valuable ideas along the way. I am also very grateful to Ken Scheve for organizing a book workshop that improved the manuscript immeasurably. His comments, along with those by the other participants—Thad Dunning, Anna Grzymala-Busse, David Laitin, Dan Posner, Jonathan Rodden, and Jessica Trounstine—were incredibly helpful. At Princeton, Joanne Gowa was always generous with her time and advice, and her frequent reminder that "books can be short" helped me get this one off the ground (though it didn't end up being so short). Raymond Hicks's assistance with all matters quantitative was equally indispensable.

Additional constructive criticism came from Claire Adida, Alícia Adserà, Quinn Albaugh, Mark Beissinger, Carles Boix, Winston Chou, Romain Ferrali, Jeremy Ferwerda, Lucila Figueroa, Dan Hopkins, Amaney Jamal, Jytte Klausen, Evan Lieberman, Grigo Pop-Eleches, Carlos Velasco Rivera, Tom Romer, Rory Truex, and Deborah Yashar. I thank them all for their helpful input. Seminar participants at George Washington University, Harvard University, MIT, Princeton University, Stanford University, Temple University, University of British Columbia, University of California San Diego, University of Michigan Ann Arbor, University of Oxford, and Yale University gave important feedback as well. Several terrific research assistants—Idir Aitsahalia, Sebastian Pukrop, and Audrye Wong—helped me gather relevant data and provided useful comments. Yotam Margalit deserves special thanks for letting me use the manifesto data we had collected together for another project.

At Princeton University Press, two anonymous reviewers provided excellent advice. Conversations with Eric Crahan improved the framing of this book, and I am also very grateful for Eric's skillful managing of the review and publication process. Jay Boggis and Debbie Tegarden offered very helpful edits.

Finally, my family has been a source of constant support, laughter, and love, and my deepest gratitude goes to my husband, Jason, and our two children. I began thinking about this book's topics when our son, Jacob, was just born. He was soon joined by his sister, Maya. I dedicate this book to the two of them.

DILEMMAS OF INCLUSION

1

Introduction

Three days before the 2015 UK General Election, the Labour Party found itself in hot water: It had to defend a Birmingham campaign event that featured separate seating for men and women. The rally, attended by a majority Muslim audience, was meant to shore up Labour support in Birmingham's ethnically diverse parliamentary constituencies, which are home to more than 200,000 Muslims. Instead of promoting its platform, the Party had to respond to accusations that in aggressively courting the Muslim vote it was turning its back on "a century or more of advancements for women's rights." As pictures of the segregated seating arrangements circulated through the news media, a Labour spokesman meekly countered that "Labour fully supports gender equality in all areas of society and all cultures."[1] Most of the charges were made by political opponents seizing an opening to damage the party just before polling began, but they stung for a reason: Over the last several decades, the Labour Party has made strong appeals to Muslim voters, and in its pursuit of votes it has chosen to empower patriarchal, traditional forces much more than it has promoted egalitarian, progressive voices.

What explains these outcomes? When do parties include groups that provoke opposition from core voters? And when does the inclusion of new groups cause parties to compromise fundamental ideological commitments?

These questions are highly relevant across diverse democracies. In the United States, Republicans and Democrats struggle with how to best respond to a growing Hispanic electorate. Across American cities, already fragile elec-

---

1. The first quote comes from Nigel Farage, former leader of the UK Independence Party (UKIP); Tory candidates also condemned the event and called into question Labour's commitment to gender equality (Walker 2015).

1

toral coalitions between whites and blacks are being further tested as this new group enters the fray.[2] In Canada and Australia, both traditional immigration countries, immigrant-origin ethnic minorities remain significantly underrepresented in politics. The same is true in most European countries.[3] Here, problems related to immigrants' sociopolitical incorporation have been very salient. More than 50 million residents living in Western Europe today were born abroad, and many hail from outside Europe.[4] Immigration has transformed the continent's ethnic and religious make-up, and it has stoked fierce controversies about how to best address this new cultural diversity.

The main object of these debates has been the "Muslim Question." Europeans fret that Muslims will not integrate into domestic societies and politics. Because of their religiosity, communalism, social conservatism, and illiberalism, critics allege, Muslims are not ready to participate in the politics of advanced liberal democracies.[5] Anti-Muslim prejudice among voters also runs high.[6] At the same time, parties face growing electoral incentives to garner Muslim support. In many Western European countries, the largest group of naturalized citizens originates from countries where Islam is the dominant religion (see Figure 1.1), a trend that recent refugee inflows from Syria, Afghanistan and Iraq will only reinforce. Muslims are thus beginning to constitute sizable portions of domestic electorates, especially at the subnational level. In Britain, 17 municipalities have Muslim populations that exceed 15 percent of the population, and in 2016 the city of London elected its first Muslim mayor.[7] In Berlin, one in four residents has a migration background, and among this population those with Turkish roots form the largest group. In Cologne, 120,000 residents are estimated to be Muslim, while in Vienna this number stands at roughly 216,000. In Amsterdam and Rotterdam, Muslims make up about 12 percent of the population.[8] In Brussels, nearly one in five residents is of Muslim faith.[9]

---

2. Abrajano and Hajnal (2015); Edsall (2015).

3. Bloemraad (2013).

4. These figures are from the year 2011; see OECD (2013). Here and below I define Western Europe as countries belonging to the EU-15 (i.e., Austria, Belgium, Denmark, Finland, France, Germany, Greece, Ireland, Italy, Luxembourg, the Netherlands, Portugal, Spain, Sweden, and the United Kingdom), as well as Norway, and Switzerland.

5. For discussions and counterclaims, see, for example, Cesari (2013), Joppke (2004), Klausen (2005), Modood (2009), Norton (2013), Parekh (2008), Sniderman and Hagendoorn (2007), and Sniderman et al. (2014).

6. See, e.g., Adida et al. (2014, 2010), Bleich (2009), Ford (2011), and Helbling (2012).

7. These figures are based on the 2011 UK census.

8. On Berlin, see Rockmann (2011); on Cologne, see von Mittelstaedt (2009); on Vienna see Aslan et al. (2014, 20); on Amsterdam and Rotterdam, see CBS (2009, 130).

9. This number refers to the Brussels Capital Region; see Fadil (2013, 100).

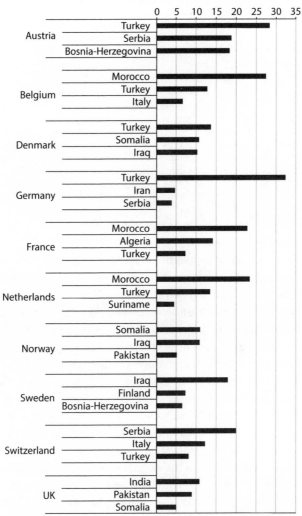

Percentage of all citizenship acquisitions (2001–2011)

FIGURE 1.1. Citizenship Acquisitions in 10 Western European Countries, by prior Nationality (2001–2011)

Note: For each country, this figure shows the percentage of citizenship acquisitions by applicants' prior nationality for the three groups with the largest number of citizenship acquisitions. The selected countries are the ten West European countries that have received large-scale migrant inflows since the 1960s. *Source:* OECD (2013).

TABLE 1.1. Muslim Political Representation in Municipalities across Countries

	Austria	Germany	Great Britain	Belgium
Muslim Parity Ratio	0.13	0.39	0.74	0.83
Muslim Population (%)	10.83	8.31	8.50	10.17
Major National Origin Groups	Turkey	Turkey	Pakistan	Turkey
	Bosnia-Herzegovina	Bosnia-Herzegovina	Bangladesh	Morocco

Note: Parity ratios divide the percentage of elected local politicians who are Muslim by the percentage of Muslims in the population. Parity ratios refer to the year 2014 for Austria and Germany. For Great Britain, they cover 2002 through 2013, and for Belgium they include 2006 through 2012. Parity ratios and Muslim population shares are based on approximately 70 municipalities per country. See Appendix A for more information on how these estimates were derived.

If demography is political destiny, parties should take a keen interest in this new electorate. Yet, we observe remarkable variation. Table 1.1 displays Muslim parity ratios across municipalities in Austria, Germany, Great Britain, and Belgium. Parity ratios are measures of representation that divide the share of elected politicians who are Muslim by Muslims' share in the population (i.e., numbers below one indicate underrepresentation, those above one denote overrepresentation). In Austria, parity ratios approach zero. In Belgium, they are close to one. These differences are not driven by the relative size of the Muslim population, which is similar across countries. They are also not the result of varying nationality groups. In Austria, Germany, and Belgium, many Muslim voters have Turkish roots, for instance. In Britain and Belgium, where inclusion rates are high, Muslims have various backgrounds (see Table 1.1). Further, in all four countries Muslim integration has generated fierce controversies, and hostility towards Muslims is widespread.

In addition to differences in the extent of electoral incorporation, parties respond differently to the ideological challenges connected to Muslim inclusion. While some select Muslim candidates who are staunchly secular and egalitarian, others pursue candidates who are decidedly less so. In British cities, for instance, community elders with roots in Pakistan and Bangladesh have for years been winning elections for the major parties on the basis of patriarchal clan and kinship structures. In these contests, men often fill out the electoral registration papers and postal ballots of their wives and adult children, who remain altogether invisible in party politics.[10] Comparable events transpire in the Netherlands. A Kurdish-origin candidate running for the *Islam Democraten* in The Hague explains his party's recruitment strategy: "Once we have the word of the head of the household, the rest of the family also votes

10. Sobolewska et al. (2015).

TABLE 1.2. Muslim Female Representation in Municipalities across Countries

	Austria	Germany	Great Britain	Belgium
Elected Muslims who are Women (%)	46.3	40.6	14.4	36.4
Muslim/non-Muslim Female Representation Ratio	1.37	1.20	0.43	0.94

Note: The Muslim/non-Muslim Female Representation Ratio divides the percentage of Muslim elected politicians who are female by the percentage of non-Muslim elected politicians who are female. See Table 1.1 and Appendix A for more information on how these data were derived.

for us. In our culture we do not go against the will of the *pater familias*."[11] The major parties have at times followed a similar playbook.

In Berlin, by contrast, political parties have been faulted for selecting Turkish-origin candidates who are too secular and too progressive to connect with the city's more pious and traditional Turkish-origin electorate.[12] Likewise, when Lale Akgün, born in Istanbul and raised in Germany, served in the Bundestag for the Social Democrats (SPD), she declared on her website that "religion is a private matter" (*Religion ist Privatsache*), even though she was the party's official "Islam representative" (*Islambeauftragte*).[13] The SPD had adopted this radically secular slogan at the end of the nineteenth century, only to drop it in 1959 in an effort to reach out to churches and religious voters.

These differences in candidate types have implications for parties' gender balance. Controversies surrounding gender equality are central to the "Muslim Question," so we might expect that parties would be careful in balancing Muslim inclusion with gender parity. Yet, Table 1.2 shows that this is not so. It presents the gender balance among Muslim elected candidates and female representation ratios, that is, the percentage of Muslim local politicians who are female divided by the percentage of non-Muslim local politicians who are female, across countries. While parties in some countries appear to seek out female Muslim candidates, others prefer them to be male. Why?

The Argument

This book develops an argument that addresses how parties respond to changing electorates and draws out the implications of these responses for the nature of party politics. First, it explains how and when parties include new groups who are disliked by a set of existing voters and whose values and

11. Zeegers (2014).
12. Karakoyun (2011).
13. Mirbach (2008, 172–73).

preferences conflict with those of others. Second, by underscoring the trade-offs that arise when confronting such a group, I show how parties' short-run inclusion strategies undercut their ideological coherence and electoral performance in the long run.

Much of this book deals with inclusion dilemmas—the notion that efforts to reach out to new voter groups will please some and upset other members of a party's existing coalition. When deciding about the inclusion of ethnic minority groups, parties in today's advanced democracies consider the reactions of ethnocentrists who do not want to be members of multicultural coalitions and of cosmopolitans who do. The Right's core constituency contains ethnocentrists but few cosmopolitans. The Left is comprised of both, but it has become increasingly dependent on the support of cosmopolitans. Though they tend to have high incomes, cosmopolitans' liberal views on gender, sexuality, and diversity have helped bind these voters to social democratic and green parties.[14] Yet, Muslim inclusion presents the Left with an added challenge: On a range of issues, the socially liberal views of cosmopolitans are incompatible with those of Muslims.[15] On top of alienating ethnocentrists, including Muslims can therefore antagonize voters who typically favor inclusiveness.

This book reveals how European parties are resolving these dilemmas. I argue that the incorporation of Muslim candidates into European parties is primarily driven by votes. Only when parties—on the Left and the Right—calculate that the net vote gains from inclusion exceed losses, will they incorporate Muslim candidates and voters. Initially, when the relative size of the minority electorate is small, parties *exclude*. Even if their rhetoric is one of equality and antidiscrimination, parties will only bring in minority candidates when they believe associated vote gains to be positive.

The nomination of minority candidates will increase minority votes but also trigger defections among those who dislike diversity. It is when the former surpass the latter that parties will opt for inclusion. Once net vote gains are no longer negative, but minority votes are not yet critical, parties engage in *symbolic inclusion*: They select a small number of minority candidates that please cosmopolitans who value diversity, but that do not necessarily appeal to a large number of minority voters. Symbolic inclusion signals that the party is mindful—but not too mindful—of the minority electorate and of the need to diversify its ranks. When parties include symbolically, I contend that they not only target minority voters; their intended audience also consists of sections of the majority electorate. Parties intend to signal to cosmopolitans that they

---

14. On this point, see, e.g., Hellwig (2014), Inglehart (1990) Kitschelt (1994), and Kriesi et al. (2008).

15. See Koopmans (2015) and Chapter 3.

support diversity and nondiscrimination and that they promote minority integration. To do so, they select candidates who adopt values and preferences that are in line with those articulated by core voters and party platforms.

When the minority grows large enough that it outnumbers its detractors and becomes a pivotal electoral player, parties enter the next phase of minority incorporation and pursue *vote-based inclusion*: Parties privilege minority candidates who can attract sizable portions of the minority electorate. Vote-based inclusion is associated with a greater degree of representational parity; the share of minority politicians will be higher when parties include primarily on the basis of minority votes than when they include symbolically. However, when pursuing the Muslim vote, European parties, particularly those on the Left, confront sharp trade-offs: Pivotal Muslim voters, this book demonstrates, live in spatially concentrated urban enclaves, and their views on religion, sexuality, and gender roles are considerably more conservative than are those of Muslims as a whole and especially those of the Center-Left's secular, progressive base. Minority candidates who excel at mobilizing the enclave vote tend to be the most ideologically distant from the Left's cosmopolitan core. On the Right, recruiting traditional Muslim electorates can be compatible with these parties' stances on social conservatism, but it will not sit well with ethnocentrists.

Several predicaments emerge when parties go for vote-based inclusion, and they are most vexing for the Left: First, the types of candidates that maximize minority vote shares and the minority electorates that sustain electoral coalitions do not generally embrace socially liberal values and therefore undermine the Left's ideological coherence. Second, though vote-based inclusion leads to religious parity, it diminishes gender parity. Muslim candidates who can rally the co-ethnic vote are plugged into ethnoreligious networks, connected to religious institutions, and enjoy high social standing within their communities. Such candidates are almost always men. If parties do not compensate for the ensuing decline in female candidates, religious parity will come at the expense of gender parity. Third, seduced by the quick and effective delivery of ethnoreligious bloc votes, the Left misses its opportunity to build cross-ethnic, class-based coalitions and thereby contributes to its own defeat. In vote-rich Muslim enclaves where Muslims are both poor and pious, class cleavages are replaced by ethnic and kinship cleavages; economic concerns are no longer tied to partisan attachments; and left parties ultimately end up losing seats they should have captured: The ethnic vote they have cultivated is not tied to partisan labels.

The crowding-out of class opens up opportunities for the Right. Economically deprived areas that should be out of reach for fiscally conservative center-right parties are in play when minority voters prize personalistic over programmatic politics. But the Right has to tread carefully, for it, too, has a brand to protect: Core voters who value the Right's traditional emphasis on cultural homogeneity may not feel at home in ethnically diversifying parties. In fact, the more common account is one in which the Right benefits from a diversifying Left; staying true to its ethno-cultural roots, right parties scoop up working-class voters who don't want to form leftist coalitions with minorities.[16] But in races where the Right can only win with minority support it will have to decide whether ethnic homogeneity is worth electoral irrelevance.

Implications

The story I tell in this book produces several implications that cast a new light on research about electoral coalitions and minority representation.

First, my argument challenges coalition accounts that highlight the importance of ideological proximity. Three decades ago, Przeworksi and Sprague noted that parties have to dilute their ideological purity when they are forced to expand their electoral coalitions. In their account, the perennial numerical minority status of the manual working-class forces socialist parties to make their platforms more palatable to middle-class voters.[17] Indeed, mainstream parties usually have to balance reaching out to independent voters without disappointing loyal supporters. In most accounts, however, unattached voters are ideological centrists. In trying to appeal to these voters, parties on the Left or the Right will consequently move closer to the middle.[18] The politics of Muslim inclusion, by contrast, causes parties to select candidates with social issue preferences that are considerably more conservative than those of centrist voters and that diverge severely from those of some loyal leftists. This occurs even though European Muslims as a whole prioritize leftist issues such as unemployment and social spending.[19] Yet, the salience of socially conservative positions among those Muslim voters whose spatial concentration and capacity for mobilization turns them into pivotal electoral forces, pushes vote-seeking parties to include candidates and electorates who, especially in case of the Left, are ideologically most distant from one of their core support bases.

Second, by examining how this disjuncture between ideological fit and electoral incentives plays out in local races, the book forces us to rethink accounts that emphasize parties' ability to reshape national cleavages by assembling diverse coalitions. On the national stage, social democratic parties seek

16. See, e.g., Carmines and Stimson (1989) and Huckfeldt and Kohfeld (1989).

17. Przeworksi and Sprague (1986).

18. See, e.g., Downs (1957) and Rohrschneider and Whitefield (2012). Moreover, it is not the case that the electoral entry of religious actors necessarily moves parties away from centrist, secular positions; see Kalyvas (1996).

19. On issue priorities, see, e.g., Brouard and Tiberj (2005), Laurence (2013), Laurence and Vaisse (2006, 204), and Mirbach (2008, 223).

to marry competing interests: They court middle-class cosmopolitans by stressing commitments to social liberalism and universalism while holding on to low-income voters susceptible to ethnocentrist movements by offering re-distributive policies.[20] Subnationally, however, parties' short-run strategic incentives collide with these goals. Inclusion decisions that are rational for local parties or individual MPs hurt the party collectively by managing to alienate both cosmopolitans *and* ethnocentrists. This development is hastened by political opponents who capitalize on their adversaries' dilemmas. For instance, a number of Conservative candidates were eager to condemn the Labour Party's sanctioning of gender-segregated seating arrangements mentioned earlier: "Labour are completely desperate. They are selling their values in exchange for a few votes," proclaimed a Conservative MP up for reelection. Competing in North West Leicestershire where the Far-Right is strong (UKIP obtained 17 percent of the vote in 2015), another Tory MP remarked, "On the one hand, Labour is preaching about feminism and equality for women, and on the other hand they are happy with a segregated audience. . . . This shows Labour talking out of both sides of its mouth—as usual."[21]

In addition to inflicting such short-run costs, inclusion strategies can also backfire in the long run as parties' incorporation of electorally influential minority voters on the basis of personalistic rather than programmatic ties creates a floating voting bloc that is not loyal to a particular party.

Third, the dynamics I explain are also difficult to square with other prominent accounts of minority electoral inclusion. Studying the incorporation of ethnic minorities in American cities, Shefter notes that the integration of new groups is also "a struggle over precisely who will assume leadership . . . extrusion of ideologically unacceptable contenders for the leadership of previously excluded groups . . . is a characteristic aspect of the process of political incorporation."[22] In line with this thinking, in the recent past the national Democratic Party has had little incentive to cater to the interests of African Americans when these have conflicted with the party's pursuit of other voting blocs the party is targeting. But parties might not always have the luxury of selecting candidates and recruiting electorates that are "ideologically acceptable" to existing voters and party elites. This book underscores that the neglect

20. On social democratic strategies and voter responses in the face of multiple cleavages, see, e.g., Beramendi et al. (2015), Cronin et al. (2011), Kitschelt (1994) Kriesi et al. (2008), and Roemer et al. (2007).

21. The first quote is from Julian Smith, Conservative MP of Skipton and Ripon; the second statement was made by Tory MP Andrew Bridgen (Martin and Robinson 2015). See also Chapter 6 on this point. Across Europe, even the Far-Right has capitalized on this tension. Recognizing leftist dilemmas, far-right parties are presenting "themselves as the only true defenders of western identity and western liberties" (Polakow-Suransky 2016).

22. Shefter (1994, 197).

or exclusion of ideologically incompatible minorities typically occurs when minority electorates have few outside options. African Americans, for instance, are captured by the Left; the Right has been less interested in their vote.[23] This capture leaves blacks with relatively little leverage within the Democratic Party. By contrast, I study how parties incorporate minorities when outside options do exist. As the following chapters will make clear, European Muslim voters are not a monolithic voting bloc, and in many contexts, especially sub-nationally, no single party can take their vote for granted. This status allows pivotal group members to influence both election outcomes and parties' ideological profiles. The findings of this book therefore have implications for how the inclusion of noncaptured groups will reshape politics. Such groups include, for instance, Hispanics or Asian Americans in the American two-party system and immigrants more broadly in European multiparty systems.[24]

Fourth, by examining the causes and consequences of different inclusion types I contribute to research on minority representation. Scholarship on the political representation of ethnic minority groups is still in its early stages, and research "on minority representation in Europe is in its infancy."[25] Most work that does exist tends to investigate one country, highlighting, for instance, whether and how features of the local context, such as electoral rules or minority spatial concentration, affect the chances of minorities getting into office.[26] I build on this work, but I also make the case that without paying attention to varying inclusion types the emphasis on election outcomes—that is, how many group members hold elected office—can't tell us much about the nature and consequences of minority political incorporation.[27]

I demonstrate instead that different inclusion types yield different candidate types. The notion that the representation of groups can take various forms has been well articulated by Hannah Pitkin.[28] However, much of the empirical

23. Frymer (2010).

24. In the 2000s, less than 50 percent of Hispanics and Asian Americans identified with a party (Hajnal and Lee 2011), though more recently these groups have voted disproportionately for the Democrats. In Europe, immigrants are more likely to vote for left parties (Bird et al. 2011a), but this link is not as tight as it used to be and, moreover, even within the Left, they can generally choose among several electorally viable parties.

25. Bloemraad and Schönwälder (2013, 572).

26. See, e.g., Dancygier (2014), Dancygier et al. (2015), Michon and Vermeulen (2013), Schönwälder (2013), Togeby (2008), and Trounstine and Valdini (2008); for an exception, see Garbaye (2005), Maxwell (2012), and Ruedin (2013), and for a comparative approach, see Bird et al. (2011b). Dancygier et al. (2015) additionally investigate the effects of individual-level candidate characteristics on election outcomes.

27. See also Dunning and Nilekani (2013) on how minority candidates' links to parties explain the relationship between descriptive and substantive representation in India. Celis et al. (2008) also argue for a more encompassing approach to women's representation that moves beyond the central assumption that "numbers matter."

28. Pitkin (1967).

research on minority representation fails to connect how party objectives critically shape *who* among the minority electorate gets represented and how this selection affects both the nature of minority inclusion and of party politics. I take Pitkin's insights as a starting point and clarify when minority political representation is likely to occur at all, what forms it is likely to take, and what political consequences it is likely to produce.

Finally, this book questions popular narratives that depict European Muslims as alienated from mainstream political institutions. Unable to bridge the gap between the traditional, conservative norms of their countries of origin with the modern, liberal cultures they experience in the West, European Muslims—the story goes—withdraw from majority society and institutions.[29] Not only do Europe's Muslims actively participate in elections, however; this book demonstrates that embeddedness in traditional ethnoreligious communities actually enhances their chances of becoming central players in subnational party politics. Moreover, parties of all stripes operating in different national contexts have recognized the usefulness of these cultural ties and ethnic linkages in the electoral sphere. The evidence I present therefore casts doubt on arguments that stress the importance of national multiculturalism policies in shaping sociopolitical incorporation.[30] Hard-nosed electoral calculations drive parties towards inclusion or exclusion and determine the salience of ethnoreligious electoral recruitment, no matter the policy regime (see also Chapter 4 on these points).

Empirical Approach

To explain the causes and consequences of Muslim electoral inclusion in Europe, I adopt a comparative approach. I chose countries based on the potential importance of the Muslim vote, which, in turn, will influence whether parties pursue exclusion, symbolic inclusion, or vote-based inclusion. To do so, I focus on the permissiveness of citizenship regimes and local electoral institutions. To avoid ambiguous cases, I select countries that are either permissive or restrictive on both counts.[31] I do not aim to disentangle which of these institutions (citizenship or electoral rules) is more influential in determining incorporation outcomes. Rather, I select institutional contexts that I hypothesize should, on average, be associated with distinct inclusion goals.

29. For a discussion and critique of this view, see Gest (2011).

30. This result is consistent with Wright and Bloemraad (2012) who largely find null effects of these regimes on immigrants' sociopolitical integration.

31. Note that France is such an ambiguous case: its citizenship code is relatively liberal, but its local electoral system—e.g., at-large elections, the absence of preference votes, a semiproportional allocation of seats, and the prominence of entrenched "local barons" (Bird 2005)—tends to be difficult to penetrate for minority voters and candidates.

In Austria and Germany, comparatively restrictive citizenship regimes combine with local electoral laws that make it difficult for minorities to capitalize on their concentration or capacity for mobilization. Local elections are held in municipalities at-large according to proportional representation (PR) rules, and the impact of preference votes is rather limited.[32] Preference ballots allow voters to support specific candidates within party lists, and minority groups have used them to boost the ranking of favored co-ethnics. Furthermore, non-EU citizens cannot vote or run in local elections. The potential electoral impact of the Muslim vote in Austrian and German municipalities is therefore, on average, small, and hence I predict that exclusion should be common, followed by symbolic inclusion.

In Belgium and Britain the opposite is true: Permissive citizenship legislation coexists alongside local electoral institutions that provide incentives for minority mobilization. In Belgium, elections are also held at-large and feature PR, but here preference votes can substantially improve the election chances of individual candidates. Moreover, noncitizens can vote (but not compete) in local elections. In Britain, local elections take place at the ward level according to plurality rule, providing spatially concentrated groups with electoral leverage. Noncitizen residents from Commonwealth countries are allowed to cast ballots and to stand for office. On average, then, Belgian and British municipalities are more likely to be home to electorally influential Muslim communities, which should generate greater degrees of vote-based inclusion and increased rates of representation as a result.

Though the overall size of the Muslim population is estimated to be similar across countries, its electoral significance (and the associated net vote gains that accrue due to inclusion) are not. This difference in the importance of the Muslim vote generates variation in religious parity and gender parity across countries.[33] Additionally, I show that my argument travels when we hold the national setting constant: It explains variation in inclusion outcomes across parties and municipalities within these countries. To test my claims, I gathered

32. When municipal elections are held according to PR and at-large, a party's seat share in parliament is based on its vote share in the municipality as a whole (e.g., a party that wins 20 percent of the municipal vote obtains approximately 20 percent of the seats). In at-large elections, the municipality is not divided into districts. In district-level plurality elections, by contrast, voting takes place in several districts across the municipality, and candidates with the highest number of votes within a district win seats.

33. Table 1.1 shows that Muslim population percentages are similar in my municipal sample. They are also at similar levels nationally. According to estimates of the Pew Research Center, the percentage of the population that is Muslim (in 2010) is 5.7 in Austria, 6.0 in Belgium, 5.0 percent in Germany, and 4.6 in the UK (see http://www.pewforum.org/2011/01/27/table-muslim-population-by-country/). According to the UK's 2011 census, 5.2 percent of those who answered the religion item identified as Muslim (in England and Wales). Statistik Austria estimates that 6.8 percent of the Austrian population was Muslim in 2012; see Aslan et al. (2014, 20).

information on the selection and election of Muslim candidates in close to 300 municipalities (approximately 70 per country; see Appendix A for more details). In Belgium and Britain (where I expect more considerable cross-municipality variation in the size of the Muslim electorate compared to Austria and Germany), I collected data on all candidates—winners and losers—which allows me to gain deeper insights into parties' selection strategies. In Belgium, I furthermore coded candidates' list rankings by religion and gender. In all, I coded the backgrounds of well over 80,000 candidates.

To establish group preferences and voting intentions I complement these election materials with several opinion surveys, and to assess parties' relevant ideological positions I developed an original coding scheme to examine how general election manifestos discuss the treatment of immigrants and Muslims.[34]

Additionally, I rely heavily on local news coverage (both conventional print sources and online sites such as election blogs) that reports on the campaigns of minority candidates and on the actions of elected minority representatives. Wherever possible, I also consult existing case studies about minority inclusion in specific localities, though this literature still remains very small. Together, these sources provide information about candidates' style of mobilization, the electorates they seek to recruit, and their behavior once in office. In some cases, these sources also comment on the assumed motivations that drive party leaders to select particular candidate types. Party gatekeepers typically do not divulge the inner workings of their parties, and it is very difficult to get political elites to talk candidly about their inclusion motives. When researchers try to engage with party elites to open up about these matters, they can usually study only one or two cases in depth, and even then it is unclear whether strategic politicians are sincere when discussing selection aims. Though I draw on such case studies and a plethora of local news reports, I have opted for an alternative research design that allows me to test my propositions across a variety of contexts and, in doing so, to rule out competing explanations having to do with party-, city-, or country-level variables.

Moreover, focusing on subnational elections offers several advantages. First, many of the issues that are relevant to ethnic minority electorates have particular salience at the local level (e.g., accommodating religious or linguistic differences in schools or public services), and understanding differences in local representation is important as a result. Second, inclusion outcomes and their determinants vary considerably across cities within countries. This variation permits me to test my argument while controlling for national-level variables that might also influence inclusion decisions. Third, by examining

34. This project was carried out with Yotam Margalit; see Chapter 4 and Appendix C for details.

subnational elections I reduce the chances that electoral inclusion generates open citizenship regimes or electoral rules. Citizenship reforms are hammered out by national political actors, often following protracted partisan negotiations, whereas the inclusion decisions I examine are taken at the municipal level. When considering which candidates to place on the ballot and whose votes to court, municipal party gatekeepers confront a fixed institutional setting. In the long run, local inclusion dynamics may prompt national politicians to reconsider these laws (though existing research points to alternative explanations)[35] but in the short term subnational party leaders and office-seekers must play with the institutional cards they are dealt.

While my empirical strategy varies minority electoral clout, I hold constant the minority group in question, and most of this book addresses the political behaviors and inclusion of European Muslims. Why Muslims? First, even before the onset of the more recent refugee migration, throughout Western Europe Muslims have been the largest and fastest-growing ethnoreligious minority group, and sizable shares of first and later generation immigrants are of Muslim faith. In addition to size, a spate of highly visible events, ranging from terrorist acts to honor killings, has raised public scrutiny and skepticism of this group, and debates about immigrant integration typically revolve around Muslims. Any study that deals with minority integration in Europe must therefore take note of this population.

Second, given that I expect that varying electoral incentives affect different short-term and long-run outcomes across countries, cities, and parties, it is helpful to limit the investigation to a group who shares similar features across these contexts. More pragmatically, since we currently lack systematic cross-national or even cross-city data on ethnic-minority politicians—let alone on candidates who do not end up winning—I concentrate my data collection efforts on one group.

Focusing on a group that shares a common religion and varying national and local contexts, the book does not seek to isolate a "Muslim effect." It instead investigates how the bundle of attributes that characterize this population—such as their social organization, settlement patterns, and political preferences—shapes their political inclusion. Through clever research designs, others have indeed presented convincing evidence of a "Muslim effect" and have documented that European Muslims do encounter increased discrimination and integration hurdles when compared to non-Muslim migrants with otherwise similar characteristics.[36] These findings underscore the importance of studying Europe's Muslim residents across contexts.

---

35. See, e.g., Brubaker (1992), Howard (2009), and Janoski (2010).
36. Adida et al. (2015).

At the same time, I do not treat Muslims as one homogenous entity but consider how variation in Muslim preferences across and within electoral districts influences parties' incorporation strategies. Following others, I build on the idea that groups who share a common, politically salient, identity can simultaneously embrace other identities.[37] Like any other group, Muslims identify along a number of dimensions, including, for example, their national, regional, or kinship backgrounds. Some of these will matter significantly during elections, an issue that I address explicitly (see Chapter 5). Specifically, the small geographic scale of British electoral wards in conjunction with Muslims' spatial concentration serves to highlight the importance of identity attributes on which Muslims differ, namely tribe and kinship. These attributes are meaningful markers in the sending regions and continue to be salient in social life and electoral politics today.

Yet, a sense of belonging to other groups exists alongside an encompassing Muslim identity. Across Europe, Muslims tend to believe that Muslims in their country "have a very or fairly strong sense of Islamic identity" and, further, that this identity is growing.[38] Muslims' attachment to their religious identity often supersedes other attachments. In Britain, for instance, only 6 percent of Muslim respondents surveyed in 2010 stated that they thought of themselves as black or Asian first, while 60 percent prioritized their religion.[39] Similarly, among second-generation migrants of Turkish origin across European cities, substantial majorities stated that "Being a Muslim is an important part of myself."[40] Finally, European Muslims' faith in contexts where majorities have traditionally been Christian, and are increasingly secular, has prompted specific claims related to the accommodation of religious practice in the public sphere.[41] In such a context, Islam—though hardly monolithic—is associated with the articulation of interests and policy concerns in ways that

37. For expositions on how this constructivist insight shapes ethnic politics, see Chandra (2012) and Posner (2005).

38. See Pew Global Attitudes Project (2006, 9). The survey also shows that large shares of Muslims state that they first think of themselves as Muslim rather than as a citizen of their country.

39. Thirty-four percent said they identified equally as Muslim and as black or Asian. These data are based on the 2010 Ethnic Minority British Election Study; see EMBES (2010). Note that in Britain, the "black" label used to be commonly employed to categorize all nonwhites.

40. Concretely, the mean answers to this question (with a range of 1, "totally disagree," to 5, "totally agree") were 4.31 in Amsterdam, 4.28 in Berlin, 4.20 in Brussels, and 4.55 in Stockholm; see Fleischmann and Phalet (2012, 329). Scholars studying a diverse set of European countries have also noted that in later generations, Muslims' religious identity rises while those tied to their ancestors' country of origin tends to recede (cf. Pędziwiatr 2010, 40).

41. On the rising but not uniform accommodation of cultural and religious rights of immigrant-origin populations across Western Europe, see, e.g., Fetzer and Soper (2005), Koopmans et al. (2012), Laurence (2012), and Tatari (2010).

ethnonational identities might not be. In short, European "Muslims share strong religious beliefs, identity and policy concerns that could lead Muslim voters to support Muslim candidates."[42]

Additionally, even when religious beliefs or interests do not come into play explicitly, Muslim identity is nevertheless relevant in political affairs. "Muslim identity," Sinno clarifies,

> is hard to escape in the context of today's politics. . . . Politicians who define themselves as "culturally Muslim" or even as "secular Muslim" find themselves dealing with "Muslim" issues and being considered as "Muslim" by their own political parties when they wish to emphasize their diversity, by minority constituents who feel connected to them or who do not trust them, by jealous rivals wishing to discredit them, by the media when they need "Muslim" voices, and by civil society's organizations. . . . Even if someone from a Muslim background wishes to do so, it is not easy to escape being a "Muslim" in the West anymore.[43]

Though this book rests on a similar premise, I also illustrate that the questions that arise with respect to the Muslim presence in Europe are neither particular to Muslims nor to Europe. Rather, the political inclusion of ethnic minorities in other democratic contexts can exhibit similar dynamics and confront parties with analogous trade-offs. The theoretical arguments I develop in Chapter 2 are formulated in a general way and can thus be tested among other groups and countries. Learning about Muslims' electoral incorporation and its effects on the nature of political competition is therefore meant to also illuminate a more general phenomenon.

Last, when examining the consequences of inclusion, this book studies the nature of electoral campaigns, election outcomes, and the effects of inclusion on another marginalized group, female candidates. But I do not systematically examine policy effects. Rather, my goal is to show how *even without* considering policies that are enacted due to minorities obtaining elected office we observe substantial transformations in the ways in which elections are fought and won as well as in the social bases of party support. As I will suggest in the conclusion, if minority incorporation generates policies that further divide existing coalitions, this realignment will be even more dramatic. Nonetheless, identifying policy effects goes beyond the scope of this book. To credibly trace policy change back to minority representatives one has to be sure that it is indeed the presence of minority politicians—rather than other characteristics of the legislature, electorate, or the district that give rise to minority elected officials—that is doing the work. Research can exploit official regulations or

---

42. Fisher et al. (2015, 889).
43. Sinno (2009, 2).

natural experiments that lead to minority candidates being elected across legislatures in an as-if-random fashion. These remain rare in the European context, but present an area ripe for future study.[44]

Chapter Outline

The following chapters proceed as follows. Chapter 2 develops the main arguments. I explain when and why parties will pursue exclusion, symbolic inclusion, or vote-based inclusion and discuss how each inclusion type is associated with distinct candidate and mobilization types. I also address how the distribution of minority and majority preferences will influence the kind of candidates and voters that parties will seek to recruit, and I specify how variation in partisanship, electoral geography, mobilizational capacity, and political competition affects the causes and consequences of minority inclusion.

The structure of the empirical chapters is organized around *causes* of inclusion (Chapters 3, 4, and first half of Chapter 5) before turning to the *consequences* of inclusion (second half of Chapter 5 and Chapter 6). Chapter 3 delineates the preference landscape that parties confront when they contemplate inclusion strategies. In essence, parties face a minority electorate whose preferences and attributes present them with an uneasy ideological fit, but whose votes can swing elections. I argue that disagreements over social values and norms between non-Muslims and Muslims are greatest where parties face the strongest inclusion pressures, namely in vote-rich neighborhoods in urban areas. Additionally, these areas are most likely to raise conflicts over economic resources, thereby intensifying inclusion dilemmas. I first review the processes that have led to this preference distribution, explaining how selection mechanisms of the migration process, available housing stock, and enclave formation have served to replicate in Europe's cities the social networks and norms that structure communal life in the sending towns and villages.

I then turn to survey data to illustrate that both sorting and polarization converge to produce a notable clash in values in these areas. Across Western Europe, sorting processes have caused more socially conservative members of Muslim communities and more socially liberal members of the non-Muslim population to reside in the same urban space. Furthermore, employing individual-level panel-data from Britain, I show that polarization is at work: Over time, non-Muslims espouse increasingly liberal views on gender roles as they become exposed to Muslim populations in their municipality. Though Muslim and non-Muslim preferences are diverse, this chapter draws on several

---

44. For research that is able to isolate the effects of minority representation on policy by examining variation in the implementation of quotas, see, e.g., Chattopadhyay and Duflo (2004) and Dunning and Nilekani (2013).

pieces of evidence to demonstrate that it is precisely in locations where parties will want to recruit the Muslim vote that the preference gap is at its peak.

One might presume, then, that the deck is stacked against Muslims' electoral inclusion. Preference divergence and prejudice, along with material conflicts, could come together to thwart incorporation. Chapter 4 investigates whether two countervailing forces—ideological commitments to equal treatment and the potential electoral leverage of the Muslim vote—can nevertheless lead to representational parity. To answer this question, I examine how parties' commitments to equal treatment and nondiscrimination on the one hand and the potential importance of the Muslim vote on the other correlate with inclusion outcomes across countries. Here, I draw on two original sources of data. The first source measures the salience of parties' programmatic pledges on issues related to the immigrant and Muslim presence in Europe, as expressed in manifestos. In the chapter, I focus on positions related to the equal treatment of immigrant-origin, minority populations as well as on parties' stances toward religion and Islam. The second original source consists of my datasets measuring Muslim descriptive representation across cities and parties in Austria, Belgium, Germany, and Great Britain.

I show that across these four countries, the Left is indeed much more tightly wedded to principles of equal treatment than is the Right, but proactive rhetoric in this domain does not predict inclusiveness. Though, within countries, center-left parties are always more likely to recruit Muslim candidates than are center-right parties, this is not true across countries; parties only feature significant shares of Muslim candidates when local Muslim electorates can deliver substantial votes. Absent electoral incentives pushing towards inclusion, parity ratios remain well below one, regardless of parties' ideological commitments. In short, electoral incentives trump ideological considerations.

Chapter 4 provides a macroperspective on the causes of inclusion, but readers may be concerned that the selected countries differ in other, unmeasured characteristics that may drive these causes. Chapter 5 therefore drills down to the microlevel and studies candidate selection and election outcomes in English municipalities. It confirms that parties are primarily interested in pursuing votes and think about the ideological repercussion later. In England, ward-level elections allow us to get a sense of how the distribution of Muslim and non-Muslim preferences affects parties' calculations of the anticipated gains and losses that they associate with Muslim inclusion. Studying thousands of ward elections over time, the chapter demonstrates that these calculations significantly influence parties' inclusion decisions. Parties are less likely to put Muslim candidates on the ticket in wards where they anticipate a considerable non-Muslim backlash. However, once the size of the Muslim electorate reaches a critical threshold, inclusion chances rise substantially.

Having demonstrated that inclusion outcomes are consistent with the notion that parties are mainly motivated by a desire to win seats, I next consider the consequences of this approach for the nature of political competition. Because parties have time and again favored the efficient mobilization of ethnoreligious bloc votes over the establishment of cross-ethnic, class-based coalitions, the electoral incorporation of Muslims has transformed party politics in Muslim enclaves, leading to candidate-centered campaigns in which partisan alignments are an afterthought. As a result, election outcomes become much more volatile: Muslim voters in enclaves switch their support on the basis of ethnoreligious kinship, no matter the party label, and the Labour Party eventually ends up losing seats that it would have easily captured had it established class-based linkages with Muslim candidates and voters. Moreover, these aggregate election outcomes are replicated at the individual level: Though class is strongly related to partisan identification among Muslims overall, in urban Muslim enclaves the link between income and partisanship is much weaker.

Chapter 5 thus draws out how parties' vote-based inclusion strategies serve to undermine the class cleavage and, along with it, the electoral performance of the Left. In Chapter 6, I turn to another consequence that emerges when parties' primary concern is to maximize votes: balancing religious parity with gender parity. A salient concern, voiced across the political spectrum, is that multicultural inclusion empowers conservative male community leaders at the expense of women. Chapter 6 inquires whether electoral inclusion can produce similar outcomes. I argue that different inclusion goals should be associated with different outcomes with respect to gender and religious parity. When parties are mainly interested in symbolic inclusion, they will select Muslim candidates who can signal to non-Muslim voters that they are well-integrated and abide by the norms and values of the majority population. The simplest way for parties (and non-Muslim voters) to assess how candidates fare on this score is to look at their gender: Just by virtue of running for office, Muslim women (especially if they do not wear a headscarf) signal that they are not bound by conservative, patriarchal constraints in ways that men—even if they shared the same belief system—cannot. When parties are interested in vote-based inclusion, by contrast, they will prioritize candidates who are enmeshed in religious networks that can dispense sizable vote shares on Election Day. These candidates are predominantly male.

The consequences of these inclusion motives are substantially different gender balances across countries and municipalities. In Austria and Germany, where due to Muslims' reduced electoral strength symbolic inclusion is more common than is vote-based inclusion, parties feature a disproportionate number of Muslim women (relative to non-Muslim women). Furthermore, parties here are more likely to include female Muslim politicians than are their counterparts in Belgium and Britain where vote-based inclusion is much more widespread. Across countries, gender parity clashes with religious parity.

To investigate these dynamics in a more fine-grained manner, I then explore variation in the representation of women and Muslims across party lists in Belgian municipalities and expose similar trade-offs. When parties seek to mobilize the Muslim vote, they systematically privilege Muslim male candidates, placing them on more attractive list positions than women, both Muslim and non-Muslim. Muslim voters, in turn, award these candidates with the highest number of preference votes. Both party and voter mechanisms therefore lead to a relative overrepresentation of Muslim male politicians, which comes at the expense of the election of female candidates overall. This trade-off between religious parity and gender parity results just as much from top-down decisions to favor men and disadvantage women as it does from bottom-up processes: Because party gatekeepers in charge of devising inclusion strategies are mainly driven by the pursuit of votes, their inclusion motives end up undermining their ideological commitments.

The concluding chapter takes a more speculative stance and considers what conditions make it more or less likely that minority political incorporation has significant impacts on intergroup relations, the identities of parties, and the electoral alignments underpinning party systems. The discussion highlights that parties' recruitment strategies can meaningfully affect majority perceptions of the minority, minority views about the political system, and minority social integration. It also emphasizes that the waning of traditional structures of mobilization—in particular the decline of trade unions—raises the relative attractiveness of minority bloc votes and associated ethnically based campaign styles. Larger, more slow-moving, political and economic forces that shape linkages between the majority electorate and political parties thus also help determine whether and in what ways minorities are brought into the party system. The chapter concludes by positing under what circumstances this incorporation will trigger electoral realignments and, in the process, generate a reordering of European party systems.

2

Defining and Explaining Inclusion

This chapter presents an overview of the book's central arguments. I begin with a brief discussion of why I focus on the inclusion of minority candidates by political parties and next highlight the dilemmas that parties face when considering the electoral inclusion of Muslims. I then review three central inclusion outcomes—exclusion, symbolic inclusion, and vote-based inclusion—and argue that symbolic and vote-based inclusion are each associated with specific candidate types. The chapter proceeds by explaining that anticipated net vote gains lead to differences in inclusion outcomes. These net vote gains are, in turn, based on differences in party type, electoral geography, and minority mobilization. Specifically, I maintain that the more religious and traditional members of ethnoreligious minority groups are both more likely to settle in urban enclaves and to be more easily mobilized during elections. I discuss how these dynamics influence parties' recruitment strategies, emphasizing how the short-term benefits that parties derive from running campaigns on an ethnoreligious basis can undermine their ideological cohesiveness and electoral performance in the long run. I also clarify some of the assumptions that generate these outcomes, namely that parties try to maximize votes and that minority voters are not captured by one party.

Minority Political Inclusion

The following pages consider parties' inclusion of minority candidates and the consequences that flow from this inclusion. Why focus on minority candidates? The selection of candidates is one of the core activities that a political party undertakes.[1] Who is included—and excluded—in the pool of selected

1. E.g., Gallagher and Marsh (1988); Hazan and Rahat (2006); Schattschneider (1942).

candidates sends a message to party members, minorities, and the electorate at large. In systems with party lists, the overall composition and candidate order of the list can visibly signal the balance of power of groups within a party and, by implication, within the electorate. In single-member districts, the "candidate becomes the public face of the party . . . and the fortunes of the individual and the party become inseparably linked."[2] Across electoral systems, a party's choice of candidates "raises central questions about the ideological and sociological identities of the party as a whole. . . . Collectively, [a party's candidates] . . . manifest the demographic, geographic, and ideological dimensions of the party."[3]

Accordingly, the inclusion of candidates belonging to minority groups is one important tool that parties can deploy when they seek to expand or reshape their electoral coalitions. This is especially so when changes in descriptive representation lead to changes in turnout levels and vote choices, both among newly represented minorities who reward parties for inclusion and among segments of the majority population who may do the opposite.[4] Because of these important functions and effects, some go so far as to declare that internal selection battles are "generally even more intense than the struggle for control over the party manifesto."[5]

The selection of candidates thus critically defines what and whom a party stands for. As such, candidate selection is directly tied to minority political inclusion. Much research indicates that elected representatives who share descriptive traits with voters may be more willing and able to represent these voters.[6] In the United States, for instance, black state legislators have been found to be more proactive in responding to inquiries from black voters than are their white counterparts, irrespective of partisanship and electoral incentives.[7] In ethnically diverse societies around the globe, voters routinely rely on candidates' ethnicity to make inferences about the policy decisions these candidates will make once in office. A widely shared assumption is that candidates will favor co-ethnics in the distribution of goods and services, espe-

2. Murray (2008, 540).

3. Katz (2001, 277–78).

4. On the effects of descriptive representation on political participation, see, e.g., Banducci et al. (2004), Barreto et al. (2004), Barreto (2007), Fisher et al. (2015), Gay (2001), Wolfinger (1965), Zingher and Farrer (2016).

5. Gallagher (1988, 3).

6. A lot of research on this question has been carried out in the United States with reference to African American voters and politicians; see, e.g., Canon (1999), Grose (2011), Preuhs (2006), and Tate (2003).

7. See Butler and Broockman (2011) and Broockman (2013). Specifically, examining legislator responses to emails from a putatively black alias asking for help in obtaining unemployment benefits, Broockman (2013) finds that black legislators are more likely than white legislators to answer these emails when the sender does not live within the politician's district.

cially in patronage democracies.[8] Beyond ethnicity, scholars have found that the election of female candidates is associated with the implementation of policies that better represent women's preferences.[9]

In the context of immigrant-origin populations, having "one of their own" in office provides immigrant communities with access points to an unfamiliar political system that they can otherwise find difficult to penetrate.[10] Local politicians can offer vital assistance in helping migrants navigate state bureaucracies such as housing departments, naturalization offices, or employment exchanges. With respect to Muslims, co-religionist elected representatives have helped in securing zoning permits for mosques, in allocating burial grounds, or in providing halal foods in schools.[11] While these efforts help Muslims feel at home in their new environments, Muslim councilors have also been charged with slowing down integration. Some have been alleged to "defend and reinforce traditional attitudes from above," by, for instance, failing to cooperate with law enforcement in the persecution of honor-based violence being perpetrated in pockets of their communities or by "block[ing] the activities of women's groups."[12] In these ways, then, local politicians can be at the forefront of minority incorporation *and* isolation. Because they are members of internally diverse communities, their actions are likely to benefit some group members more than others.[13] The propositions I develop below discuss how parties' selection decisions can influence this balance.

This book, then, examines parties' inclusion of candidates belonging to minority groups because in diverse societies candidate selection constitutes a crucial political activity. Moreover, it influences minority sociopolitical integration and shapes the identity of political parties and, by extension, of electoral democracy.

Inclusion Dilemmas

Given the critical role of candidate selection, parties have to take into account how existing party members and constituents view the entry of newcomers.

8. On the ethnicity-policy link, see, e.g., Chandra (2004), Ferree (2006), Franck and Rainer (2012), Lieberman and McClendon (2012), and Posner (2005).

9. See, e.g., Chattopadhyay and Duflo (2004) on such effects in Indian villages and Bratton and Ray (2002) on the election of women and the provision of municipal child care in Norway. For a review of findings in this area, see Paxton et al. (2007).

10. E.g., Bloemraad (2006); Dancygier (2010); Solomos and Back (1995).

11. Dancygier (2013); Gale (2005); Tatari (2010).

12. Cited in Brandon and Hafez (2008, 79 and 105); the authors investigate how honor-based violence is sustained in the UK.

13. For this reason, Dovi (2002, 729) points out that "some descriptive representatives are preferable than others" and goes on to argue that "Preferable descriptive representatives have strong *mutual* relationships with *dispossessed* subgroups" (emphasis in original). For a related point on representing the interests of minority women, see Htun (2014).

Here, mainstream parties come up against a series of dilemmas. First, they have to confront the fact that sections of the electorate dislike diversity while others appreciate it. Parties that diversify too much risk losing the support of ethnocentrists, while those that remain too homogenous may push away cosmopolitans and minorities.

Parties across diverse democracies face this balancing act, and it is very relevant when it comes to the electoral incorporation of European Muslims. Anti-Muslim prejudice and concerns about Muslim integration are widespread. In 2010, only 33 percent of West Europeans thought that Muslims were integrating well, while 58 percent felt the opposite was true.[14] One year later, 58 percent considered relations between Muslims and Westerners to be "poor"; 70 percent were concerned about Islamic extremists in their country; and 61 and 48 percent, respectively, associated being Muslim with being "fanatical" and "violent."[15] These sentiments intensify and can spill over into anti-Muslim assaults, especially in the aftermath of Islamic terrorist events, such as 9/11 or the 2015 Paris attacks.

Notwithstanding these tensions, the growing size of the Muslim electorate may compel parties to reach out to this group, even if it entails forsaking ethnocentrist support. But here parties encounter another dilemma: The inclusion of religious, traditional electorates may also drive away secular, progressive cosmopolitans. To the extent that left parties are more likely to feel pressures to incorporate minorities *and* to please cosmopolitans, this dilemma is especially pronounced among the Left, and it is one that strikes at the core of the European Left's identity as a champion of secular universalism.

Many European center-left parties have anticlerical roots. Their leaders were "visibly, and often militantly, godless," and their followers have come to adopt preferences that conflict with religious doctrines.[16] For example, religious education and reproductive rights have been key issues that have divided religious and secular politicians and publics.[17] Though cosmopolitan leftists may be more willing than ethnocentrists to tolerate religious difference, they

14. These findings are based on a survey by the German Marshall Fund (2014, 17) that sampled residents in France, Germany, Italy, the Netherlands, Spain, and the UK.

15. These responses refer to cross-country averages, based on surveys conducted in Britain, France, Germany, and Spain; see http://www.pewglobal.org/. See also Bleich (2009) and Helbling (2012).

16. Hobsbawm (1984, 34); see also De La O and Rodden (2008) and Lipset and Rokkan (1967). Part of the Left's anticlericalism was based on the church's role in upholding authoritarian orders and on its rejection of the religious electoral cleavage. Religious doctrine (especially caring for the poor) is not, by definition, incompatible with the Left's preferences and goals, and religious faith has historically played a more important role among socialists than has been commonly assumed. On this point, see, e.g., Heimann and Walter (1993), Knox (1988), Linden (1932), Reitz (1983), and Smith (1993).

17. See Minkenberg (2002) and Norris and Inglehart (2004).

are nevertheless concerned that Muslims will roll back the hard-wrung achievements of the modern social contract by bringing back religion and conservatism into secular and liberal public spheres and policy debates.[18]

The following complaint by a Dutch councilor in the city of Utrecht about Muslims' tendency to rely on religious figures to solve day-to-day problems is emblematic of this concern:

> Surely, you have other links. You don't just have your imam. I am also a member of a religious community, my parish also has its minister. But I don't go to him when I have a housing problem. Then I go to the housing department, I don't go to the minister. That was how it used to be done in the old days. I mean, those days are gone.[19]

Antwerp's mayor raised a similar theme when discussing the controversies surrounding the wearing of the headscarf in public schools:

> We have had a period of 40 or 50 years when the role of religion in general has diminished in the public realm. Now we are confronted with the fact that one specific religion is becoming much more important in the public domain. So a lot of teachers feel we are going . . . 30 or 40 years back in history . . . we are going through the same growing pains all over again.[20]

The reason why debates about veiling have been so widespread is not only because the headscarf visibly signals religion in the public sphere. Controversies persist because they go to the heart of the multicultural dilemma faced by liberal cosmopolitans: How can proponents of diversity recognize groups that they perceive as internally illiberal?[21]

Leftists and social liberals have historically disapproved of the customs and social orders that religious groups adopt because they associate them with tradition, backwardness, and illiberalism.[22] Today, these objectionable customs take the form of patriarchal structures and unequal gender relations that are more pronounced among pious Muslims. As a result of these traditions, many Europeans who do not fall in the ethnocentrist camp nevertheless consider Islam "a symbol of . . . illiberalism, and premodernism."[23] Even leftist parties whose relationship with religion has historically been less fraught

18. Bowen (2007); Cesari (2013); Norton (2013).

19. Cited in Rath et al. (2001, 129).

20. *The Economist* (2009).

21. European feminists have been particularly divided on questions related to veiling; see, e.g., Rottmann and Marx Ferree (2008) and Korteweg and Yurdakul (2014). Outside the electoral sphere, political theorists have addressed problems related to the multicultural dilemma; see, e.g., Barry (2001), Kymlicka (2012), Okin (1999), Shachar (2001), and Song (2007).

22. See discussions in Parekh (2008) and Rath et al. (2001); see also Zetterbaum (1893).

23. Bramadat (2009, 6); cf. Parekh (2008).

(such as British Labour) confront this clash because they operate in a political environment where commitments to universalism and, in particular, to egalitarian gender norms, have become one of the Left's defining features.[24] They allow social democratic parties to reach out to affluent cosmopolitans who do not have much to gain from leftist redistributive policies.

Ethnic diversity also presents the Right with challenges. The exclusion of ethnic minorities from electoral coalitions does not generally undermine programmatic pledges, for center-right parties do not tend to campaign as champions of minority rights and equal treatment. If anything, a candidate pool that is too ethnically diverse will upset voters who ally with the Right precisely because they value its emphasis on maintaining a common ethnocultural heritage. Yet, when the exclusion of minorities dooms any chance of electoral success, right parties will have to decide whether the price of ethnic homogeneity is too steep.

How, then, do parties resolve these multicultural dilemmas? One logical response would be for party gatekeepers to select Muslim candidates who align well with their parties' core supporters. Europe's Muslims are internally diverse, and parties therefore have some flexibility here. Many less observant Muslims, for instance, seek to distance themselves from their more pious co-religionists. They often identify as "secular" or "cultural" Muslims, rather than shed their religious identity altogether and would therefore be a good match for the Left. The embrace of traditional family values could in turn be the common thread binding Muslim electorates and candidates to the Right. These differences are reflected within Muslim electorates; in many Muslim families, a "chronic struggle [takes place] over the interpretation of Islam and over what it means to be a good Muslim."[25] Such cultural and generational differences can come into view when internally diverse Muslim populations seek to settle on political representatives.[26] Some subgroups will feel more closely represented by a candidate who understands the discrimination that Muslims experience in the labor market while others will want to ensure that their can-

24. Though the salience of gender equality has risen over the last several decades, the belief that religion subjugates women goes back to at least August Bebel, one of the founding figures of German Social Democracy, who declared that Christianity's "doctrines contain the same disdain of women that is met with in all the religions of the Orient. It commands her to be an obedient servant to man" (Bebel 1910, 58). Bebel wrote at a time when European publics were, for the most part, still deeply religious and when traditional gender roles were entrenched. Marx and Engels also wrote about the "Woman Question," but thought that the main reason for women's oppression was the capitalist system of production.

25. Brubaker (2013, 4).

26. See, for instance, Akhtar (2013) and Baston (2013). On generational differences in ethnic and religious attachment among Dutch Muslims, see Maliepaard et al. (2010). On the importance of religiosity in predicting conservative gender views and behaviors among German Muslims *across* generations, see Diehl et al. (2009).

didate is sensitive to their religious needs or protective of existing social structures.

Despite these internal fissures, I argue that electoral incentives—rather than concerns about ideological fit—systematically push political parties toward certain candidate types. The evidence presented in this book will demonstrate that when it comes to the competitive politics of candidate selection and election, the Left's inclusion strategies reveal it to be neither as supportive of gender equality nor as apprehensive of ethnoreligious communalism as its rhetoric might suggest, while the Right strives for cultural homogeneity among its candidates only when it makes electoral sense to do so. The next sections spell out the logic behind these outcomes.

Inclusion Types and Candidate Types

When confronting inclusion, political parties do not merely make a simple binary decision of whether or not to welcome minority candidates in their midst. Parties also have to identify what goals they want inclusion to accomplish, and, having settled on these goals, they will next have to determine what type of candidate will be best suited to fulfill them.

INCLUSION TYPES

Political parties may decide not to incorporate minority candidates at all. The inclusion of newcomers often pushes out existing politicians, generating internal conflicts.[27] Further, it can lead to defections among existing voters. Having a limited number of slots at their disposal and a host of subgroups to satisfy, party selectorates may therefore consider inclusion too costly and opt for *exclusion*.

By contrast, parties engage in *symbolic inclusion* to send a message that they support minority integration into sociopolitical life. In diverse democracies, questions of inclusiveness and equal treatment arise frequently, especially when minority status coincides with social, economic, or political disadvantage. Parties may want to convey that they believe in successful integration, and their selection of minority candidates is an efficient and visible way to do so. As Mansbridge notes, the presence of minority legislators can create "a social meaning of 'ability to rule' for members of a group . . . where that ability has been seriously questioned." By doing so, this presence can also enhance the legitimacy of the party and of the political system as a whole.[28]

27. See Chandra (2004) on how parties that want to include new groups tackle this problem.

28. See Mansbridge (1999, 628) and Phillips (1995). Because what are commonly labeled

Symbolic inclusion is meant to shape a party's image. It signals that the party accepts and explicitly recognizes the group in question, but this acceptance and recognition occurs on the party's own terms. Symbolic inclusion, I argue, is neither designed to produce significant prominority policy concessions, nor to effect major shifts in electoral coalitions. It occurs when parties are beginning to tap into the still comparatively limited electoral potential of minority voters, and when they expect inclusion to yield a small-to-moderate return in terms of minority votes. As a result, minority groups may dismiss these acts as empty gestures that are relatively costless for the party and that have few tangible effects for the group in question.[29]

In many European cities, party officials field symbolic candidates because they "do not want to be perceived as racist or discriminatory . . . public opinion and the media expect party lists to be diverse." Parties put so-called Alibi Alis on the list because it is "about the media and the image that will be created," suggested an ethnic-minority candidate in Belgium.[30] By contrast, the maintenance of all-white, all-native lists would make parties appear out-of-step with demographic realities and progressive preferences.

Indeed, I maintain that when parties include symbolically, they do not simply aim for the minority vote. Parties that include symbolically also want to convince cosmopolitans who value equality and diversity that they do not give in to ethnocentrist impulses while simultaneously making some headway among minority voters. Observing that the party incorporates underrepresented groups as candidates, cosmopolitans and some minority voters view inclusion as "a public acknowledgement of equal value."[31] Because parties have two audiences in mind when including symbolically, it may be the case that it is chiefly majority voters who recognize and accept the symbolization, but that the minority electorate remains somewhat more skeptical.[32]

Moves toward symbolic inclusion take place when the minority electorate is not pivotal. Parties often opt for symbolic candidates to shape their brand and win over majority voters. For instance, smaller parties (such as the Greens)

"symbolic" acts can have real consequences—psychological and otherwise—Mansbridge argues that it is best not to use the term "symbolic." On symbolic legislation in the context of African American representation, see Tate (2003).

29. On token immigrant representatives, see, e.g., Bird (2005), Geisser (1997), and Geisser and Soum (2012).

30. Eelbode (2013, 140).

31. Phillips (1995, 40).

32. Though Pitkin (1967, 105–111) does not differentiate between minority and majority audiences, she also emphasizes that a particular audience must understand and accept the symbolization. In Pitkin's definition the symbols themselves have little meaning without such acceptance (e.g., a flag can symbolize a country but only if citizens agree with and recognize this symbolization). See also Escobar-Lemmon and Taylor-Robinson (2014) and Mansbridge (2003) for discussions of different types of minority representation.

that nominate sizable shares of minority candidates can peel away social democratic voters by advertising their superior record of minority inclusion and progressive universalism more generally. Center-right parties can also use symbolic inclusion to pick up high-income cosmopolitans whose social values otherwise drive them to the Left. For example, in Germany the Christian Democrats were the first party to select a Muslim to be minister in a state parliament. Aygül Özkan, a woman with Turkish roots, was appointed minister of social affairs in Niedersachsen, a highly publicized move designed to make the party more competitive among cosmopolitans and migrants alike.[33]

Parties can also go for symbolic inclusion to compensate for their drift towards antiminority positions in other realms. Featuring minority politicians within their ranks provides parties with some cover; it permits them to make inroads among the minority electorate and to appeal to cosmopolitans while at the same time holding on to positions that are more closely in line with diversity skeptics. Such motives appeared to be at work, for example, in the aftermath of the "Sarazzin-Affair" in Germany. Thilo Sarazzin, a prominent member of the Social Democrats, wrote a highly publicized anti-immigrant book that spawned a heated debate about minority integration that dominated the media for months. Despite many requests, the SPD decided not to expel Sarazzin. Aware that the issue had cost the SPD support among ethnic minorities and undermined its cosmopolitan credentials, the party responded to its critics by announcing plans to increase the number of politicians with a minority background.[34]

French president Sarkozy's selection of women of North African descent to high-profile cabinet positions can also be understood in this light. As interior minister, Sarkozy had condemned rioting youths of immigrant-origin as "scum," but as president he included an unprecedented number of ethnic minority women. Similar dynamics may apply to the U.S. Republicans' appointment of African Americans to prominent positions. Such appointments can bring affluent social liberals disillusioned with the party's record on race relations back into the fold. With a minority-friendly Right in play, these voters would not have to choose between their material interests and their postmaterial values.

Symbolic inclusion thus takes place when parties want to respond to voter preferences for diversity and equality, and when election outcomes do not hinge on the voting behavior of minority voters. Conversely, parties pursue

33. Reimann (2010).

34. Many immigrant-origin ethnic minorities were dismayed at the party's failure to expel Sarrazin. In his bestselling 2010 book, Sarrazin argued that immigrants lacked the innate ability and willingness to integrate into Germany's economy and social fabric, a claim that was hotly debated in the media for months. See "SPD plant parteiinterne Migrantenquote." *Die Zeit*, May 2, 2011.

vote-based inclusion once minority electorates can significantly influence election outcomes.[35] Here, parties put minority individuals on the ballot in the hopes of attracting the minority vote. To send a credible signal that the party takes the minority electorate seriously, it will include a larger number of minority candidates than it does when including symbolically. In party-list proportional representation systems, minority candidates will be placed on electable list positions rather than occupy spots that have no chance of delivering a seat. When competing for a single seat in plurality systems, minority candidates will be selected to run in districts that the party has a good chance of winning.[36]

Vote-based inclusion is not intended to send a message to the majority electorate; the main audience is the minority electorate. This applies irrespective of majority voters' preference for equality and nondiscrimination. Realizing that securing a large number of seats will only be possible with a significant degree of minority support, parties will include minority candidates who are best equipped to rally the co-ethnic vote.

Note an interesting tension here: When parties include symbolically it is actually *less* likely that minority voters will consider minority candidates to be "one of their own," but this function is often ascribed to symbolic representation. It is when parties nominate candidates to maximize minority votes that minorities are more likely to feel connected to their representatives. This disjuncture occurs because parties also have preferences of the majority electorate in mind when recruiting symbolically. Put differently, it is precisely when parties are *not* interested in the symbolic messages that representation can send and instead are after minority votes that minority representatives are more likely to be accepted as such by minority voters. This is so because each inclusion type is associated with distinct candidate types.

CANDIDATE TYPES

If parties pursue different inclusion goals, they also use different types of candidates to fulfill these objectives.[37] In the case of symbolic inclusion, where an important target audience belongs to the majority electorate, selectors will

35. On electoral appeals to minority voters and minority representation based on the relative size and electoral leverage of the minority electorate, see, e.g., Dancygier (2010, 2014), Trounstine and Valdini (2008), and Wilkinson (2004).

36. See Dancygier (2014) on variation in the desirability of seats based on the size of the minority electorate and the electoral system.

37. For an alternative, but complementary, take on candidate types, see also Canon's (1999) study of black representation in the United States. Canon distinguishes between minority candidates who highlight common interests with whites from those who emphasize intergroup difference and argues that the presence or absence of white candidates will influence what type of black candidate will be successful.

pick candidates whose values and preferences are in line with those of the party and the party's electorate at large. When minority candidates espouse preferences that hew closely to those of core supporters, the party conveys that it accepts the "right" type of assimilated minority individual. Because the selection of minority candidates is not expected to produce substantial minority votes, symbolic candidates should alienate as few majority voters as possible. Choosing a candidate who is assimilated and whose preferences on major issues are easily compatible with a party's core constituency is meant to accomplish this goal.

The preference fit between the party and the candidate is especially important with respect to issues that have been politicized in debates surrounding minority integration and stoke fierce reactions across the political divide. For instance, if a minority group is known for advocating foreign policy positions that are well beyond those of the median voter or party supporter, selectors will want to make sure to settle on a candidate whose views on these questions are more in keeping with mainstream opinion, and, moreover who can credibly signal to the majority electorate that this is the case.

In the case of European Muslims, much debate has revolved around this group's involvement in terrorist activity, its social conservatism, and its promotion of Islam in the public sphere. Parties that seek to include symbolically will therefore select candidates who can convey to voters that they adopt the "correct" stance on these issues. These stances will in turn vary a bit by party type. Parties on the Left will find it more important that candidates not be socially conservative (see also Chapter 6), while parties on the Right will want to make sure that a candidate's Muslim roots will not come into conflict with what are perceived to be traditional Christian values.

Symbolic inclusion therefore carries some risks because minority candidates may deviate from their assigned roles. For example, when Aygül Özkan, the state minister appointed by the CDU, called for eliminating crucifixes in public schools her fellow Christian Democrats responded with a firestorm of criticism, publicly questioning whether Özkan belonged in a "Christian" party. Their fierce reaction in turn exposed the motives behind her selection: "Party elites want to use Özkan to reach new voter segments in the big cities. . . . [But a] token migrant with her own opinion? That goes too far for the CDU."[38] While Özkan's proposal for banning crucifixes would not have upset the more secular support base of the Left, it was less compatible with the core constituents of Germany's Center-Right, many of whom want to uphold the country's Christian heritage.

To summarize, symbolic inclusion is intended to send a message to minorities and cosmopolitans that a party welcomes diversity. It is supposed to

---

38. For a discussion, see Reimann (2010).

mobilize these voting blocs without alienating existing constituencies. To achieve this objective, symbolic candidates cannot stray too far from party orthodoxy, especially with regard to issues that raise doubts about minority assimilation to relevant norms.

This strict adherence to majority conventions can compromise the legitimacy of symbolic candidates in the eyes of the minority community. Debates about African American representation have pointed to this tension. Here, some contend that black candidates "who are handpicked by the 'establishment,' or who must appeal to white voters in order to get elected . . . are unlikely to be authentic because they are not elected as the representatives of choice of the black community. In addition, these officials are often marginal community members whose only real connection with black constituents is skin color."[39]

By implication, when capturing the minority vote is the main objective parties must pick "authentic" candidates. Though they would of course like to settle on a candidate who fits well with established party norms and preferences, they will have to prioritize the candidate's ability to mobilize fellow group members on Election Day. Failure to obtain large shares of the minority vote when the group represents a sizable voting bloc may spell electoral defeat in single-member races and reduced seat shares in PR-list systems. As a result, party selectors will want to pick candidates who are appealing to minority voters. These candidates' preferences should therefore not deviate too much from those adopted by the minority population whose vote is being courted. Furthermore, selected candidates should have connections to minority voters and be embedded in community networks to facilitate the delivery of votes. Ideally, candidates who excel at vote mobilization also share the values and interests of the majority electorate. Yet, as I will show in the remainder of this book, this preference fit often eludes political parties. Before doing so, I will explain in greater detail what determines parties' inclusion decisions in the first place.

NET VOTE GAINS AND INCLUSION TYPES

I maintain that parties' foremost concern is the maximization of their vote shares and that calculations about the net vote gain that minority incorporation is likely to yield (when compared to exclusion) will determine parties' inclusion decisions. The voting behavior of both minorities and majorities will come into play here because sections within both groups can join or defect from parties in reaction to inclusion decisions. In other words, minorities, ethnocentrists, and cosmopolitans are not captured by a single party, a point I will return to below. When the increased minority votes that the presence of minority candidates is thought to bring about is too small to outweigh de-

39. Guinier (1991, 1103–4).

fections among the existing electorate that minority inclusion is thought to trigger, exclusion will prevail.

Symbolic inclusion takes place when the minority electorate's vote is not yet sizable enough to compensate for significant vote losses among the majority, but when the minority presence is large enough that parties expect segments of the majority and minority electorate to value or push for inclusiveness. Parties do not expect large net vote gains when they include symbolically, but hope to secure a foothold among the minority electorate while also courting cosmopolitans. Vote-based inclusion, by contrast, unfolds when the net vote gain associated with inclusion is clearly positive, and when failure to recruit the minority vote threatens a party's performance at the polls. Minority voters reward parties that select co-ethnic candidates with substantial votes, and these votes exceed the losses parties anticipate due to majority defections that this inclusion induces. Though I argue that inclusion decisions are primarily based on parties' calculation about net vote gains, in what follows I discuss that differences in these anticipated net vote gains are a function of partisanship, electoral geography, and mobilization.

PARTY AND CANDIDATE EFFECTS

Figure 2.1 captures the importance of the net vote gain and also indicates that voters' responses to minority inclusion are conditional on party and candidate type. The argument represented in these figures is based on the following assumptions. First, all else equal, there is a positive relationship between the size of the minority population and the amount of majority opposition to it. This opposition can be based on material and cultural threats. Majority voters may fear that an increase in the minority presence will also cause an increase in resource shifts away from the majority and towards the minority. Likewise, to the extent that a larger minority population is associated with a more visible minority cultural presence, a growing minority population will evoke greater cultural fears among segments of the majority electorate. Both types of threats will be magnified if minority groups can elect co-ethnics who successfully lobby for economic and cultural goods once in office. The greater the minority population, the greater the threat associated with the representation of minority interests, cultural, economic, or otherwise.[40] Second, in line with much existing research,[41] I assume that center-right parties target, on average, voters that are more ethnocentrist and less accommodating of diversity than do

40. For a detailed account of how minority political representation can prompt majority backlash, see Dancygier (2010, 2013) and Chapter 5. On the importance of group size in generating antiminority behavior, see also Adida et al. (2015), Blalock (1967), Hainmueller and Hangartner (2013), and Hewstone et al. (2002).

41. For instance, see Kitschelt (1996), Häusermann and Kriesi (2015), McLaren (2001), Sides and Citrin (2007) and Street (2014).

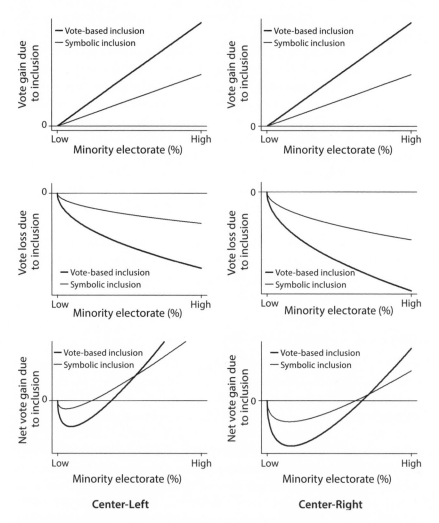

FIGURE 2.1. Vote Gains and Losses Due to Minority Inclusion

center-left parties. As a result, center-right parties foresee greater losses among their typical support base when selecting minority candidates than do those on the Left, though both types of parties will incur losses among ethnocentrists. Third, minority and majority voters and candidates have outside options; they are not tied to one particular party.

Figure 2.1 presents stylized approximations of the net vote gains parties anticipate at different levels of the minority population, and of the inclusion outcomes these are likely to produce. The top panel of Figure 2.1 depicts vote gains across parties. These gains increase with the size of the minority population, and they do so more rapidly in the case of vote-based inclusion, the inclusion type designed to maximize minority votes. Symbolic inclusion produces gains among cosmopolitans, but it yields fewer votes among the minority population. The middle panel presents vote losses that are caused by ethnocentrist departures. When the minority population is small, the backlash is still muted, but it begins to rise with the size of the minority electorate. However, not every majority voter will be susceptible to ethnocentrist appeals, and the rate of growth of defections therefore starts to decline: At intermediate levels of the minority population a relatively smaller additional share of the majority electorate moves into the antiminority camp. Vote losses are more pronounced among the Right than they are among the Left. Moreover, vote-based inclusion generates greater losses than does symbolic inclusion, because vote-based candidates are less likely to align with the preferences of existing voters than are symbolic candidates.

The bottom panel combines vote gains and losses. When the minority electorate is very small, majority opposition will not be sizable but both types of parties will still face net vote losses since the minority electorate is too small to counterbalance defections among the ethnocentrist electorate. At intermediate levels of the minority electorate, symbolic inclusion is more profitable, but as the minority electorate becomes more sizable so too do the net gains that accrue due to vote-based inclusion. At high levels of minority concentration, vote-based inclusion is the better bet for parties seeking to maximize votes. Across inclusion types net vote gains turn positive sooner for the Left than they do for the Right. It is only when the minority electorate is very sizable that minority inclusion will be a net winner at the polls for center-right parties.[42]

Parties may pursue both inclusion types simultaneously. For instance, at given levels of the minority electorate a party will realize that it can only be a viable contender if it receives considerable minority support, and it will therefore engage in vote-based inclusion. Nonetheless, it may additionally still want inclusion to send symbolic messages and to relay to the majority electorate that the party appreciates the *right type* of diversity. Parties can try to achieve these dual aims by selecting different types of candidates, but they may not always be successful in doing so. A more realistic scenario is one in which parties respond to a minority electorate that is growing over time by sequentially moving from symbolic inclusion to vote-based inclusion.

42. Note that the outcomes are similar if we assume that the selection of minority candidates prompts a higher minority vote for the Left than for the Right; in this case, the difference across parties in the size of the minority electorate associated with net vote gains will just be larger. Though in most contemporary democracies ethnic minority voters lean towards center-left parties (Bird et al. 2011a; Dancygier and Saunders 2006; Dawson 1994; Saggar 2000), this link is at least in part caused by the Left's higher rates of minority inclusion. I therefore present figures in which inclusion generates similar minority vote gains across parties.

Note that Figure 2.1 is silent on turnout and the effect of descriptive representation on turnout. If minorities and majorities (as well as ethnocentrists and cosmopolitans within the latter group) turn out at equal rates, and, moreover, if the selection of minority candidates is equally salient in determining turnout across these groups, the demographic balance between various subgroups will determine at which size of the minority electorate the net vote gain turns positive. By contrast, if minorities turn out at higher rates than do voters who are hostile to them and their political incorporation, and, relatedly, if minority inclusion triggers a higher turnout among minorities than it does among other voters, minority inclusion will generate more votes than it costs at lower levels of the minority electorate. The same is true when members of the majority population who reward parties for minority inclusion turn out at higher rates than those who will punish parties for featuring minority candidates on their lists. By the same token, when minority individuals are more difficult to get to the polls than are their detractors, minority political inclusion will require a larger minority electorate (all else equal).

Note also that when dealing with immigrant-origin residents, the minority electorate will be smaller than the minority adult population. Voting eligibility rules and citizenship regimes will therefore be important in translating numerical presence into electoral strength. All else equal, as the stringency of eligibility rules and citizenship laws decreases, a larger share of immigrant-origin residents will adopt the nationality of the new country. Criteria for citizenship can include, for instance, the existence of *jus soli* (i.e., citizenship based on the place of birth); the length of residence; the renunciation of prior citizenship; language competency; civic integration; sociocultural assimilation; and economic standing. As a vibrant literature has shown, the openness of citizenship regimes along these dimensions varies greatly across countries and within countries over time.[43] In light of this variation, incentives for electoral inclusion should differ significantly across countries as well.

ELECTORAL GEOGRAPHY EFFECTS

The previous section highlighted that the behavior of different constituencies will affect anticipated net vote gains. This implies that the ways in which these groups sort across electoral districts will shape inclusion strategies. Figure 2.1 depicts net vote gains in a district where the distribution of preferences mirrors that of the electorate at large. Yet, such a district might not be the typical district in which inclusion pressures arise. For example, local parties will not engage in symbolic inclusion if their electorates do not value diversity, even if parts of national electorates and party platforms do. Similarly, local parties

---

43. See, e.g., Brubaker (1992), Goodman (2014), Howard (2009), and Janoski (2010).

will be less afraid of a backlash if their districts contain few ethnocentrist voters.

Whether or not minority voters share the same electoral arena with cosmopolitans or ethnocentrists depends on the settlement patterns of each of these groups and on the ways in which electoral boundaries aggregate them into districts. In many advanced industrialized democracies, low-income voters, who generally exhibit above-average levels of ethnocentrism, cluster in cities. At the same time voters who espouse more cosmopolitan and minority-friendly positions and have higher income and education levels also choose to live in urban environments.[44] The same is true for ethnic minority voters. To the extent that minorities are disproportionately poorer than the majority population, they may reside in similar neighborhoods as do low-income majority voters. The balancing act of minority inclusion will thus depend at least in part on whether electoral districts are large enough to group together those who favor minority political incorporation with those who are less eager about being members of multiethnic coalitions.

Electoral geography helps determine not only whether inclusion occurs, but it will also influence the inclusion type. For instance, if the electoral arena is small and comprises mainly low-income majority and minority voters, parties may forgo symbolic inclusion altogether—few cosmopolitan votes are up for grabs here—and they will opt for vote-based inclusion at relatively higher shares of the minority electorate. We should observe the opposite when electoral districts are large. Here cosmopolitans who are in favor of minority incorporation constitute part of the electorate, but minority voting strength will be diluted in larger districts compared to smaller-sized districts (assuming some degree of spatial concentration).

Figure 2.2 illustrates the importance of electoral boundaries in aggregating voters of different types. The two rectangles each represent a city in which settlement patterns are identical in size and distribution; the overall electorate is composed of 10 cosmopolitans, 10 ethnocentrists, and 3 ethnic minorities. The only difference is that City A conducts at-large elections whereas City B is divided into nine electoral districts. In both cities, those favoring minority inclusion outnumber those who oppose it, and, if we assume that preferences about minority inclusion are central to voters' party choices, selectorates of most mainstream parties will opt for minority inclusion in City A: an alliance between cosmopolitans and minorities beats the ethnocentrist coalition. In districts that contain minorities within City B, by contrast, voters supporting minority inclusion never exceed those who oppose it. Minority voters are numerically sizable in the inner city, but they are outnumbered by ethnocentrists. Furthermore, in City B ethnic minority voters do not live in the same

44. Rodden (2010).

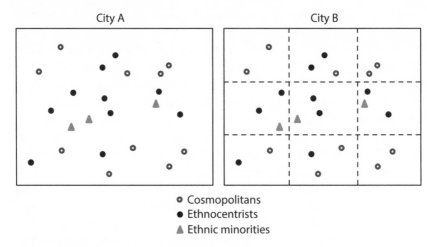

FIGURE 2.2. Electoral Geography and Voter Groups
Note: In City A elections are held at-large; the whole city forms one electoral district. In City B elections are held in 9 districts within
the city.

districts as do cosmopolitans. Symbolic inclusion is thus unlikely, though vote-based incorporation could unfold if minorities can demonstrate that their turnout is at least twice as high as that of their detractors. Finally, though Figure 2.2 compares two cities, we can also think of it as contrasting national with subnational elections. National elections should produce symbolic candidates at a higher rate than do subnational contests.

Figure 2.2 is, of course, an oversimplification: The electorate contains additional voter groups, and party stances on minority inclusion do not influence all voters in the same way. The figure serves to highlight, however, that electoral geography is critical for minority inclusion. While ward-level elections have generally been shown to boost the electoral leverage of spatially concentrated groups, the presence of ethnocentrists within the same ward can undermine this leverage. The importance of electoral geography has been key to debates about redistricting, race, and representation in the United States. It should be at least as salient in Europe, where a greater number of parties compete for the votes of specific voter groups such as cosmopolitans and ethnocentrists.

So far I have discussed how the composition of the electorate can influence inclusion outcomes, but I have not differentiated minority voters. However, it is plausible to assume that minority individuals who settle close to fellow co-ethnics evoke more opposition than those who do not live in minority enclaves.[45] Minorities that cluster together may do so because they speak the

45. Nonetheless, migrant enclaves in which residents are culturally similar to natives can also

minority language and adhere to the group's traditional customs. As a result, they generate greater hostility among ethnocentrist voters than do more assimilated minority individuals who may have left the enclave. Additionally, such concentrated minorities may create unease even among majority voters who are typically supporters of diversity and inclusiveness. Specifically, when minority preferences and traditions clash with the socially liberal preferences of voters who otherwise embrace cultural diversity, parties may hesitate to bring minorities into the fold, even if they generally (and perhaps sincerely) champion diversity and minority rights. This tension between multiculturalism on the one hand and liberalism or feminism on the other presents a dilemma that has long occupied political theorists,[46] but it also plays itself out daily on the streets and city halls of Europe. Squeezed from the left and the right, parties may surmise that minority inclusion does not pay at the polls.

In party politics, the multicultural dilemma, I argue, is particularly pronounced when it comes to ethnoreligious minorities because their traditionally minded and pious members are more likely to concentrate in urban areas than are less observant co-religionists. The tendency of religious minorities to live in cohesive spatial units arises from at least two reasons: the requirements of their faith and the social structures commonly associated with religious minority groups.

First, the daily activities related to religious practice are much more easily carried out in a dense urban space. Describing the settlement patterns of Orthodox Jews in the United States, Heilman explains:

> Orthodox Jewish practices and religious commitments were more easily satisfied in a geographically contained urban environment. Because of their adherence to strict Sabbath observance, for example, Orthodox Jews need to have synagogues within walking distance of their homes. They insist on their own schools. They demand places where kosher food can be obtained, along with holy books and other ritual articles. Neighborhoods that concentrate large numbers of Orthodox Jews in a relatively small territory can more easily sustain such schools and establishments. . . . Put differently, Orthodox Jews cannot easily live as isolated individuals scattered throughout a region.[47]

Muslims' settlement in urban Europe shares many parallels (see Chapter 3). Proximity to prayer rooms and mosques, the availability of halal foods, or access to religious schooling is much more easily realized in dense enclaves.

---

fuel resentment, because this similarity can threaten the status of natives. See Adida (2014) on this point.

46. See, e.g., Barry (2001), Kymlicka (2012), Okin (1999), Shachar (2001), and Song (2007).

47. Heilman (2000, 20).

Thus, even in the absence of negative constraints such as housing discrimination, for many groups religious observance and spatial concentration go hand in hand as a matter of necessity.

Second, and relatedly, members of ethnoreligious minority groups often display tight social linkages that both cause and further cultivate spatial concentration. Some of these networks are directly tied to religious practice. For instance, communal prayer can promote social interactions, while the provision of charitable services by religious communities can make it easier for co-religionists to engage in religious behaviors that would otherwise be too costly, particularly in a largely secular market economy.[48]

Finally, if densely populated urban space favors the settlement of observant religious groups, it may also help sustain these groups' traditional customs. The small geographic scale of urban neighborhoods facilitates the monitoring of behavior. Norm transgressions, such as failure to wear traditional dress or religious symbols, or contact with the opposite sex, are more easily observed in small, densely populated urban areas where group members encounter one another on city streets, buses, and markets than they are in more sparsely populated areas where such contact is rarer.

To sum up, if the distinctiveness of ethnic and religious traits rises in minority enclaves, districts that are conducive to minority inclusion based on the size of the minority electorate are also districts where the characteristics of the minority group are likely to evoke opposition and to do so in a way that can extend across the political spectrum.

MOBILIZATION EFFECTS

When minority spatial concentration correlates with increased and broad-based majority opposition, parties confront significant inclusion dilemmas. Yet, voters have multiple identities, and their interests span issue dimensions. Successful parties build on this multiplicity by constructing coalitions that bring together diverse groups under a common banner. If parties calculate that they could stand to benefit from minority inclusion if they reduced the ethnocentrist backlash or increased cosmopolitan support, they could highlight issues that unite these different constituencies and downplay issues that polarize them. For instance, most immigrant-origin minorities in Europe tend to be economically disadvantaged.[49] Leftist parties could therefore build elec-

---

48. For example, the long years spent studying in the Yeshiva deprives Ultra-Orthodox men of market wages, but the local religious community provides support in turn (cited in Grzymala-Busse 2013). On why and how local religious communities provide networks of material and emotional support, see Grzymala-Busse (2013).

49. See, e.g., Dancygier and Laitin (2014).

toral coalitions by drawing attention to the common experience of economic insecurity faced by low-income voters.[50] To do so, they would pick minority candidates that campaign on redistribution and economic justice and that liaise with workers' and welfare organizations. Such candidates should be more agreeable to low-income or socially liberal majority voters than those who run on their ethnoreligious identities and social conservatism.

Though a class-based strategy appears to be safe at first blush, it is in fact quite risky, at least in the short term. First, existing research suggests that building cross-ethnic, working-class coalitions is difficult: Prejudice and suspicion can undermine working-class solidarity and raise the attractiveness of ethnocentrist appeals.[51] Second, when resources are finite, it can be difficult for parties to satisfy economic demands across groups. This is especially true at the local level where material goods (e.g., schools, housing, or neighborhood renewal grants) are quite targeted and are likely to benefit some groups more than others, particularly when groups are spatially segregated.[52] Focusing on economics can therefore deepen intergroup conflict.[53] Third, when parties calculate that they can maximize their chances of winning by mobilizing the minority electorate, they will want to be sure to select candidates who can guarantee to deliver the co-ethnic vote. Candidates who are enmeshed in traditional social structures, I argue, are best able to accomplish this. When parties rely on the minority vote for electoral success, they will select candidates whose reputations are rooted in their local communities and whose social standing helps them get out the vote. In the case of ethnoreligious groups, such candidates will therefore reflect the social conservatism and piety of the local minority electorate.

I argue that when faced with the multicultural dilemma in vote-rich enclaves parties come down on the side of culture. I later demonstrate that this mobilization preference shapes contemporary inclusion outcomes of Muslims in Europe, but this development is not unique to this group. The fact that cultural traits that cause unease among parties and voters can also be usefully exploited for electoral gain has been a source of tension in other contexts. In Europe, such tensions came to the fore with respect to the "Jewish Question." Beginning in the nineteenth century, leftist intellectuals expressed contempt for practices related to mysticism, superstition, and Jews' general lack of assimilation to modern values. They were disdainful of Orthodox Jews' continued use of Yiddish, their belief in "miracle rabbis" (*Wunderrabbis*), and their

50. See Przeworski and Sprague (1986) on parties' construction of class-based political identities.

51. See, e.g., Alesina and Glaeser (2004), Huckfeldt and Kohfeld (1989), and Roemer et al. (2007).

52. Trounstine (2016).

53. Dancygier (2010).

shtetl mentality.[54] Rosa Luxemburg, for instance, saw "The Jewish 'nationality' in Tsarist Poland . . . [as] a product of social backwardness . . . and the narrowness of *shtetl* existence."[55] However, while leftists widely condemned the cultural and religious separateness of the Jewish proletariat and feared that Judaism could undercut socialism, leftist thinkers and organizers were acutely aware that ethnoreligious ties and traditions could be deployed for the socialist cause. In the early twentieth century, Russian and Polish Socialists realized that, notwithstanding their general preference for assimilated, modern Jews, it was much easier to enlist the Jewish proletariat if socialist literature and mobilization materials were written in Yiddish. The Galician Social Democratic Party even founded a Yiddish language journal (*Der Arbeter*) so that religious Jews could more easily join the class struggle.[56] One trade-off inherent in this mobilization strategy, however, is that it brings in political leaders (and followers) whose religiosity and traditionalism may clash with the preferences of existing party members and elites.

Inclusion Types and Political Consequences

Mobilization strategies that exploit ethnocultural traits, I contend, can therefore leave deep imprints on party politics. This book addresses how the vote-based incorporation of Muslims can replace a system largely built around class-based cleavages with one where partisan alliances are rooted in ethnoreligious kinship. These developments represent a general phenomenon that goes beyond the case of European Muslims. The personalistic religious vote is widespread in liberal democracies whose electoral politics are not otherwise structured around ethnicity or religion. For instance, Ultra-Orthodox (Hasidic) Jews in New York City deliver bloc votes to candidates who promise to help maintain religious traditions, even if such traditions conflict with stated party principles and average voter preferences. Hasidic views on matters like abortion, gender relations, or Middle East politics are quite different from those adopted by other core constituents and party leaders. Yet, because of the Hasidim's propensity to "vote in blocs according to the wishes of a sect's grand rabbi," politicians take note of their demands.[57] Requests for female lifeguards at municipal swimming pools, segregated seating by gender on public buses, or state funding for religious education—issues that echo flashpoints arising from Muslim inclusion—would be ignored were it not for the electoral leverage wielded by this group. In fact, officials at the local and state level have hired Hasidic advisers in the hopes of courting "that vote more aggressively

54. See, e.g., Beer (1893–94) and Wistrich (1982).
55. Wistrich (1982, 144).
56. Balakan (1905), Wistrich (1981).
57. Berger (2014).

over the more diffuse traditional [non-Orthodox] Jewish vote."[58] As with other religious minorities, spatial diffusion weakens the electoral leverage of less devout members of the group, and inclusion dilemmas follow.

Because local parties follow electoral incentives, electoral geography and mobilizational considerations can come together to create major disjunctures between the preferences of included constituencies and the principles that are expressed in party platforms. British parties' mobilization of the Irish Catholic vote provides another example. In several late nineteenth- and early twentieth-century English and Scottish constituencies, local branches of the Labour Party heavily relied on this vote.[59] This affiliation had policy implications because local Labour politicians in districts with a large Irish presence turned out to be more flexible on religious education or the role of the church in public life than the rhetoric of their party's national leadership would have warranted. However, "any threat to the electoral loyalty of this group [the Irish], whether from association with Communism or Spanish Republicanism, or from advocating secularism or birth control, was inevitably opposed by those in the party who were primarily concerned with maximizing the party's electoral support."[60]

The electoral incorporation of Irish Catholics in early-twentieth-century Glasgow presents striking parallels to contemporary Muslim inclusion. In Glasgow, Irish Catholic support

> for Labour was always conditional: questionnaires were sent to Labour candidates to determine their attitudes to moral, religious and international matters. Silence was demanded from Labour on issues such as abortion, birth control, desegregation of schooling, and so on . . . And in spite of occasional protests from Labour members worried at the close identification of Labour with Catholicism and the consequent alienation of Protestant voters, the fear of losing the Catholic vote was too great for Labour to renounce sectarian alliances. This meant that whole areas of socialist debate concerning the family and gender relations were deliberately obfuscated. . . . Although the Catholic vote never amounted to more than 30 per cent of the total electorate in the industrial wards of Glasgow, it was extremely powerful, as in most three-cornered fights it held the balance of power. This power was further reinforced by the fact that on average the turn-out at municipal elections was never more than 60 per cent, yet the Catholic votes polled varied, according to the Catholic Union, from 70 to

---

58. Cited in Berger (2014). See also Berger (2013), Heilman (2000), Nathan-Kazis (2010), and Rivera and Otterman (2012).

59. See, e.g., Fielding (1993), Flinn (2005), and McHugh (2006).

60. See Flinn (2005, 114). This quote refers to Labour's strategy in Oldham and Bolton in the 1930s. These two northern towns now have a large Muslim presence.

90 per cent. Moreover, this vote was organized more systematically by the Catholic Union, than the Protestant vote.[61]

Then as now, calculations about turnout trumped ideological considerations and left their mark on the Labour Party: Writing about the varied appeals made by local branches, Pugh states that "In time, as Labour reflected the needs of Catholic communities in northern and Scottish constituencies, its local parties gradually became socially conservative and remained so for the rest of the century."[62] The national party, though not pleased, understood these trade-offs: "Whilst the Parliamentary leadership was irritated by some of the consequences of Irish participation, it realised that in numerous constituencies their support was vital."[63]

These examples illustrate that electoral geography and turnout can come together to undermine party positions and cleavage structures. On the surface, however, not much appears to have changed, at least in the short run: Poor minorities that settle in urban areas are recruited by left parties that are both pro-poor and, in more recent decades, pro-minority. Yet, when there is little actual connection between parties' official platforms on the one hand and their local mobilization strategies on the other, minority voters are less likely to develop attachments to a particular party. Their allegiance will remain with authority figures who are prominent in their local communities. In contexts where minorities can vote for and enter more than one party, this implies that minority voters will be likely to switch their partisan allegiance on the basis of ethnic or religious ties. They will cast ballots for candidates who command authority in local minority communities, irrespective of partisan labels. In late-nineteenth-century Britain, for instance, constituencies with a high share of Irish Catholic voters could experience large swings simply as a result of "instructions of a local priest [to] the Irish vote."[64] Parties that maximize vote shares by cultivating personalistic relationships with candidates who can deliver minority votes en bloc may thus end up losing votes once additional parties vie for the minority's vote. In this way, short-term local incentives collide not only with party and voter positions nationally, they also imperil party performance in the long run.

In brief, spatially bound enclaves have the potential to turn their inhabitants into influential voters, while intragroup ties can realize this potential on Election Day. Thus, even if substantial segments of the minority electorate were to prioritize secular, economic policies it does not automatically follow that these types of concerns are channeled through the political process or

61. Knox (1988, 622–23).
62. Pugh (2002, 528).
63. Fielding and Geddes (1998, 63).
64. Pelling (1967, 246).

that their elected representatives are equally interested in lobbying for these issues. More secular and less traditional voters, even when they outnumber their more religious counterparts in the aggregate, commonly do not live in enclaves, and their collective votes therefore do not translate as easily or visibly into collective electoral leverage. Because parties are primarily interested in increasing vote shares, minority incorporation in such settings can severely strain the ideological coherence of electoral coalitions and, in the process, transform the nature of party politics.

Vote Maximization and Political Competition

The story I have told thus far assumes that parties want to maximize vote shares and that minorities' demographic size translates into electoral leverage. Yet, other accounts of ethnic politics are based on the idea that parties favor building minimum winning coalitions,[65] and research on minority political behavior has in turn found that minorities can be disengaged from the electoral process.[66] Group size and electoral influence therefore do not necessarily go hand in hand, in part because parties may prefer to govern with the support of smaller, more homogenous coalitions. These logics, I argue, do not generally comport with subnational politics in advanced, economically developed democracies for three reasons: (1) the comparatively decreased importance of targeted economic goods by local parties; (2) the uncertainty introduced by the small electoral arena and by the low cost of entry; and (3) the political agency of enfranchised minority groups.

First, the linkage between ethnic politics and minimum winning coalitions is prevalent in economically less developed patronage democracies.[67] It depends heavily on the notion that the winning party limits distribution of the finite spoils of victory to its supporters, and that voting behavior is primarily motivated by access to these goods. Adding more voters to a given coalition therefore shrinks each supporter's piece of the pie, leading voters and parties to seek out ethnically based coalitions that easily distinguish winners from losers and that are just large enough to win office but not so large as to make victory unprofitable. Though patronage and pork certainly play a role in European local politics,[68] nonpartisan bureaucracies and needs-based allocation principles make it more difficult for parties to target individual voters with material goods.

65. Chandra (2012), Fearon (1999), and Posner (2004).
66. On variation in political participation among immigrant-origin voters, see, e.g., Dancygier (2010), Hajnal and Lee (2011), Maxwell (2012), and Segura (2013).
67. Chandra (2004) and Posner (2005).
68. On this point, see Dancygier (2010) and Kitschelt (2000).

Furthermore, expansive welfare states and increased affluence reduce voters' reliance on such targeted distribution. In relatively rich democracies, voters do not cast ballots on the basis of material goods alone. "Postmaterialist" values (e.g., protecting the environment, promoting gender equality, advocating for LGBTQ rights, or enhancing personal liberties) and ethnocentrist motives also loom large.[69] Among minority voters, ethnoreligious goods such as zoning permits for religious buildings or culturally sensitive child care institutions can be just as important in influencing vote choices as is access to economic benefits (especially where such access is a matter of state regulation rather than local discretion). More generally, minimum winning coalitions are not prevalent when "policy payoffs" (rather than the division of fixed spoils) are at stake.[70]

The political economy of many advanced democracies therefore makes it less likely that subnational politicians will strive for minimum winning coalitions. Nonetheless, why should (winning) parties want to include new groups when this inclusion upsets the status quo? To answer this question, we have to consider both the context of local politics and the political agency of minority groups. When electoral districts comprise a relatively small number of voters, slight changes in turnout or voter preferences can change election outcomes. In light of this uncertainty, relying on coalitions that are expected to just barely deliver victory is a risky and potentially unwise strategy, even when elections are mainly about the distribution of patronage. For instance, though aware that larger coalitions meant smaller per capita spoils for their supporters, parties operating in the context of U.S. machine politics in the early twentieth century much preferred comfortable margins of victory.[71] This should apply even more when patronage is not at the heart of electoral politics.

In plurality ward-level local elections in Britain, for example, the difference between winning and losing is often a matter of a few hundred votes. In at-large PR-systems across Europe, lists whose percentage of the vote never exceeds the low single digits routinely send candidates to the city council and can deprive larger parties of pivotal votes. For instance, in 2012 Lhoucine Aït Jaddig was elected to the city council in the Brussels' municipality of Molenbeek on the ticket of the "Islam Party," whose founder envisions that the country will eventually be governed by sharia law. The party garnered 1,478 votes (3.8 percent) in an election where the Center-Left beat the Center-Right by only 663 votes. Since participation requirements faced by new, aspiring en-

---

69. See, e.g., Bechtel et al. (2014), Hellwig (2014), Inglehart (1990), Kitschelt (1994), and Kriesi et al. (2008).

70. Laver and Shepsle (1996).

71. It was only once their majority status was clear and assured that political machines fixed the system in their favor (i.e., by instituting rules or corrupt practices that deterred entry) and stopped trying to maximize votes. See Trounstine (2008) on this point.

trants such as the Islam Party are not too onerous—that is, campaigns do not have to be financed with large sums of money, and incumbents generally do not engage in illicit intimidation—established parties will prefer larger over smaller winning margins.

Given the uncertainty that small electorates and low-cost entry generate, I assume that subnational European parties want to maximize vote shares. Even so, this goal could still lead parties to exclude minorities. After all, minority inclusion can trigger the defection of existing voters and set off divisive internal battles. For minorities to become electoral partners whose votes sustain party success, they have to flex their electoral muscle. Whether or not vote-eligible minority groups participate in electoral politics varies, and is ultimately an empirical question that depends on the actions of both parties and minority groups themselves. Parties can actively seek to demobilize minorities through, for instance, the implementation of strict voter identification laws. This strategy has been employed to depress turnout of ethnic and racial minorities in the United States.[72]

Parties can also respond to the emergence of a new group by colluding to exclude. Preferring the status quo over the construction of new coalitions and the internal wrangling that would probably ensue, leaders from different parties can strike deals whereby they each agree to refrain from minority inclusion.[73] However, if new candidates and parties can enter the fray and win votes without too much trouble, a strategy of collusion is not easily sustainable. In the contemporary European case, subnational vote-based inclusion indeed often occurs after immigrant-origin voters demonstrate their electoral leverage by fielding their own independent candidates or by linking up with smaller parties. In East London (Tower Hamlets), for instance, the Labour Party, which was initially closed to Bangladeshis, began running Bangladeshi candidates in the early 1980s once this group had successfully nominated and elected one of their own running as an Independent and defeating Labour in the process. In Leicester, Gujarati immigrants reminded the local political establishment of their electoral strength by proposing new local parties.[74] In Belgium, Muslim voters have cast their ballots for a number of parties. Though social democratic parties tend to do well among this group, center-right and far-left lists obtain significant vote shares, and Muslim candidates run for a large variety of parties (see also Chapter 5 for a similar pattern in England).[75]

72. Key (1949) and Mickey (2015).

73. See Shefter (1994; Chapter 6) on this strategy in the context of mid-twentieth-century New York politics.

74. Dancygier (2010).

75. According to exit polls conducted in Francophone Brussels and Wallonia at the 2007 federal election, 53.6 of Muslims supported the main center-left parties (43.1 percent voted for the Socialist Party and 10.5 supported Écolo) while 33.5 percent cast ballots for the main center-right

In Germany, Muslim voters who don't feel welcome in the country's major parties have founded their own party, the "Coalition for Innovation and Justice" (*Bündnis für Innovation und Gerechtigkeit*, BIG). Its campaign posters featured a strong message that the SPD was hostile to Muslim interests and urged Muslim voters to consider alternatives. The posters displayed a picture of SPD-member Thilo Sarrazin with the slogan "the SPD gets rid of itself" (*SPD schafft sich ab*), a play on words: Sarazzin's bestselling anti-immigrant book is entitled "Germany gets rid of itself" (*Deutschland schafft sich ab*).

BIG has won seats in local races and has prompted established parties to reconsider their approach to the Muslim electorate.[76] In the northwestern city of Duisburg, home of Germany's largest mosque, Gürsel Dogan left the center-right Christian Democrats in 2004 because the party placed him on an unwinnable list position. Along with several other migrants who felt that the larger parties did not give them a fair shake, he founded the "Duisburger Alternative Liste" and managed to get elected. He later rejoined the CDU and was awarded a list position that secured him a seat on the city council.[77] Similar events transpired in Munich. Here, immigrants had threatened to put up their own list after having been placed on list positions that were sure to be losers. During the next election cycle, all major parties included immigrant-origin candidates, aiming to appeal to "immigrant communities whose ties to the SPD are not nearly as tight as they once were."[78]

In short, if vote-eligible minority groups can mobilize co-ethnics and coordinate successfully to challenge the status quo, and if parties have incentives to maximize vote shares, there should be a positive relationship between a group's relative size and its electoral influence. To be sure, it may take minorities, especially those of immigrant origin, some time to learn the ins-and-outs of the political system, thereby delaying their potential political impact. Furthermore, in rare cases, parties' winning margins may be so large that they truly do not need additional votes or can continue to win in the face of minority competitors. Alternatively, electoral margins may be so narrow that minorities can influence elections at relatively smaller sizes (though note that the

---

parties (18.7 percent for the Centre Démocrate Humaniste (CDH), and 14.8 percent in favor of the Mouvement Réformateur (MR)) (Amjahad and Sandri 2012).

76. At the time of writing, the party had secured two seats in Bonn and Gelsenkirchen, respectively. Observers have linked the party to Recep Erdogan's similarly named "Justice and Development" party; see Popp and Sehl (2011).

77. Ernst (2009).

78. *Merkur Online* "Parteien umgarnen Migranten," January 19, 2014, http://www.merkur -online.de/lokales/kommunalwahl/muenchen/parteien-umgarnen-migranten-3321295.html, accessed April 22, 2015. See also *Merkur Online* "Mehr Migranten in den Stadtrat," June 23, 2009, http://www.merkur-online.de/lokales/regionen/mehr-migranten-stadtrat-368868.html, accessed April 22, 2015.

size of winning margins can be a result of the minority presence and its effect on different voter groups and parties in the first place). On the whole, however, I posit that minority agency and party objectives generate a positive relationship between the size of the minority electorate and its electoral impact.

By contrast, if minorities lack the interest or capacity to mobilize, increases in the size of the minority electorate will not easily translate into increases in its electoral leverage.[79] The same will be true when they are captured by one party because no other party will have them, and when entry costs are high. Minorities recognize that being too closely linked to one party is not in their interest. As Malcom X admonished his followers, "Either party you align yourself with is suicide . . . once you are aligning, you have no bargaining power."[80] Nevertheless, in the United States a two-party system with high barriers to entry has coincided with partisan racial divides to produce just such an alignment. In Europe, the following chapters will show that minority alignments and subnational party strategies remain more fluid.

Scope Conditions

I expect my overall arguments to travel to advanced democracies that contain minority populations and whose electorates cast ballots on the basis of multiple cleavages. Specifically, for my arguments to hold, segments of the majority population have to make their views about ethnic diversity—be they positive or negative—part of their vote choice. Existing research indicates that in most advanced democracies, issues that go beyond the economic domain have become increasingly salient in electoral politics. Additionally, the arguments should generalize more readily to parties in which gatekeepers play an important role in deciding candidate selection, [81] and where the cost of entry for new parties or independent candidates is not high. The parts of my argument that deal with the ideological challenges of minority inclusion will travel to contexts in which minority groups have significantly different preferences from those of large sections of the majority electorate on a salient dimension, while the stipulations concerning the spatial settlement patterns of ethnoreligious minorities and how these shape parties' recruitment strategies should extend to democratic settings more broadly.

79. On the concept of capture in the case of African Americans, see, e.g., Dawson (1994), Frymer (2010), and Frymer and Skrentny (1998).

80. Cited in Hajnal and Lee (2011, 103).

81. Party elites are decisive in this regard across virtually all major parties in Western Europe, even at the subnational level, and in many other democracies. On the significance of party selectorates, see Gallagher and Marsh (1988) and Norris (1997).

Conclusion

This chapter has furnished the building blocks on which the remainder of this book rests. I have clarified how electoral incentives are connected to different types of minority inclusion and how these varied types in turn give rise to different kinds of candidates. When confronting questions of minority inclusion, parties routinely face trade-offs. This chapter has introduced the generic trade-offs faced by parties operating in diverse societies, and it has also highlighted the specific dilemmas that arise when parties consider the inclusion of Muslim candidates and voters in Europe. That the more religious and traditional group members often live in concentrated urban settlements that can be electorally influential sharpens inclusion dilemmas. These group members, I maintain, are also well equipped to supply large vote shares with ease—provided citizenship and electoral institutions allow them to do so—and can therefore sway vote-maximizing parties to overlook notable conflicts over social values and cultural practices. These calculations end up undermining ideological coherence in the short run and electoral success in the long run. In the next chapter, I delve more deeply into the social geography of Muslim preferences and how this preference distribution compares to that of their non-Muslim neighbors. Residential sorting and preference polarization confront political parties with electorates who, though sharing the same urban space, are deeply divided over social issues.

3

The Social Geography of Migration and Preferences

The previous chapter has argued that the distribution of minority and majority preferences across electoral districts plays an important role in determining inclusion outcomes. In this chapter, I provide evidence on these spatial patterns, and I focus my discussion on European Muslims. The integration of Muslims has been a salient and controversial topic across Europe. European publics and elites grapple with the Muslim presence in part because the political integration of Muslims is said to test values and behaviors that have become defining features of European states. According to this interpretation, Muslims reintroduce religious claims into largely secular public realms and, in doing so, challenge some of the liberal democratic achievements that characterize contemporary European societies. Europe's Muslims, many fear, privilege communalism over individualism; patriarchy over egalitarianism; and obscurantism over rationality. These characteristics not only drive a wedge between Muslim minorities and non-Muslim majorities, they also, so the narrative goes, encourage the spread of fundamentalist beliefs and Islamic terrorism on Europe's streets.[1]

This stylized account essentializes Muslim minorities as much as it does non-Muslim majorities. Both groups are quite heterogeneous in their belief systems and behaviors, and religion has not disappeared from Europe's public places. In fact, one common critique leveled against those who express concerns about the Muslim presence is that European publics are portrayed as much more secular, progressive, and egalitarian than they really are. By the

1. Cf. Casanova (2007), Cesari (2013), Norton (2013).

same token, Muslims in Europe vary a great deal in their levels of religiosity and in their embrace of tradition and patriarchy. Only a small minority endorses terrorist violence committed in the name of Islam.

How does this heterogeneity affect inclusion strategies? What is the extent and nature of the purported values clash when parties hope to recruit Muslim candidates and voters? This chapter argues that the preference divergence across groups is large and that it is most consequential where incentives for vote-based incorporation are greatest. The social geography of migration and settlement has heightened the potential for conflict and has sharpened the inclusion trade-offs that political parties face. Thanks to a combination of chain migration, available housing stock, and ensuing enclave formation, areas of Muslim concentration are more likely to feature conservative and religious Muslims, and they are commonly found in urban city centers. By contrast, among the non-Muslim majority city residents are more likely to be socially liberal and secular.[2] As a result of these dual processes, the potential for a values conflict is greatest in Europe's cities. But it is also in these cities that parties encounter the strongest inclusion pressures. To the extent that electoral geography favors spatial concentration, parties thus confront a situation in which the social preferences of minority groups who have electoral leverage diverge significantly from those of the majority. When low rates of citizenship deprive these groups of electoral clout, vote-seeking parties facing such preference conflicts will likely opt for exclusion.

The goal of this chapter is to convey the contours of the preference landscape that parties face when devising inclusion strategies. To do so, I draw on several sources. First, I illustrate the processes that have led to the formation of relatively religious and traditional enclaves in West European cities, making use of secondary sources that trace the migration process and ensuing enclave formation. Though these pathways are not identical across countries, they share many parallels that ultimately lead to very similar outcomes, namely to the formation of traditional, socially conservative enclaves in cities. Next, cross-national survey evidence reveals Muslims to be substantially more religious and less socially liberal than non-Muslims, and this preference divergence is especially pronounced among city residents. The ways in which Muslims and non-Muslims have settled in space consequently magnifies the preference divergence as it manifests on the ground.

In addition to these sorting processes, I argue that preferences polarize: Living near growing Muslim populations causes non-Muslims to become more steadfast in their social liberalism. In a setting where debates about patriarchy

2. For a detailed account of how the political preferences of voters differ by the degree of urbanization within advanced democracies, see Rodden (2011), who shows that political preferences in urban districts are typically more homogenous and more leftist than are those in nonurban districts.

and fundamentalism have been highly salient, these belief systems serve to draw a sharp line between minority and majority populations. Longitudinal surveys accordingly show that the presence of Muslims has contributed to preference polarization: Non-Muslims who are exposed to Muslims in their municipalities come to be more supportive of gender equality over time. Both sorting and polarization widen preference gaps across groups.

Social Geography of Migration among West European Muslims

The cultural constraints presented by enclaves—as opposed to by ethnicity or religion per se—are nicely illustrated by Naila Kabeer's study of women's labor market experiences in Bangladesh and the UK. Kabeer contrasts female garment workers in Dhaka (Bangladesh) with those in the East End of London.[3] While, in the 1990s, Bangladeshi women worked in factories alongside men in Dhaka, in London norms of purdah—the physical seclusion of women from men—prevented many women from entering the formal labor market and instead compelled them to do poorly paid piecework within the confines of their homes. Along this metric of female employment, Kabeer noted, Dhaka appears to be considerably more progressive than London even though, in both cases, women were migrants moving to cities. Yet, in Bangladesh women left behind their families, larger kinship networks, and village communities, pursuing gainful employment and independence in the city. In Britain, by contrast, entire kinship groups were transplanted from rural parts of Bangladesh to East London, bringing with them social conservatism and patriarchal social structures.

This comparison illuminates three aspects that are central to understanding the social character of Muslim communities in Western Europe today: selection, chain migration, and settlement. Specifically, initial labor migration, which represented the first entry pathway for many Muslims arriving in Western Europe in the postwar years, was characterized by a select type of migrant who was often embedded in tight family and village networks back home. This embeddedness in turn facilitated chain migration, while a combination of housing availability, immigrant preferences and discrimination led to these migrants' settling in inner-city areas that non-Muslim natives were beginning to abandon for more desirable spaces. Together, these processes have helped shape urban Muslim enclaves that are marked by religiosity, tradition, and communalism.

Family-based chain migration from rural villages in developing countries to the urban centers of advanced economies is, of course, neither new nor

3. Kabeer (2000).

restricted to Muslims headed to Europe.[4] Moreover, tightly knit enclaves often characterize the immigrant experience. Among migrant communities in the United States, kin clans that dominate these enclaves have helped uphold traditional customs and have sanctioned those who introduce progressive change, sometimes with implications for gender hierarchies. Research on Latin American and Chinese migrants in American cities, for instance, has found that the social networks underpinning migrant enclaves may help the socioeconomic advancement of men, but that these benefits elude immigrant women.[5] Understanding the distribution of preferences of Europe's Muslims and their electoral repercussions therefore yields implications for immigrants' political inclusion more broadly.

MIGRATION PROCESS AND ENCLAVE CONSERVATISM

Many migrants hailing from Muslim-majority countries were recruited during the 1950s and 1960s to work in low-skilled, manual jobs in the manufacturing sector. Most of these migrants intended to return home once they had earned enough money, though large portions ended up staying. That guestworkers and colonial migrants became permanent settlers is well known. What is less often appreciated is that this type of migration—that is, migration from rural villages in poor countries with the intention to accumulate and remit money before making the journey back home—is associated not only with certain skill profiles but also with specific social structures. Migrants for whom the primary goal of migration is to improve the lot of their families in the home country are, by definition, tied into kin structures. In fact, these migrants' ability to even make the journey and to leave behind their relatives, land, and property is usually based on strong networks of support.

These networks enable migrants to embark on prolonged journeys as family members back home take care of spouses, children, and land. Thus, Straube notes in her ethnographic study of Turkish life in Germany, "it is the traditional relationships in Turkey that facilitate emigration to Germany in the first place. Only the existence of intact, solidary relationships in the home country makes it possible to emigrate."[6] Ballard comes to the same conclusion when summarizing the South Asian migration experience in the UK.[7] Remittances of postcolonial migrants were used to invest in property in the home country or to furnish a female relative with a more attractive dowry. "Hence the initial objective of most migrants, especially peasant-famers, was to raise their fam-

4. There is a large literature about the role of social networks in structuring migration. See, e.g., Boyd (1989), Massey et al. (1987), and Palloni et al. (2001).

5. See, e.g., Hagan (1998) and Portes and Sensenbrenner (1993).

6. Straube (1987, 76).

7. Ballard (1994, 11).

ily's standing in the local social hierarchy. In such a context migration is a far less individualistic activity than is often supposed. . . most migrants regarded their continued membership of their extended families as axiomatic." Shaw also notes that "Pakistani migration to Britain was never that of self-propelled individuals intent upon creating new lives for themselves, but of migrants as representatives of their *biradaris* [endogamous kin networks based on patrilineal descent], intent upon improving the position of their *ghar* (household) and other close relatives 'at home.' "[8] For many Muslims, then, individual migration to Europe was a collective endeavor. Permanent emigration and independence from former kin and social ties were not the goals.[9]

Once in the destination country, village-kin networks significantly shaped paths of chain migration, as is common across migration streams around the globe. Young men were often sent to live with members of the same family or small village who had already found their bearings in an unfamiliar environment.[10] Information about jobs, housing, and the everyday logistics that natives take for granted was most easily obtained through these ties. Even in Germany, where employers, unions, and the state had embarked on a well-organized guestworker system, a 1972 survey of migrants in Duisburg, located in the country's industrial heartland and home to a sizable Turkish population, suggested that the majority of migrants had been more likely to hear about job opportunities from family and friends than through official channels (e.g., through the *Bundesanstalt für Arbeit*).[11] At the same time, employers themselves tapped into family networks to recruit foreign labor.[12] Chain migration was thus encouraged, and it contributed to the overrepresentation of rural migrants. In Germany, "Turkish migration became the migration of families, relatives, and friends. Strong and extended family ties and kin relationships in rural Turkey made the practice almost exclusively a channel of rural migration."[13]

It is not surprising, then, that many Muslims in Europe today trace their roots to a small number of regional clusters. For instance, over 90 percent of Bangladeshis in Tower Hamlets (East London) originate from the Sylhet region, while nearly all of Bradford's Pakistanis are from the Mirpur district in Azad Kashmir.[14] Most of Belgium's Turkish population originates from the district of Emirdağ, located in the Anatolian province of Ayfon, whose central

8. Shaw (2001, 328).

9. See also Engelbrektsson (1978) and Holtbrügge (1975).

10. See Ballard (1994), Engelbrektsson (1978), Gitmez and Wilpert (1987), and Samad (1996, 91).

11. Holtbrügge (1975, 80).

12. See Akgündüz (2008, 91–92), Böcker (1994, 88), and O'Loughlin (1980, 264).

13. Gitmez (1991, 121–22).

14. Samad (1996, 91).

town counts about 20,000 residents, many of whom live in houses that are owned by relatives living in Western Europe.[15] Among Sweden's Turkish population, the largest group hails from the town of Kulu, located in Central Anatolia. Even though only 8,905 residents lived in Kulu in 1965, by 1975 the town had sent an estimated 4,000 of its own to Sweden. These migrants have mostly settled in the Greater Stockholm area. Half of the migrants who came to the Netherlands from Elazığ in Eastern Anatolia settled in The Hague.[16] Likewise, settlements of Berlin's East Anatolian and Kurdish populations originate from a small number of villages.[17]

Though contemporary European public debate highlights the religious background of immigrant communities hailing from Muslim-majority countries, family and village-based chain migration suggests that these communities' religion is but one of many salient identity markers in the destination country. At the more local level, narrower identifications based on neighborhood, caste, sect, or kinship group come into play. Among Pakistanis in Britain, such identifications significantly structure social relations and, as we will see in later chapters, electoral politics.[18] Indeed, rates of cousin-marriage have remained high and have been estimated to be significantly higher among British Pakistanis than among Pakistanis living in Pakistan.[19] It is therefore not surprising that kinship links remain highly salient. Among Turks in Western Europe, the social reference group of the highest importance consists of the husband's extended family.[20]

These social networks of kin and clan have deeply affected the character of Muslim enclaves in European cities. Muslim families began to reconstitute the social norms and behaviors of the home village as concepts of family honor and social standing—often the main motivators for what was intended to be temporary migration—remained of vital importance in the new setting.[21] Information about behaviors in the new country could be easily transmitted to friends and families back home, while the dense settlement of the enclave meant these could be monitored in the first place. As the years progressed, the establishment of shops, cafés, tea rooms, and mosques reinforced pre-existing social norms. In some Turkish restaurants in Germany, for example, separate

15. Timmerman (2006, 132).

16. Akgündüz (2008, 90–92).

17. Gitmez and Wilpert (1987, 95).

18. Akhtar (2013), Saifullah Khan (1976), Shaw (2000).

19. Shaw (2000) relies on a sample of 70 marriages between Pakistani-origin migrants in Oxford and finds that 41 (59 percent) are between first cousins while only 6 consist of spouses from different *biraderis*. See also Muttarak and Heath (2010) who, examining ethnic groups in Britain, find the highest rates of co-ethnic marriage among Indians, Pakistanis, and Bangladeshis but also increased exogamy in the second generation.

20. Straube (1987, 75).

21. For a review about the social implications of transnational kinship ties beyond the Muslim European experience, see Levitt and Jaworsky (2007, 137–39).

sections are closed off for families so that women do not encounter men from outside their kin group.[22] Though these institutions serve many functions, they also make it possible to observe and sanction violations of tradition and honor. Some Muslim women may therefore not leave the home unaccompanied, as this could invite rumors with repercussions in the home village.[23] Writing about gender roles among Pakistanis in West Yorkshire in the 1980s, Afshar concludes that "cultural ties and the moral economy of kin have proved remarkably firm" with familial control remaining intact even after several decades of settlement.[24] Similarly, strong "transnational ties between Turkish communities in Flanders and in the region around Emirdağ . . . enable 'transnational social control,'" and leave their mark on gender relations in the destination country.[25] The reconstruction of village networks and norms thus had a strongly conservatizing impact on the enclave. Indicators of this development have been, for instance, the increased intensity of religious practice and concerns about the education and conduct of girls.[26]

Representative opinion surveys match up with these more local accounts. When asked "How religious are you?" on a scale from zero to 10, European Muslims gave an average response of 7 compared to native non-Muslims whose average score was a 4.7 (see Figure 3.1).[27] Muslims also adhere to more conservative gender norms: 60 percent of European Muslims and 39 percent of non-Muslim natives believe that a woman should be willing to cut down on gainful employment for the sake of her family. Whereas close to a third of Muslims do not think that gays and lesbians "should be free to live their own life as they wish," this is true for only one in ten non-Muslims. Though both groups are quite diverse in their views, based on these responses Muslims are considerably more religious and socially conservative than non-Muslim Europeans. Note, however, that the opinion gap is much smaller when it comes to redistribution (see Figure 3.1), a subject that is highly salient in

22. Straube (1987, 62).

23. Afshar (1989), Dale (2002), Straube (1987, 82–83).

24. Afshar (1989, 211).

25. Timmerman (2006, 128).

26. Shaw (1994), Werbner (1990), Nielsen (1999, 28–29).

27. These figures are based on the European Social Survey (2013; covering years 2002–2010), with the sample restricted to the EU-15, Norway and Switzerland. The ESS is a good resource because it asks pertinent questions about religion and social values, and it does so every other year covering a wide range of European countries. Yet, there are drawbacks. The survey does not specifically sample Muslim or immigrant minorities, and it is administered in the language of the survey country. As a result, we miss respondents who do not speak the country language and who are presumably less assimilated and perhaps more religious and conservative. The results may therefore be an underestimate of the religiosity and social conservatism of Europe's Muslims (and are therefore biased against finding the kind of effects that I anticipate), but previous studies do find that immigrant populations, including those originating from Muslim-majority countries, are relatively well sampled in the ESS (Just et al. 2014, 132).

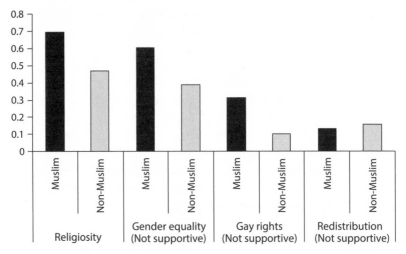

FIGURE 3.1. Religiosity and Preferences by Religion (EU-15, Norway, and Switzerland)
Note: The y-axis measures respondents' religiosity and the proportion of respondents that do not support a given policy, respectively. The religiosity measure asks respondents how religious they are on a scale from 0 to 10 (and is divided by 10). See Appendix B for variable descriptions.

European politics and that shapes partisan attachments. Only small minorities in each group disagree with the idea that the government "should take measures to reduce differences in income levels" (see Appendix B for the exact question wording).

Taken together, this distribution of preferences implies that Muslims do not make logical constituents for leftist parties, the more typical political agents of minority inclusion. Muslims are more conservative on social issues, and they are not substantially more supportive of government intervention aimed at reducing income differences. Indeed, Figure 3.2 further demonstrates that European Muslims' levels of religiosity and positions on social issues align more closely with non-Muslims who place themselves on the right side of the political spectrum than they do with those that identify with the Left.[28] It is only in the area of government redistribution that Muslims take a relatively centrist position.

While migrants, especially of the second and third generation, also acculturate to the environment of the host society, the enclave dynamics outlined just above slow down this process.[29] The dense infrastructure of the enclave— combined with native prejudice—makes it less likely that natives and migrants

28. The item tapping ideology reads: "In politics people sometimes talk of the "left" and "right." Using this card, where would you place yourself on this sale, where 0 means the left and 10 means the right?" Respondents who answered 0–4 were coded as identifying with the Left; respondents who responded 6–10 were coded as identifying with the Right. Those who selected 5 are excluded here.

29. On acculturation processes, see Maxwell (2013).

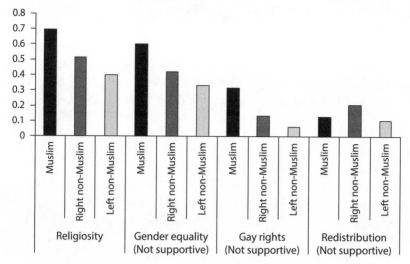

FIGURE 3.2. Religiosity and Preferences by Religion and Ideology (EU-15, Norway, and Switzerland)

Note: The y-axis measures respondents' religiosity and the proportion of respondents that do not support a given policy, respectively. The religiosity measure asks respondents how religious they are on a scale from 0 to 10 (and is divided by 10). See Appendix B for variable descriptions.

will interact. By the 1990s, for example, a survey of Berlin's Turkish-origin youth (aged 16 to 25) documented that 30 percent only very rarely came into contact with German youth, and 34 percent had no such contacts.[30] Already back in the late 1970s, a study of the Turkish population in Nuremberg (southern Germany) found that two-thirds of the city's Turks only had Turkish neighbors and most lived in extended families and followed Turkish cultural practices and norms, leading the author to conclude that "Little Turkey has taken root in Germany."[31] A young man born in Germany with parents originating from a Kurdish Alevi village in eastern Anatolia described the situation in Berlin as such: "Social relations are only with people from the same village.... Everyone is related to everyone else anyway.... Everything which happens to us here, every new event, is immediately known back in the village. That's why people are very careful here."[32]

Berlin is home to one of the largest, most densely concentrated Turkish populations in Germany. Examining the Turkish-origin population as a whole and looking at more recent trends, it is clear that intergroup contact has increased. A 2008 survey of individuals with Turkish roots living in Germany shows that only 9 percent have no contact with the German-origin, non-Turkish population and that when contact occurs it is most often in one's

30. Çağlar (1995, 310).
31. Bostanci (1982, 84).
32. Cited in Gitmez and Wilpert (1987, 95–96).

neighborhood. The same survey reports that 42 percent of Turks had regular or daily friendly interactions with Germans in their leisure time. Nonetheless, nearly one-third stated that such contact occurred rarely or never.[33] A survey of Antwerp residents similarly indicated that 40 percent of Muslim residents had daily or weekly interactions with "ethnic others" in their free time, while 19 percent had no meaningful contact with outgroups.[34] In Paris (18th Arrondissement), patterns of intergroup contact are very similar: 43 percent of Muslims answered that they met with members from other ethnic groups on a daily or weekly basis, but 21 percent said they did so "at least once a year" (but less than monthly) or never.[35]

Overall, then, the general trend is one of increased societal integration amid continued separation of a significant minority. Though most research concludes that alarmist notions of segregated, "parallel societies" (*Parallelgesellschaften*) are overstated, several processes nevertheless help preserve the closed-off nature of the enclave.[36] The fear or experience of discrimination and racist violence, for instance, keeps many in the relative safety of the enclave.[37] Additionally, the arrival of marriage partners from abroad can further sustain traditional structures, especially as girls who are brought up in Europe are less likely to accept social hierarchies that place women at the bottom.[38] Survey evidence corroborates this idea: Among Turkish and Moroccan women in Belgium, "imported brides are apparently recruited among the more conservative segments of the population in the sending areas," and their views on purdah, on the wearing of the headscarf, as well as their preference for having boys over girls, are more in line with older, first-generation migrant women than they are with second-generation females in the same age group.[39] In Germany, the 2008 survey likewise found that Turkish marriage migrants were less likely to establish contacts with Germans than, for example, those of the second generation or those with high levels of education.[40]

In an immigration policy context where non-EU labor migration is increasingly difficult, marriage migration represents one of the few available legal

33. Sauer and Halm (2009, 83–86).

34. Open Society Foundations (2011a, 57).

35. Open Society Foundation (2012, 100). On residential diversity and its effects on social relationships in France, see Algan et al. (2016).

36. In its summary report, based on research in 11 EU cities, the Open Society Institute ([OSI] 2010, 23) concludes that its survey "results run contrary to the view that Muslims live parallel or segregated lives, or do not feel a sense of belonging or attachment to the city or country where they live." On the relationship between residential segregation and integration, see, e.g., Phillips (2010). Using British survey data, Heath and Demireva (2014) reject the idea that the integration of ethno-religious minority groups has failed.

37. Cf. Dancygier and Laitin (2014), Open Society Foundations (2011).

38. Lesthaeghe and Surkyn (1995), Straube (1987), Timmerman (2006).

39. Lesthaeghe and Surkyn (1995, 17).

40. Sauer and Halm (2009, 83).

entry options, and it has remained a significant source of immigration.[41] In 2007, overwhelming majorities of Turkish-origin respondents of the second generation sampled in cities in Sweden, the Netherlands, Belgium, Germany, Switzerland, and Austria married Turkish-origin spouses, and in most of these countries (all except Germany and Sweden) these spouses were born in Turkey. Having parental roots in rural Anatolia reduces the likelihood of marrying a native non-Turk.[42]

ENCLAVE CONSERVATISM IN THE CITY

Last, enclave formation has largely occurred in cities. In many cases, the reconstruction of village networks and their attendant social norms has taken place in highly urbanized, densely populated settings. The arrival of wives and children coincided with declining industrial employment, increased joblessness and the resulting departure of many native families from Europe's inner cities. In addition to general economic downturns hitting these areas in the 1970s, much of their housing stock had not been updated in decades. Nineteenth-century terraced housing (especially in the UK) and run-down apartment buildings with outdated plumbing, no central heat, and few amenities had become unattractive to native residents. These dwellings were thus available and affordable to migrant families, many of whom maintained frugal lifestyles as they continued to invest their earnings in their home villages.[43] In Brussels, for instance, 77 percent of Turks and 80 percent of Moroccans lived in prewar buildings in 1991, compared to 41 percent of the remaining population. The same year, 22 percent of Turks and 30 percent of Moroccans lived in dwellings that did not have a bath or shower, but this was true for only 14 percent of other residents.[44] In Vienna, data from the 1990s indicate that about "95 per cent of all Turks . . . live in urban areas with a predominantly old housing stock."[45] In Paris, approximately half of the households headed by Moroccans, Algerians, or Turks are said to live in poor-quality housing, but such housing disadvantage only affects 11 percent of the general population.[46]

Many immigrants, including Muslims, have also chosen to live in social housing. They oftentimes moved into apartments that native families had started to leave behind. In France, this type of housing succession in the social

41. Böcker (1994), Shaw (2001).

42. See Huschek et al. (2012). These findings are based on "The Integration of the European Second Generation" (TIES 2007–2008) survey. The study also finds that partner choice for first-generation Turks decreases with the human capital of both parents. See also Böcker (1994).

43. See Ballard (1994), Gitmez and Wilpert (1987, 90–91), O'Loughlin (1980), Özüekren and van Kempen (1997), and Werbner (1990, 12ff).

44. Kesteloot et al. (1997, 78).

45. Giffinger and Reeger (1997, 59).

46. OSI (2010, 139).

housing sector was common. In Britain, where council housing consists of different types of housing, ranging from flats in large estates to smaller houses, competition over social housing often arose. However, outside of London most Muslim families of South Asian origin have opted for private, owner-occupied housing.[47]

Muslim migrants' housing options have thus generally been located in urban city centers, close to railway stations, or alongside industrial zones.[48] The residential patterns of Muslim communities are therefore marked by concentration and segregation, though differences in housing policies and in the availability and type of housing have led to some cross-national variation.[49] In Vienna, for example, Turks cluster in "working-class milieus," and since their initial settlement their degree of spatial segregation has increased.[50] Even where spatial clustering at the neighborhood level appears less pronounced, as, for example in German cities, early studies demonstrate that segregation "increases dramatically as the unit of measurement decreases so that almost total segregation is present between apartment buildings."[51] Further, such concentration is more pronounced among Turks than among Greeks and Yugoslavs, two groups that constitute large segments of Germany's guestworker population.[52] More recent studies show that, across European cities, migrants originating from Muslim-majority countries tend to score highest on segregation indices, ahead of migrants from other non-European countries.[53]

Preferences for living among co-ethnics combine with low incomes to explain some of these housing choices. However, discrimination by realtors and landlords—including by local authorities—and fear of racism in predominantly non-Muslim neighborhoods have also been critical. Immigrant families who did try to move into nicer neighborhoods often encountered landlords who were unwilling to rent or sell to migrants,[54] a practice that continues to impede socio-economic integration and to foster segregation.[55] In Sweden, for example, research has shown that landlords are less likely to rent apartments to applicants with Arabic-sounding names than to applicants whose names denote a Swedish background.[56] Surveys of self-perceived discrimina-

47. Dancygier (2010).

48. Dasetto (1996, 285), O'Loughlin (1980).

49. Differences in the measurement of geographic units and of migrant groups (e.g., by nationality or by country of birth) make cross-national comparisons difficult (van Kempen 2005; Musterd 2005, 2012).

50. Giffinger and Reeger (1997, 59).

51. O'Loughlin (1980, 275).

52. This assessment is based on a study of Düsseldorf; see O'Loughlin et al. (1987).

53. For a discussion, see Koopmans (2010).

54. O'Loughlin et al. (1987).

55. Cf. EUMC (2006).

56. See Ahmed and Hammarstedt (2008), Ahmed et al. (2010), and Bengtsson et al. (2012).

tion also show that respondents born in non-OECD countries (in Africa, Latin America, and the Middle East) report more instances of discrimination than those born in OECD countries.[57] Similar forms of housing discrimination have been documented across Western European countries.[58]

In brief, the migration and settlement patterns that characterize the Muslim presence in Western Europe have led to the replication of village and kin networks in European cities. Many Muslim migrants hail from rural villages in developing countries where religiosity and patriarchy are the norm. It is therefore not surprising that Muslims exhibit higher degrees of religiosity and are more supportive of conservative social norms than is the non-Muslim European population. To be sure, Europe's Muslim population is quite heterogeneous in its social values and behaviors. A significant portion espouses preferences and religious behaviors that mirror those of the non-Muslim majority population, especially when considering the second generation.[59] Yet, the residential patterns of both groups serve to exacerbate the values gap as it occurs in the localities of settlement.

When breaking down responses to the survey questions cited above by urban vs. nonurban residence, we find that religious and socially conservative Muslims and secular and socially liberal non-Muslims are both found in cities (see Appendix B for statistical analyses). Whereas Muslim urbanites are considerably more religious and espouse significantly more conservative views on gender equality and gay rights, this is not true for non-Muslims residing in big cities.[60] Further, when restricting the sample to citizens (who can participate in elections), these gaps do not diminish. Urban settlement coincides with progressivism among the non-Muslims electorate, and with religiosity and conservatism among Muslim voters.

MUSLIM ECONOMIC DISADVANTAGE

Ethnic minorities and liberal members of the majority population often join forces in politics,[61] but these ideological differences significantly complicate parties' coalition-building efforts. Yet, whereas Muslims' comparatively conservative views make for an uneasy fit with the Left, we might nevertheless

57. Lange (2000), Myrberg (2007).

58. EUMC (2006), OSI (2010).

59. See, for example, McAndrew and Voas (2014). Studying members of the Turkish-origin second generation across four European cities, Fleischmann and Phalet (2012) find mixed support for the secularization hypothesis.

60. Since I am interested in the distribution of Muslim preferences across space—not across individuals with different characteristics—I do not control for other individual-level covariates such as education. Nonetheless, when controlling for respondents' highest level of education, results remain largely similar.

61. Browning et al. (1984).

imagine successful coalitions based on shared economic interests. Muslims' economic position should put this group squarely within the social democratic camp. European Muslims are, on average, less economically successful than the non-Muslim population. The sources of this disadvantage are varied. Immigration regimes that focused on the recruitment of low-skilled labor; national governments and migrant groups who regarded settlement as temporary and who therefore underinvested in skill formation; the low share of Muslim women in the labor force; and discrimination in schools and labor markets are some of the reasons driving Muslims' economic position in Europe.[62]

Though it appears that Western Europe's Muslim population faces more daunting economic challenges than does the non-Muslim majority population, it is difficult to obtain exact figures because most countries do not collect data on the basis of religion. As a result, researchers tend to rely on national origins to draw inferences about the labor market position and welfare use of Muslim residents.

When using national origin as a proxy, it is apparent that Muslim unemployment rates are substantially higher than are those of the native, non-Muslim populations. In the Netherlands in 2009, for instance, those originating from Turkey and Morocco registered unemployment rates of 10.0 and 12.3 percent, respectively, while less than 4 percent of the native Dutch were unemployed. As a result, these groups are also much more likely than natives to receive social assistance. Among Turks, 8.3 percent are recipients of such benefits, compared to 12.1 of Moroccans, and only 1.6 percent of the native Dutch population.[63] In Denmark, Turks and Iraqis are four and six times more likely, respectively, to be unemployed than is the overall population. In France, first-generation Algerians have an unemployment rate triple that of the native French population (30.1 vs. 10.1 percent), while one in four Moroccans and Turks is without a job.[64] The unemployment rate of Turkish nationals in Germany is twice as high as the national average. Moroccans and Turks in Belgium are a staggering five times more likely to be jobless than the average Belgian, leading to similarly extreme differences in poverty: In 2001, 10 percent of native Belgians and close to 60 percent of Turks and Moroccans lived in poverty.[65]

---

62. On the link between migration types and labor market performance, see Constant and Zimmermann (2005). On employer discrimination against Muslims, see Adida et al. (2010). For an extensive discussion and a review of the literature on the labor market disadvantages faced by immigrant-origin minorities in Europe, see, Zimmermann et al. (2008) and Heath and Cheung (2007).

63. Gijsberts and Dagevos (2010, 143 and 150).

64. These figures refer to the population aged between 18 and 40; see Zimmermann et al. (2008, 15–16).

65. OSI (2010, 112); Van Robaeys and Perrin (2006).

Immigrants from Muslim-majority countries not only face difficulties find-ing employment, but are also paid less than native workers. In the Netherlands, the hourly wage of Turks and Moroccans is approximately 70 percent that of the Dutch majority population. In Denmark, Turks earn two-thirds and Iraqis make only about half of what the average Danish population earns.[66] A similar picture of disadvantage emerges in Britain where Muslims exhibit the lowest activity rate, the highest unemployment rate, and the lowest earnings among all religious groups. Muslims' low labor market participation is in part driven by the fact that less than a third of Muslim women work, but even Muslim men are less likely to be in the labor force than men of other faith groups.[67] In line with their position in the labor market, British Muslims are also overrepre-sented in neighborhoods that suffer from economic deprivation.[68]

The economic position of European Muslims should make this group a natural ally of the Left and an unlikely partner for the Right. At the same time, leftist parties may hesitate to incorporate Muslims on an economic basis: non-Muslim low-income voters may fear that including Muslims in class-based, interethnic coalitions will erode their claims to economic resources. Anti-immigrant and anti-Muslim forces have skillfully exploited such fears, and the competition over economic goods—real and perceived—is a central element in the non-Muslim backlash against Muslims' electoral inclusion.[69] Though the preference fit between Muslims and center-left parties along the economic dimension may be high, the ways in which economic interests play out on the ground can put leftist parties in a bind, particularly since divergent social pref-erences further undermine coalition-building efforts. Conversely, traditional social norms are less of a problem for center-right parties. Yet, these parties will be reluctant to accommodate ethnic minority constituents because of identity-based concerns among their core voters.

Preference Polarization

Up to now I have described how settlement and sorting generate vast prefer-ence gaps between groups. Though segments of the Muslim population as-similate, the rest of this chapter shows that non-Muslims more firmly embrace

---

66. Zimmermann et al. (2008, 15).

67. See Hills et al. (2010, 149) and findings from the UK Census, available at www.nomisweb .co.uk (my calculations). For additional evidence of Muslim economic disadvantage in the UK, see Saggar (2009).

68. Peach (2006).

69. For detailed accounts of materially driven confrontations between immigrant-origin mi-norities (including Muslims) and natives in Europe, see, e.g., Dancygier (2010, 2013), Eade (1989), and Ouseley (2001). McCarty et al. (2006) also note that natives might resist joining forces with immigrants in the United States if this leads to a decrease in per capita goods distribution.

their social liberalism as they are exposed to a conservative minority group. This polarization in turn slows down the closing of preference gaps.

It may well be true that some (rightwing) critics of the Muslim presence are insincere in their defense of gender equality and gay rights, but it is also plausible that the immigration of groups with significantly more conservative views and the ubiquitous political debates that follow have served to reinforce progressive values among non-Muslim natives.[70] If this liberalization occurs, we would expect this process to apply to views about gender equality. The role of women is a particularly salient topic in the debate about Muslim integration, and about minority groups more generally. As Phillips and Saharso note, politicians and media outlets typically cite disagreements about women's rights as the

> main example of value divergence. . . . Abuses of girls and women figure high in the daily chit-chat through which people represent or misrepresent minority cultures, as in accusations that "they" don't encourage their girls to continue in education, that "they" punish sexual transgressions in females while tolerating similarly transgressive behaviour in males, that "they" expect their wives to be docile and submissive, or don't allow women to work outside the home . . . the preoccupation with oppressive gender relations in minority cultural groups is also increasingly evident in policy initiatives across Europe, where there is now a considerable amount of legislation and intervention designed to protect the rights of girls and women in minority groups.[71]

Irrespective of the fact that non-Muslim majorities are not uniformly united behind the goal of gender equality, the settlement of Muslims has raised the public salience of this issue, and positions on gender roles increasingly serve as dividing lines that differentiate both groups. As a result, majority societies may become more supportive of gender equality as they are confronted with relative gender inequality. Such trends would illuminate some facets of the divisive debate about multicultural integration: Defenders of multiculturalism accuse its detractors of wrongly depicting the majority society as overly progressive, and they further charge that highlighting gender inequities in minority cultures allows the majority to divert attention from the hierarchies that govern its own gender roles.[72]

To help address whether gender norms change when non-Muslims encounter Muslims, I turn to developments in Britain where we can examine longitudinal surveys that track the same individuals over the course of nearly

70. This mechanism is consistent with tenets of self-categorization theory, whereby individuals have a tendency to differentiate in-groups and out-groups on a salient dimension (Fiske 2010).
71. Phillips and Saharso (2008, 294).
72. Gressgård and Jacobsen (2003), Pitcher (2009, 120ff).

two decades. Every other year these surveys include questions about gender equality and therefore allow us to investigate processes of change.[73] Britons' views about gender equality fall somewhere in the middle of the European distribution. Drawing on the same Europe-wide survey cited earlier,[74] in the EU-15, Norway, and Switzerland, 39 percent of non-Muslim natives agree with the statement that women should be prepared to cut down on paid work for the sake of family, while 40 percent disagree (the rest are undecided). In Britain, 38 percent agree and disagree, respectively (by comparison, 60 percent of native non-Muslim Swedes reject traditional gender roles and 16 percent support them). Unlike in Sweden or Denmark, where the overwhelming majority favors gender equality, in Britain there is still considerable room for opinions to shift in a more (or less) egalitarian direction.

As in other European countries, the question of whether or not minority communities—and especially Muslims—endorse equal rights for women and men has been in the political and media spotlight in Britain. Horrific instances of honor violence and examples of abusive forced marriages have appeared in the headlines and have been discussed at the elite level.[75] Figure 3.3 depicts trends in the number of articles, published in the *Times of London* between 1990 and 2012 (by year and by month), that discuss the unequal treatment of Muslim women abroad and in the UK. Table 3.1 breaks types of gender inequality down into (not mutually exclusive) categories. (I repeated the analysis with the *Guardian,* a left-of-center publication, and the trends are very similar.) Overall, 1,471 articles were published that mention gender inequality in the context of Muslim women (note that this represents nearly all—that is, 99.98 percent—articles that mention the words "women and Islam" or "women and Muslim"). Two-thirds of articles cover foreign countries, and the remainder relates these issues as they unfold in the UK. One-third of the domestic articles make specific reference to migrants from Pakistan and Bangladesh (most domestic articles do not refer to a country of origin). The majority of Muslims in the UK hails from these two countries.

Interestingly, the spike in 2006 represents the controversy that erupted when Labour MP Jack Straw suggested that Muslim women in his constituency, but also in the country as a whole, should consider removing full-face veils to foster communication and integration. The media firestorm that ensued exemplifies the tensions that politicians face when confronting

73. Specifically, the British Household Panel Survey (BHPS) carried out interviews from 1991 to 2009 (see University of Essex 2010). The average number of individuals per survey is 13,277. The survey includes local area identifiers so that individuals can be placed within localities; I can therefore test how changing minority-group contexts contribute to changes in attitudes, controlling for a host of other variables that vary at the individual and at the locality level.

74. ESS (2013).

75. Meetoo and Mirza (2011).

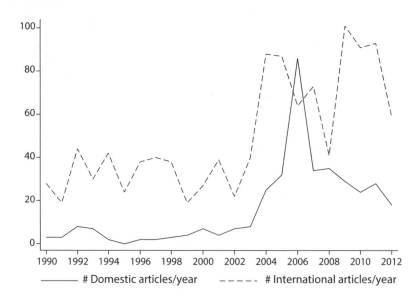

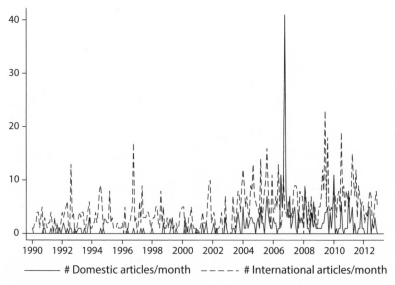

FIGURE 3.3. Yearly and Monthly Newspaper Coverage of Women and Islam in the *Times of London*, 1990–2012

multicultural dilemmas as they play out in their districts. While some perceived discriminatory intent when minority behaviors are being called into question, others welcomed an earnest debate about minority rights and responsibilities. The chairman of the London-based Islamic Human Rights Commission, Massoud Shadjareh, fell in the former camp and condemned the remarks: "It is astonishing," Shadjareh commented, "that someone as experi-

TABLE 3.1. Articles Making Reference to Women and Islam in the *Times of London*, 1990–2012 (%)

	All (N=1,471)	International (N=1,100)		Domestic (N=371)	
		All	Pakistan or Bangladesh (N=152)	All	Pakistan or Bangladesh (N=131)
Inequality and repression	62	68	77	46	48
Exclusion from education or labor market	26	30	33	14	19
Violence against women	34	36	56	27	49
Honor violence against women	12	12	18	14	16
Forced marriage	8	4	7	19	34
Female genital mutilation	3	2	1	4	5
Veiling/covering	46	46	21	46	31
Polygamy	3	3	0	5	10

Search terms: Women and (Islam* or Muslim); excludes articles that do not make reference to any of these eight dimensions and where women's issues are mentioned only peripherally.

enced and senior as Jack Straw does not realise that the job of an elected representative is to represent the interests of the constituency, not to selectively discriminate on the basis of religion." Political opponents were also quick to denounce Straw. Simon Hughes, then-president of the Liberal Democrats, stated that "Commenting on the dress of any constituent of whatever cultural background is highly insensitive. The experience of visiting their MP is difficult enough for many people without having to consider a dress code. These women have come to their elected representative for help and advice, not for recommendations on appropriate clothing."[76]

Others praised Straw for raising an issue central to both Muslim integration and women's rights. Salman Rushdie, never one to mince words, noted that Straw had been "expressing an important opinion, which is that veils suck, which they do. I think that the veil is a way of taking power away from women."[77] Saira Khan, a prominent British TV personality of Pakistani descent, said many moderate Muslim women would welcome the remarks: "This is an opportunity for them to say: 'I don't wear the veil but I am Muslim.' . . . This is my message to British Muslim women—if you want your daughters to take advantage of all the opportunities that Britain has to offer, do not encourage them to wear the veil. We must unite against the radical Muslim men who would love women to be hidden, unseen and unheard. I was able to take

76. Webster and Jenkins (2006).
77. Gledhill (2006).

advantage of what Britain has got to offer and I hope Mr Straw's comments will help more Muslim women to do the same."[78]

Though the discussions that Straw's comments unleashed were extensive, they nonetheless highlight that the Muslim presence has propelled questions of gender equality into the media spotlight and that disparities in gender norms can draw bright lines between minority and majority communities. A change in attitudes among non-Muslims should therefore be particularly likely in the British—and wider European—context where the treatment of women by Muslims at home and abroad has received considerable media attention.[79] Finally, in addition to media coverage, other visible markers of Muslims' more conservative gender norms are the very low employment rates of Muslim women, According to the 2001 census, only 31 percent of Muslim women re-siding in England and Wales were in the labor force compared to about twice that among all other ethnoreligious groups.

The social geography of migration has magnified preference divergence by slotting conservative Muslims and liberal non-Muslims in the same urban space. On top of this sorting process, I posit that polarization further sharpens inclusion dilemmas as residents who are exposed to Muslims become more supportive of equal gender roles. Even if individuals who live in diverse areas are more socially liberal to begin with or possess certain characteristics that push them towards gender equality, by examining the views of the same indi-viduals over time as the composition of their municipalities changes we can examine whether an increase in residential exposure to Muslim communities contributes to liberalizing attitude change *within* individuals. If at work, this polarization effect could help explain why gender equality has become such a key issue in debates about Muslim integration.

To measure views about gender roles I analyze answers to the following question: "Here are some questions about the family and women's role and work outside the household. Do you personally agree or disagree. . . . A hus-band's job is to earn money; a wife's job is to look after the home and family." Answers include strongly agree (1), agree (2), neither agree nor disagree (3), disagree (4), and strongly disagree (5). This question evokes more patriarchal gender roles than the earlier ESS item, which does not mention husbands, and is less strongly worded. As a result, native non-Muslim Britons are less likely to opt for the conservative answer: One in five agree or strongly agree with the statement compared to one in two who disagree or strongly disagree. A sizable share (28 percent) is undecided. Among Muslims, views are noticeably more conservative: 43 percent agree with a traditional gendered division of labor. Yet, it is also noteworthy that 30 percent of Muslims disagree with such

78. Khan (2006).

79. On the interplay between national media salience and local demographic change in the production of anti-immigrant sentiment in the United States, see Hopkins (2010).

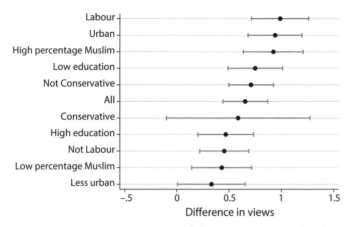

FIGURE 3.4. Differences in Views about Gender Equality across Muslims and non-Muslims in Britain, by Subgroup

Note: The circles indicate the size of the opinion gaps; the capped lines indicate the upper and lower bounds of the 95 percent confidence interval. A positive difference indicates the degree to which non-Muslim natives are more support-ive of equal gender roles than are Muslims. See Table 3.2 for the variable description.

gender roles and that 27 percent neither agree nor disagree. Though some of these results might be driven by what respondents deem to be the socially desirable answer, there is little reason to believe that Muslims would feel these response pressures less than would non-Muslims (if anything the opposite might be true).

Significant portions of the Muslim electorate reject traditional gender roles, but it is nevertheless not the case that progressive Muslims and non-Muslims make natural electoral coalition partners. In fact, as Table 3.2 and Figure 3.4 demonstrate, some of the characteristics that are associated with egalitarianism among non-Muslims are associated with patriarchy among Muslims: feeling close to the Labour Party and living in municipalities that are urbanized and that feature a high share of Muslim residents. Since religious composition was not included until the 2001 census, this variable is proxied here and in the statistical analyses below by the percentage of Pakistanis and Bangladeshis living in a municipality.[80]

These patterns suggest that inclusion dilemmas are likely to take place within the Left and in urban areas of sizable Muslim settlement, as more liberal natives and more conservative Muslims end up in the same electoral coalition. By contrast, differences in opinion among those who identify with the Conservative Party are smaller and less consistent (but note that only a small

80. In 2001, the percentage of Muslim residents in a municipality correlated with the percentage of Pakistani and Bangladeshi residents at .92; $p = .000$; see Table 3.2 for variable descriptions.

TABLE 3.2. Attitudes about Gender Roles by Religion and Subgroups (England and Wales, 1991–2008)

	Non-Muslims	Muslims	Difference	Std. Error	Non-Muslims		Muslims	
					N	unique respondents	N	unique respondents
All	3.44	2.78	0.66	0.11	75,009	16,241	551	156
Close to Labour	3.45	2.46	0.99	0.14	23,232	7,041	222	91
Urban	3.51	2.57	0.94	0.13	20,341	5,091	317	102
High % Muslim	3.46	2.53	0.92	0.15	4,450	1,283	275	79
Younger	3.83	2.97	0.85	0.11	40,358	10,512	412	129
Older	3.07	2.26	0.81	0.23	34,651	7,995	139	39
Low education	3.21	2.46	0.75	0.13	40,513	9,758	299	101
Male	3.33	2.58	0.75	0.13	34,241	7,385	298	76
Not close to Conservatives	3.51	2.79	0.71	0.11	57,096	14,064	517	149
Close to Conservatives	3.25	2.67	0.59	0.35	16,913	4,897	25	18
Female	3.55	3.07	0.48	0.18	40,106	8,194	245	72
High education	3.71	3.24	0.47	0.14	33,928	7,188	244	68
Not close to Labour	3.44	2.99	0.46	0.12	50,777	13,055	320	122
Low % Muslim	3.44	3.01	0.43	0.15	70,559	15,573	276	87
Less urban	3.41	3.08	0.33	0.17	54,668	12,277	234	59

Note: This table displays answers to the following question: "Do you personally agree or disagree. . . . A husband's job is to earn money; a wife's job is to look after the home and family."

Answers include strongly agree (1), agree (2), neither agree nor disagree (3), disagree (4), and strongly disagree (5).

Source: University of Essex (2010) (weighted data).

Subgroup Variables:

Feels close/not close to Labour (1/0)

Feels close/not close to Conservatives (1/0)

Urban/less urban: lives in a municipality with a population density at or above/below the mean population density (1/0)

High/Low % Muslim: lives in a municipality in which Pakistanis and Bangladeshis comprise at least/below 5% of the population (1/0)

High/Low education: at least/below mean education level (1/0)

Younger/Older: below/at least mean age (1/0)

number of Muslims feels close to the Conservatives, which explains the large confidence intervals). Further, additional calculations reveal that preference differences compound (not shown): 71 percent of Muslims—but only 22 percent of non-Muslims—who reside in urbanized localities with a high Muslim population and who feel close to the Labour Party favor patriarchal social orders, leading to a vast chasm of close to *50 points* across these groups.

Gender norms are generally slow to change. Liberalization may take place across age cohorts rather than individuals. Further, as people age they tend to become more conservative. Yet, change does occur: 44 percent of respondents change their views between surveys (typically two years apart) while 56 percent do not. Are these shifts partly caused by polarization? To test whether exposure to groups adhering to more patriarchal customs accounts for some of this change, I regress views about gender roles on the size of the Muslim population in the respondent's municipality, controlling for a number of other variables that can also shape these views. The regressions include individual fixed effects, meaning that the coefficients measure the effects of changes in the independent variables (that is, the percentage of Muslims living in the municipality) on gender egalitarianism within individuals over time. Individuals may possess unmeasured attributes that predispose them towards certain attitudes about gender roles—perhaps some have particularly strong mothers or had formative gender-related experiences in their youth. But by tracking the same individuals over the years and including individual fixed effects, we can be more confident that these unmeasured factors are not producing attitude shifts. I also add individual-level variables (such as getting married or becoming more educated) that can prompt a change in attitudes and local-level controls at the municipality level.[81] Specifically, the local diversity effect could simply be driven by urbanization (captured by *Population Density*); that is, as residents are exposed to city life they may become more progressive on a number of dimensions, including gender equality. It may also be the case that the extent to which women in a municipality are economically active influences views about gender roles, and I therefore add a variable measuring females' labor market participation.[82]

Figure 3.5 presents the results graphically (the regression table can be found in Appendix B). The circles indicate how a change in a given variable affects attitudes about gender roles within the same individuals over time. We

81. Including wave trends or wave fixed effects yields similar results.

82. Lastly, since values for local-level variables are interpolated linearly between decennial censuses (1991, 2001, and 2011), we might be concerned that individual respondents are assigned the same treatment multiple times. I therefore run a model where I restrict the sample so that each individual respondent appears at most three times, selecting waves that are closest to the census year. In this model, the effect of the local Muslim population remains statistically significant ($p < 0.05$), and is larger in size.

see that when the share of Muslims in a municipality rises, so does support for egalitarian gender norms among non-Muslim natives. Encountering these groups has a liberalizing effect. The top panel features contextual effects, and the bottom panel displays how changes at the individual level influence attitudes (note that the scales across figures are different, due to the large effects of education). Looking at municipality-level results, the effects are largest and most significant with respect to the share of Muslims living in a municipality. As this percentage rises, individuals come to adopt more egalitarian gender roles. By contrast, changes in the local female labor market participation rate or the in population density have no significant effects.

The substantive magnitude of the local "Muslim effect" (.009) appears modest. However, this effect must be seen in light of the fact that these opinions are rather sticky; an average change in views for a given individual between surveys is negative and stands at −.012. If the Muslim population increased by one standard deviation (2.7 percent), gender views would liberalize by .025 points. This effect is about half the effect we would observe if an individual obtained employment, and it is larger (in absolute terms) than the conservatizing effect of having additional children (−.017). The progressive effects of a two standard deviation rise (5.4 percent) in a municipality's Muslim population are of roughly the same magnitude (again in absolute terms) as is the drift towards more patriarchal gender norms that comes with getting married. If the Muslim population increased from its minimum (0 percent) to its maximum (34.2 percent) these attitudes would, hypothetically, move .31 points in the egalitarian direction. By comparison, obtaining secondary education—by far the biggest effect—is associated with a .19 increase in the egalitarian direction.

Though this chapter is interested in the distribution of preferences of Muslims and non-Muslims, one potential critique is that ethnic diversification of *any type* will lead to more progressive views. It may not be exposure to ethnic groups with conservative gender norms that prompts individuals to change their views. Rather, diversity per se may have a liberalizing effect. To test this claim, I include the shares of ethnic minority groups who feature a markedly less gendered division of labor (black Africans, black Caribbeans, and Indians, respectively). I find that the presence of these groups does not have a significant effect on gender role attitudes. In a similar vein, I examine whether individuals who live in municipalities with a rising Muslim population generally end up espousing more leftist views. Liberal shifts in gender attitudes could simply present one aspect of this trend. To test this proposition, I rerun the regressions with a different dependent variable, agreement with the position that it "is the government's responsibility to provide a job for everyone who wants one." In this test, the size of the local Muslim population has no effect,

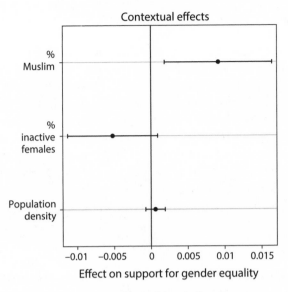

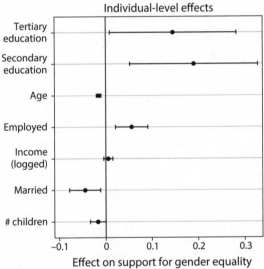

FIGURE 3.5. Effect of Contextual and Individual-Level Variables on Views about Gender Equality among British non-Muslims
Note: The circles indicate the size of the coefficients; the capped lines indicate the upper and lower bounds of the 95 percent confidence interval. Results are based on Model 2 in Table B.2 (Appendix B).

suggesting there has been no generalized shift towards leftwing positions in localities whose Muslim populations have been increasing. Finally, the main results remain substantively similar when I exclude those who espoused conservative positions when they were first surveyed, and who therefore had the most room to move on this issue.

In short, polarization is taking place: Living in municipalities that witness an increasing number of relatively more patriarchal Muslim residents induces more support for gender egalitarianism among non-Muslims. This polarization of views occurs alongside public debate, which has increasingly portrayed the social conservatism of Muslims as one of the prime impediments to their integration. While non-Muslim Europeans have become more secular and liberal on social issues, they are confronted with a group that is much less so.

Conclusion

This chapter has sought to lay out the sociopolitical landscape that parties face when making inclusion decisions. Chain migration, the formation of conservative enclaves in urban centers, and the resulting polarization in preferences confront political parties with distinct electorates whose religious behaviors and social preferences differ markedly from one another.

The social geography of Muslim migration, I have argued, has helped amplify this conflict over values. Though Muslim preferences are quite diverse, ranging from the socially liberal to the very traditional, Muslims living in urban enclaves are more religious and more conservative than the average Muslim. When it comes to non-Muslims, however, the opposite is true: Living in Europe's cities is associated with social liberalism among this group. How do political parties tackle Muslim inclusion in light of this divide? Does the magnitude of the social preference gap cause parties to exclude Muslims? Or do parties try to build class-based coalitions that bring together low-income voters across ethnoreligious groups? The next chapters provide answers to these questions.

4

Ideology, Electoral Incentives, and Inclusion Outcomes across Countries

Chapter 3 demonstrated that European Muslims are noticeably more religious and espouse significantly more conservative views on social issues than do their non-Muslim neighbors. This preference divergence is particularly striking in urban centers of Muslim concentration—areas where electoral inclusion pressures are highest. Though Muslims' social conservatism should make this group an ally of the Right, their centrist views on income redistribution and the Right's traditional reluctance to embrace minority constituencies hamper such alliances.

Left parties in Europe, the United States, and beyond have historically been more open to including ethnic minorities in their coalitions. Inclusion paths have been varied and rocky, but the Left's customary emphasis on justice and equality together with the lower-class status that often characterizes ethnic-minority communities have helped pave the way for inclusion. Further, immigrant minorities'—including European Muslims'—concentration in urban areas where the Left is usually strong[1] also means that these groups are more likely to encounter left party organizations. However, social democrats and other leftist parties confront notable disagreements on social issues when trying to incorporate Muslim voters and their interests. As revealed in the previous chapter, for example, the largest opinion gap between British Muslims and non-Muslims on gender egalitarianism arises *within* the camp of

1. See Rodden (2010).

Labour identifiers. Further, Muslims' concentration in relatively poorer districts can pit this group against other low-income voters in the competition over scarce material resources.[2] In short, the ways in which settlement patterns map onto the distribution of preferences makes European Muslims an uneasy partisan fit.

We may assume, then, that electoral inclusion is modest, at best. Preference polarization, prejudice, and resource conflicts will impede incorporation. Yet, countervailing pressures can push parties towards inclusion. Ideological commitments to equality and nondiscrimination have been bedrocks of modern social democratic parties, and large sections of leftist voters subscribe to these norms (see below). But do such principles also extend to Muslims? Do social democratic parties and their constituents adhere to these principles when it comes to concrete inclusion efforts in the municipalities they seek to govern? Lastly, when inclusion does occur, what are the implications of Muslims' more socially conservative views and social structures for party politics?

Parties on the Right confront fewer dilemmas. Traditionally less wedded to norms of antidiscrimination and egalitarianism, these parties may be faced with inclusion pressures only when the size of the local Muslim electorate is substantial. However, it is also possible that center-right parties have adapted to the demographic realities that half a century of immigration has wrought. Facing an increasingly diverse electorate, parties on the Right may have become more welcoming of migrant populations, both in their rhetoric and in practice.[3] For example, a strategy paper by the German Christian Democrats entitled "Reconquering the Big Cities" calls for a more aggressive targeting of diverse urban populations. Reaching beyond the party's "core clientele" and setting up "tight links with mosque communities" is a critical part of this strategy.[4] But does this outreach occur mainly behind the scenes, or does it indeed extend to the competitive and visible politics of candidate selection?

Guided by these questions, this chapter provides a macrolevel perspective of how party platforms, voter preferences and electoral incentives link up with parties' inclusion of Muslim candidates. I first present original data, based on a large-scale text analysis project, on parties' commitments to the equal treatment of immigrant-origin, minority populations, as stated in election manifestos.[5] Additionally, I analyze parties' positions on Islam, Muslims, and religion.

2. Dancygier (2010, 2013).

3. On the European Center-Right's approach to immigration, see, e.g., Bale (2008) and Dancygier and Margalit (2014).

4. Wegner (2014, 5).

5. These data are based on a translation and coding project, undertaken with Yotam Margalit,

Scholars have long theorized how different ideological positions as formulated in manifestos (especially the broad left-right dimension), shape legislative behavior and policy outputs.[6] Existing datasets tracking party positions as expressed in manifestos do not, however, include the manifold issues that have arisen due to postwar immigration and the ethnic and religious diversity this migration has brought about.[7] Neither do studies examine whether the candidate pools that parties assemble reflect their stated ideological positions. As a result, we know much less about how parties discuss matters related to immigration and immigrant-origin minorities and, in turn, whether party selection decisions are correlated with manifesto pronouncements.

Considering major center-left and center-right parties in Austria, Belgium, Germany, and Great Britain, I find that left parties in all four countries do emphasize principles of equality and nondiscrimination in their approach to minority groups of immigrant origin. The equal treatment of these groups is an important aspect of these parties' stated beliefs and policy proposals. In stark contrast, center-right parties hardly ever make such declarations. Furthermore, survey data confirm that majority preferences echo these differences: Individuals who identify with the Left are more likely to view measures combating racial or ethnic discrimination favorably than are those on the Right. With respect to Islam, Muslims, and religion, however, differences across party families aren't quite as striking. The Left prefers to either ignore these issues altogether or to discuss them cautiously, a strategy that hints at the inclusion dilemmas playing out on the ground. The Right also does not focus on matters revolving around Islam and Muslims, but when it does, it tends to bring up what it perceives to be the negative repercussions of the Muslim presence.

The chapter next examines whether these party pronouncements and voter preferences match up with inclusion outcomes. Drawing on a data-gathering project on Muslim representation that I carried out in close to 300 municipalities in Austria, Belgium, Britain, and Germany, I find that the picture is mixed: Though, within countries, the Left is considerably more likely to include than is the Right, across countries social democratic parties' stated adherence to equal treatment cannot account for differences in inclusion outcomes. Center-left parties in Austria, Britain, and Germany appear nearly identical with respect to their affirmation of equality and nondiscrimination in their election manifestos, and leftist voters in all four countries

---

and cover 12 Western European countries. For a more detailed description of the coding protocol, see Appendix C and Dancygier and Margalit (2014).

6. See, for example, Benoit and Laver (2006), Budge et al. (1987), and Klingemann et al. (1994).

7. For an exception, see Akkerman (2015).

strongly favor measures to combat antidiscrimination. But left parties in these countries exhibit drastically different inclusion outcomes. For instance, the Austrian Social Democrats (SPÖ) feature a paltry parity ratio of 0.14, compared to a much higher ratio of 1.14 among British Labour. Electoral incentives, I conclude, can better explain these striking cross-national differences than can aggregate voter preferences or stated party ideals. Simply put, parity ratios are higher in Belgium and Britain where many Muslims are voting citizens who participate actively in elections than in Austria and Germany where the acquisition of citizenship by immigrants, including Muslims, has been less common and where local electoral laws place less of a premium on minority mobilization. Though preference divergence, prejudice, and resource pressures may block inclusion where Muslims do not wield much electoral leverage, they appear to present smaller obstacles where parties face electoral incentives to open themselves up to Muslim office-seekers and voters.

Before proceeding, I should address two potential points of concern: First, some might be skeptical that we should expect ideology to affect local politics at all: Parks and potholes—not abstract principles—guide the behavior of local parties. Though day-to-day service issues clearly play a larger role in local politics than they do on the national stage, it is nevertheless the case that party politics, and the governing ideologies that come with it, loom large in European urban municipalities. For instance, research indicates that the views and ideological self-placement of local councilors correspond to the positioning of those of their national parties: The Left-Right distinction is very much alive at the local level.[8] Moreover, national parties have become increasingly involved in the activities of local parties, especially in urban areas. In Britain, local party manifestos are said to reflect those of the national party, and there is an expectation that local representatives "feel bound collectively by the contents of the manifesto."[9] In German cities, municipal electoral campaigns, party competition, and policy positions also mirror developments on the national stage.[10] To be sure, this correspondence is not perfect, and this chapter demonstrates that divergence indeed can occur when the pledges made in national manifestos conflict with local electoral objectives.

Second, the purpose of this chapter is not to tell a causal story that neatly separates out the effects of parties' ideological commitments on the one hand and those generated by electoral incentives on the other. Rather, the chapter aims to convey whether principles of equal treatment and nondiscrimination as put forth by national party rhetoric are put into action by local parties that in fact come face to face with ethnoreligious diversity and tangible questions

8. On this point, see De Vries (2000). The author finds clear ideological differences across local councilors based on party, but fewer distinctions when it comes to problem perceptions.

9. See Leach (2004, 77) and Rallings and Thrasher (1997, especially Chapter 6).

10. For a brief discussion, see Holtkamp (2006).

of minority incorporation. In the long run, it is of course possible that party ideology and electoral incentives influence one another. A liberal citizenship regime that is associated with a high degree of electoral participation by immigrant minorities may, over the years, prompt even the most reluctant parties to adopt more egalitarian platforms that call for an end to discrimination. Likewise, parties that are committed to equality irrespective of origin or religion have often advocated for more expansive citizenship policies,[11] and they may have done so in part because they expect to reap electoral rewards from such policies.

In the short term, however, subnational parties deal with a fixed set of citizenship and electoral institutions, and the principles that national parties promulgate in manifestos may be at odds with the electoral realities local parties encounter when trying to build winning coalitions. This chapter establishes the broad context in which parties operate when approaching Muslim inclusion, while the next two chapters flesh out more fully how these ideological and strategic tensions unfold in the electoral arena.

Party Principles and Voter Preferences

The large and growing presence of first- and later-generation immigrants in European countries has prompted parties to devise a host of principles and policies that guide the inflow, settlement, and treatment of these new minorities. Though parties were generally slow to address these matters in their official election programs, in the more recent past mainstream parties—and certainly those on the far-right—have discussed issues relating to the causes and consequences of the immigrant presence in public debates and in election manifestos.[12] Because Muslims constitute a substantial part of Europe's population with recent migration roots, parties' pronouncements in this issue area are relevant to this group as well. In fact, these pronouncements are often formulated with the economic, social, and political implications of the Muslim presence in mind.

Though the nuts and bolts of immigration policy—who can enter, how, and when—continue to be salient in election manifestos, parties on all sides of the political spectrum have begun to dedicate increasing attention to the integration of long-settled immigrant-origin minorities and to issues that are tied specifically to Muslims. An issue cluster that is of particular interest in this chapter is that of equal treatment and nondiscrimination. Discrimination by party elites presents a significant hurdle for minorities seeking to enter

11. Janoski (2010) and Howard (2009).

12. See Dancygier and Margalit (2014) on the evolution of the immigration debate as articulated in party manifestos. See also Messina (1989) on parties' earlier "conspiracy of silence" with respect to immigration.

electoral politics.[13] Ethnic-minority office-seekers, even when they possess very similar socioeconomic or educational characteristics to those of the majority population, face substantial barriers when trying to run for elected office, receiving lower returns on income and education than do natives. These penalties are particularly steep among migrants from developing countries, many of whom are of Muslim origin.[14] Yet, as we will see, the extent of descriptive representation varies dramatically across parties, suggesting that discriminatory behavior of party gatekeepers differs as well.

Do parties that devote greater attention to equality and nondiscrimination have better records of including Muslim candidates? To answer this question I first examine how center-left and center-right parties have approached matters of equal treatment and discrimination as they pertain to immigrant-origin groups in their party manifestos. In each country, I focus on the largest center-right and center-left party—for two reasons. First, to make substantial gains in descriptive representation, any minority group will have to find a home in parties that manage to obtain a significant number of seats. Second, measuring the relative salience and sentiment of the relevant stated principles and policy claims is extremely time-consuming. It requires the identification, translation, and coding of all statements that relate to immigration and its repercussions. Specifically, the text-analysis project identified 30 different issue clusters, including, for example, immigrants' impact on the labor market or welfare state, asylum and refugees, border security, law and order, language, as well as equal treatment and Islam (see Appendix C for a complete list). Each relevant statement is coded as belonging to one or more categories, and as being positive, neutral, or negative in tone.

Taking stock of the last 15 years, I analyzed party manifestos from 2000 onwards, yielding 37 manifestos. Center-left parties include the SPÖ (Social Democrats, Austria); the PSF (Francophone Socialist Party, Belgium); the SP.a (Flemish Socialist Party, Belgium); the SPD (Social Democrats, Germany); and the Labour Party (Great Britain). Center-right parties are comprised of the ÖVP (People's Party, Austria); the CD&V (Flemish Christian Democrats, Belgium); the MR (Francophone Reformist Movement, Belgium); the CDU/CSU (Christian Democrats, Germany), and the Conservatives (Great Britain). Since Belgium features two parties of each type, I take the average across two parties, respectively (Flemish and Francophone parties do not vary substantially in the attention they give to equality and discrimination).

With respect to the category "Equal Treatment and Nondiscrimination," statements are both general and specific in nature. For instance, in their 2013

13. See, e.g., Bhavnani (2013), Brouard and Tiberj (2011), Dancygier et al. (2015), and Norris and Lovenduski (1995).
14. Dancygier et al. (2015).

manifesto the Austrian Social Democrats proclaim they hope to improve the integration of migrants, and, to do so, they "oppose discrimination of all forms." The same year the German Christian Democrats pronounce: "Our goal is equal chances for everyone—regardless of gender, age or skin color" while the SPD similarly maintains to "advocate for everyone in our country and decidedly oppose discrimination and prejudice." In a section on immigrant rights, the Francophone Socialists in Belgium state in their 2003 manifesto that "Equality is at the heart of our struggles." This sentence is then followed by several more specific policy proposals, including, for example, ending nationality-based employment discrimination in the public sector (i.e., the exclusion of non-EU nationals). Likewise, the British Labour Party's 2005 manifesto declares: "We will take forward the Strategy for Race Equality to ensure that we combat discrimination on the grounds of race and ethnicity across a range of services." All of these statements are coded as having a positive tone.

To measure the relative salience of the "Equal Treatment and Nondiscrimination" cluster and because manifestos vary significantly in length, each statement that falls in this category is divided by the total number of statements that pertain to immigration and immigrant-origin residents (note that a sentence can include statements classified as speaking to more than one category, and the total number of statements reflects these multiple mentions; see Appendix C for further clarification). To avoid giving disproportionate weight to statements in very short manifestos, I aggregate statements across party manifestos, rather than taking the average of individual party manifestos (the latter approach produces very similar results, however).

Figure 4.1 displays the frequency with which parties speak about issues relating to equal treatment and nondiscrimination. It is immediately apparent that the Left addresses these topics much more frequently than does the Right. When discussing issues related to immigration and immigrant populations, statements pertaining to equal treatment and nondiscrimination comprise between 8 and 17 percent of all statements, resulting in an average of 11 percent. Social democratic parties in Austria, Germany, and Great Britain pay close to equal attention to this dimension (between 8 and 9 percent), while center-left parties in Belgium devote 17 percent to this topic. To put these figures in perspective, it is useful to note that major issues such as immigration policy, asylum and refugees, and integration constitute, respectively, 10, 12, and 11 percent of statements. Immigrants' impact on jobs, wages, and the welfare state (2, 1, and 2 percent, respectively) are comparatively much less significant. Further, when speaking about equal treatment and discrimination, the Left's approach is almost exclusively positive.

Judging by their political rhetoric, then, social democratic parties are staunch defenders of equality for all, including for migrant populations, and they decidedly reject discrimination. Based purely on these commitments

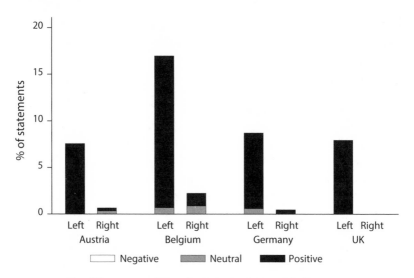

FIGURE 4.1. Equal Treatment and Non-discrimination in Party Manifestos

as voiced in election manifestos, we would expect center-left parties to treat immigrants as equals in the electoral process, and to open their gates to immigrant-origin candidates, including to those of Muslim faith.

A much different picture emerges on the Right. Center-right manifestos show very little interest in equal treatment and discrimination, at least as far as immigrant-origin populations are concerned. Though several topics are similarly central across party families—immigration policy, asylum and refugees, and integration are represented in 16, 17, and 14 percent of statements by the Right—matters of equality and discrimination are conspicuously absent; they appear in less than 1 percent of statements.

Do these differences also reflect preference divides in the electorate? Table 4.1 presents average responses to questions about antidiscrimination, broken down by respondents' ideological orientation. The two questions ask respondents to assess whether laws "against promoting racial or ethnic hatred" or "against racial or ethnic discrimination in the workplace" are "extremely bad" (0) or "extremely good" (10) for a country. Though respondents on the Left and on the Right agree, on average, that such laws would be beneficial, support is stronger among leftists. This result is not surprising as these views likely help shape ideological orientation in the first place. Yet, we also observe that these differences narrow considerably once we break them down by income: Within the Left and the Right, low-income respondents are less supportive of antidiscrimination measures than are those with higher incomes. Across ideological groups, low-income leftists are only slightly more in favor of these policies than are high-income rightists. In Britain, class appears to be even more important than ideology: Low-income respondents across the ideological divide are less enthusiastic than are richer individuals about equality-promoting policies.

TABLE 4.1. Support for Antidiscrimination Measures by Country, Ideology, and Income

HOW GOOD OR BAD ARE EACH OF THESE THINGS FOR A COUNTRY:

A law against promoting
racial or ethnic hatred
(0 = extremely bad,
10 = extremely good)

	Austria		Belgium		Germany		Great Britain	
	Mean	t-statistic	Mean	t-statistic	Mean	t-statistic	Mean	t-statistic
Left	8.02		6.91		7.86		7.61	
Right	7.14	*4.34*	6.14	*3.72*	7.20	*4.27*	7.27	*1.67*
Left, high income	8.42		7.22		8.08		8.47	
Left, low income	7.82	*−1.98*	6.60	*−1.94*	7.45	*−3.12*	6.84	*−5.46*
Right, high income	7.41		6.46		7.41		7.62	
Right, low income	7.27	*−0.37*	5.73	*−2.22*	6.82	*−2.07*	6.80	*−2.81*

HOW GOOD OR BAD ARE EACH OF THESE THINGS FOR A COUNTRY:

A law against racial or ethnic
discrimination in the workplace
(0 = extremely bad,
10 = extremely good)

	Austria		Belgium		Germany		Great Britain	
	Mean	t-statistic	Mean	t-statistic	Mean	t-statistic	Mean	t-statistic
Left	7.46		6.97		7.16		7.55	
Right	6.39	*5.29*	6.27	*3.84*	6.43	*4.85*	7.12	*2.44*
Left, high income	7.65		7.18		7.33		8.39	
Left, low income	7.41	*−0.78*	6.83	*−1.25*	6.89	*−2.15*	6.58	*−6.88*
Right, high income	6.51		6.52		6.54		7.34	
Right, low income	6.21	*−0.82*	5.91	*−2.20*	6.17	*−1.34*	6.83	*−1.94*

Note: These figures are from the European Social Survey, Round 1 (2002). The sample is weighted and restricted to non-Muslim natives. Significance tests are two-tailed.

Left-right ideology is measured with the following question: "In politics people sometimes talk of "left" and "right." Using this card, where would you place yourself on this scale, where 0 means the left and 10 means the right?" Respondents below 5 were coded as left, and those above 5 were coded as right. Income refers to household income; respondents with a household income below/above the country median were coded as having low/high incomes.

These splits allude to the inclusion dilemmas that play out in districts of migrant settlement, which I investigate in greater depth in Chapters 5 and 6. Local party elites, even if they want to act in accordance with party platforms and aggregate constituency preferences, may contend with local electorates that are less keen on extending principles of equality and nondiscrimination to ethnic outsiders. Furthermore, an additional source of tension relates to the identity of these outsiders. As previously highlighted, the Muslim electorate, especially where it is numerous, does not fit comfortably within existing patterns of partisan alignment. Muslim social preferences are especially distinct from attitudes of those who identify with the Left, and anti-Muslim hostility may further dissuade party elites from putting Muslim candidates on the ballot. Additionally, as highlighted in Chapter 2, leftist parties that fashion themselves as champions of minority rights might be much less eager to accommodate minorities that are deeply religious and traditional.

Before moving on to an investigation of inclusion outcomes, I therefore consider parties' stances on Islam, Muslims, and religion, which may already hint at these tensions. Does the Left's fraught relationship with religion carry through in its position toward Islam and Muslim populations? Center-right parties, most obviously Christian Democrats, have been more closely linked to religious bodies and doctrines. These parties may be more comfortable in addressing religious matters, but it is unclear whether this should also extend to Islam and Muslims. Figure 4.2 presents parties' positions on Islam and Muslims (top panel) and on religion (bottom panel). Statements pertaining to Islam and Muslims speak to a range of issues, including, for example, the wearing of religious symbols in schools, the establishment of, and dialogue with, national Islamic councils, the training of imams, the treatment of women in Muslim communities, or Islamophobia. Note that statements addressing Islam and Muslims may not refer to religion, but to practices associated with Muslims (e.g., forced marriage); statements categorized under religion may not be explicitly about Islam (e.g., broad statements about religious differences and religious toleration); and that statements can fall under both categories, Islam and Muslims, and religion (e.g., overseeing the training of imams). In practice, many of the statements referencing religion without singling out Muslims have the Muslim population in mind, and I therefore display results for both categories. Finally, as with the other categories, only sentences that deal with immigrant-origin populations are included. The practice of Islam in other countries or references to religious matters concerning the majority population are not part of the analysis.

As Figure 4.2 makes clear, the relative salience of these issue clusters is much lower among center-left parties than is the issue cluster pertaining to equality and nondiscrimination. (This remains true even when combining the Islam and religion frequencies.) In spite (or perhaps because) of the heated public discussions about the integration of Islam and of Muslims, the Austrian SPÖ and the British Labour Party ignore these matters entirely in their manifestos. Center-left parties in Belgium and Germany are more likely to address such topics, but do so in a rather negative light, especially when compared to these parties' unambiguous embrace of equality and nondiscrimination. The SPD is particularly critical. Almost all of its statements, many of which address forced marriage and the treatment of women, highlight negative aspects of the Muslim presence.

Left parties are somewhat more positive when discussing specifically religious aspects of Islam (versus social practices associated with Muslim com-

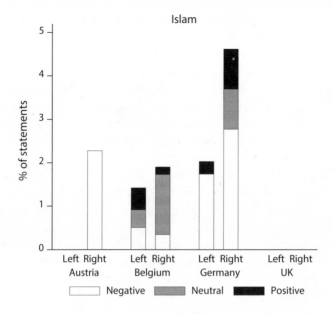

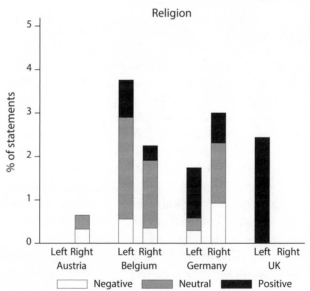

FIGURE 4.2. Islam and Religion in Party Manifestos

munities) as well as minority religion more broadly defined. The SPD thus maintains to "respect and appreciate freedom of religion and the religious and ideological diversity in Germany" (2013 manifesto). The British Labour Party's positive references to religion are in turn mainly about religiously based discrimination (and are therefore also coded as belonging to the equal-treatment /

nondiscrimination category). For example, in its 2005 manifesto the party states that it "will further extend protection against discrimination on the grounds of religion and belief." In Belgium, center-left parties devote considerable attention to secularism and the separation of church and state. Across party types, we observe fewer systematic differences in these categories when compared to the equality-and-nondiscrimination category. On the whole, the Right is more likely to make statements relating to Islam and Muslims, but, just like the Left, it rarely speaks in positive terms. No consistent pattern emerges with respect to the religion category.

Summing up, whereas the Left is unequivocal in its defense of equality and nondiscrimination in its platforms, it is much more circumspect when it comes to Islam, Muslims, and religion. In light of these competing agendas, beliefs about equality may not translate into equal treatment of Muslims on party lists. The Right, in turn, is not too concerned with equality and discriminatory behavior, and it also shows few signs of appreciating Islam, Muslims, and the religious diversity that sustained immigration has produced. Based on the rhetoric espoused in their manifestos, center-right parties' inclusion of Muslim candidates should be minimal.

Electoral Incentives

Whereas parties' and voters' lukewarm positions on Islam and Muslims probably dampen efforts to reach out to Muslim voters and candidates, Muslim electorates may nevertheless pique the interests of local parties keen on winning seats. The kin structures outlined earlier coincide with a certain set of preferences and behaviors that can hinder social integration and complicate partisan outreach, but they are also conducive to electoral mobilization. Indeed, a host of studies has highlighted the superior mobilizational capacity of candidates who trace their roots to, for instance, Morocco, Turkey, or Pakistan.[15] Drawing on networks of kin and clan, these mostly Muslim office-seekers engage in communal electioneering of a style typical of urban ethnic machines in the nineteenth- and twentieth-century United States.

Studying the electoral participation of Pakistani-origin Britons, Akhtar (2013, 62–3) writes that traditional leaders who rely on kin and religious links have come to dominate the politics of the enclave: "This type of leadership was, and is, highly personalised; it relies on a network of duties and debts, kinship and village allegiances, informed by a tradition of clientism . . . traditional leaders . . . utilise kinship networks to engineer bloc mobilization."[16] The electoral inclusion of Britain's Bangladeshis has followed a similar trajec-

---

15. For examples, see Dancygier (2010), Maxwell (2012), Teney et al. (2010), and sources cited in the next two chapters.

16. Akhtar (2013, 62–63). See also Anwar (1998) and Shaw (2000), and sources cited in Chapters 5 and 6.

tory.[17] In Brussels, Dassetto also notes that personal ties, ethnic origins, and religious identification converge to shape Muslims' electoral inclusion.[18] In Dutch cities, such mobilization was already apparent in the early 1980s. Among Turkish and Moroccan candidates and voters, Rath writes, "The role of political ideology is fairly questionable," and the candidate takes precedence over the party. Campaigns consist of "attendances at mosques, coffee-houses, tea-houses, boarding-houses, and [of] the mobilisation of friends, neighbors and relatives."[19] Migrant voters cite factors such as the candidates' regional origin, religion, "modernism," and gender among the salient characteristics influencing their vote choice.

While ethnoreligious ties are well suited for the mobilization of bloc votes, the mosque often serves as a convenient and popular campaign stop, despite remarks by religious leaders that mosques are politically off limits.[20] Mosques are expedient campaign venues that allow candidates to reach a large audience efficiently and effectively, and religious figures may advise their congregations on how to vote. The Muslim Council of Britain (MCB), for instance, sent a memo to 1,500 mosques in Britain, "urging imams to encourage their congregations to go out and vote at the local, national and European elections. . . to counter-act any gains by the far-right British National Party."[21] The East London Mosque "is seen as a key power broker in the local political arena, so much so that every local politician is obliged to speak with its leadership and publicly visit the mosque if they want to stand a chance of being elected."[22] Similarly, in Bradford the "religious arena . . . overlaps with the political sphere. Pir Maroof Shah instructs his follower to vote Labour."[23]

In Antwerp, the local mosque association representing 26 mosques came out in public support of a Moroccan-origin candidate.[24] A large mosque in Molenbeek, a Brussels municipality that has been labeled the "jihadi capital of Europe," is widely considered an "electoral machine for the socialist mayor and his Moroccan-origin running mates."[25] To get their congregants to the polls, Brussels' mosques have sent out text messages on the eve of local elections, telling voters what parties are best at defending Muslims' religious interests. One message called on voters to cast ballots for the Socialists—not the Greens or the center-right MR: "Dear brothers and sisters, we will vote this

17. Glynn (2008).

18. Dassetto (2011, 129 ff.).

19. Rath (1981, 141–42).

20. Mosque involvement also shapes the political participation of Arab Muslims in the United States; see Jamal (2005).

21. Akhtar (2013, 86).

22. Peace (2013, 311).

23. Samad (1996, 93).

24. Zibouh (2010, 81).

25. Koksal (2007, 17).

weekend Inshallah! Let us be united in our votes, let us all vote for the PS. Other parties like Ecolo or the MR do not support our religion and sometimes even cause it harm. Example: wearing of the headscarf in schools, the organization of [religious] events. . . . " The message then urged Muslims to cast their preference ballots for Moroccan candidates on Socialist lists.[26]

In the German city of Dortmund, where nearly one in three residents has non-German roots, contacts between religious leaders and mainstream parties are also common. The SPD arranged meetings with several imams a few days ahead of local elections, asking for their support during the upcoming contest.[27] In Vienna and Salzburg, mosques have also endorsed Muslim politicians, and Muslim candidates have handed out leaflets before and after Friday prayers.[28] More controversially, campaign workers supporting Turkish candidates in Austria are said to have collected postal ballots in mosques, leading to impressive electoral results in some precincts. Reminiscent of events in England (see Chapter 5), some have charged that Austro-Turkish candidates attained a large number of preference votes fraudulently, by having campaign aides fill out postal ballots on behalf of Turkish-origin voters in mosques.[29]

In brief, European parties operating in areas of Muslim concentration are faced with Muslim electorates that are not wedded to particular parties and whose ethnic networks and religious institutions coalesce to turn them into a potent electoral force. In their search for votes, local party elites will find these realities hard to ignore. Some may even welcome the ease with which enclave votes can be drummed up. As a result, they may incorporate large numbers of Muslim candidates and voters on an ethnoreligious basis, notwithstanding ideological tensions or non-Muslim opposition.

Are electoral incentives more important than party principles in determining inclusion outcomes? To provide a first cut at this question, Figure 4.3 shows how Muslims' potential electoral significance varies across countries on the basis of citizenship and electoral institutions. The four countries studied in this book differ in the openness of their citizenship regimes and in the extent to which local electoral laws empower minority groups. To avoid cases that would yield ambiguous predictions, I select countries that are either permissive along both dimensions or restrictive along both dimensions. I therefore do not seek to examine the relative importance of citizenship regimes versus electoral rules in determining inclusion outcomes, but instead pick cases in which the effects of both types of institutions on minority electoral power point in the same direction.

26. Corinne De Permentier, a Brussels politician for the center-right MR, took issue with these appeals; see LaLibre.be (2012).

27. Migration in Germany (2009).

28. Beig (2010); Profil Online (2013).

29. Pink (2013) and Schwaiger (2013).

Liberal citizenship regime

	More	Less

More	Great Britain
	  Single and multi-member wards
	  Plurality
	  Non-citizen voting/running
	  CPI: 5
	
	Belgium
	  At-large PR
	  Strong potential impact of
	    preference votes
	  Non-citizen voting, not running
	  CPI: 5.5	

Less		Germany
		  At-large PR
		  Moderate to no impact of
		    preference votes
		  Non-citizens cannot vote/run
		  CPI: 2
		
		Austria
		  At-large PR
		  Moderate to no impact of
		    preference votes
		  Non-citizens cannot vote/run
		  CPI: 0

Local electoral laws empower minorities

FIGURE 4.3. Country Case Selection by the Potential Importance of the Local Minority Vote

Note: The CPI (Citizenship Policy Index) is based on Howard's (2009) coding of citizenship regimes (0 is the most restrictive, 6 is the most permissive).

In Germany and Austria, citizenship laws are comparatively restrictive, and consequently many immigrant-origin minorities have not been naturalized. Even though Muslims in Austria (mostly originating from Turkey and the former Yugoslavia) have lived in the country for decades, according to the 2001 Austrian census (the last one to enumerate religious background) 71 percent of the country's Muslim population were not Austrian citizens. In municipalities with sizable Muslim populations (that is, where Muslim voters could potentially have some electoral influence), this share tends to be even higher.[30] Based on Howard's (2009) index of citizenship policies (CPI; measured in 2008),[31] Austria's citizenship policy index receives a zero (six being the highest potential score). Germany liberalized its citizenship code in the late 1990s, but its regime still remains relatively closed, reaching a score of two (the mean/median score in Howard's sample is 3.1/4.2).[32] Though a sizable

30. This assessment is based on my analysis of Viennese districts using census data.

31. This index is based on three domains: (1) the existence of *jus soli*; (2) the length of residency requirements; and (3) the possibility of dual citizenship. Howard's index is highly correlated with indices developed by other scholars (see Helbling 2011; Koopmans et al. 2012), and I therefore only rely on Howard's ranking here.

32. The 1999 reform included a limited version of *jus soli*, a reduction of residency requirements to eight years, and dual citizenship for minors (Howard 2012).

number of Muslims, many of Turkish origin, have been naturalized, the limited options for dual citizenship have deterred many.[33]

In both countries, local electoral rules also do not tend to empower minority voters. Noncitizens from outside the European Union do not have the right to vote or run in local elections, and even in localities where a sizable share of Muslims does have the vote, electoral laws do not reward concentration: Elections are held at-large using proportional representation. Spatial concentration within cities therefore does not translate into electoral leverage. In some cases, however, electoral laws facilitate collective mobilization via preference votes. Preference votes allow voters to deviate from the ranking of candidates as devised by the party and to cast ballots for specific candidates. The adoption of preference vote systems varies across Austrian and German *Länder*.[34] In some municipalities it is therefore conceivable that Muslim candidates who are placed on low list positions would garner sufficient personal votes to be moved up on the list and win a seat. However, in practice this happens rarely (though with increasing frequency); Muslim candidates and voters have to be citizens, and the initial placement on the party list remains critical. In both Austria and Germany, then, on the whole Muslims do not wield much electoral power in local elections.

The picture is different in Belgium and Great Britain. Here, open citizenship laws and local electoral rules combine to turn ethnic minorities into potentially powerful electoral constituencies. As one Belgian politician put it, perhaps somewhat hyperbolically: "Elections in every large city will be won or lost with the ethnic vote."[35] Minimal residency and integration requirements and the toleration of dual nationality made Belgium's nationality laws quite permissive and prompted criticism that citizenship had been devalued to a "mere confirmation of one's residence."[36] Large shares of Turks and Moroccans have naturalized. Between 1999 and 2007, these groups accounted for over half of all the individuals acquiring citizenship. Accordingly, 80 percent of those born in Turkey are Belgian citizens.[37] Though Britain's citizenship code has been tightened over the decades, it still remains relatively open, permitting *jus soli* and dual citizenship. When large numbers of postcolonial migrants settled in the 1950s and 1960s, they generally arrived as British citizens. This expansive

33. According to Aktürk (2010, 74–75), in the late 2000s, about three-quarters of Turks living in Germany had not sought German citizenship because they did not want to give up their Turkish nationality. In 2014 a new law was enacted that made it easier for those born in Germany (but not before 1990) to have two nationalities.

34. Leß (2012), Tiefenbach (2006), and van der Kolk (2007).

35. Celis et al. (2014, 45).

36. Foblets and Loones (2006, 91). In 2010, some of these liberalizations were reversed, and, in line with many of its European neighbors, Belgium implemented tougher criteria, including language tests.

37. See Knott and Manço (2010, 283); the authors note that immigrants from Morocco and the Democratic Republic of Congo show similar trends.

understanding of citizenship was reined in over the years, but in 2008 Britain's CPI was still at the high end of the spectrum, scoring a 5 (down from a 5.5 in the 1980s, mainly due to slightly stricter residency requirements).

In addition to liberal citizenship regimes, local electoral laws can boost the electoral influence of minorities. In Belgium, nationals of any country can vote in local elections, as long as they have fulfilled a five-year residency requirement. In Britain, residents who are citizens of Commonwealth countries (which include Bangladesh and Pakistan) can vote and stand in local elections. Further, though the two countries' electoral systems differ, they are both conducive to coordination along ethnoreligious lines. In Belgium, as in Austria and Germany, at-large local elections operate according to PR. In all Belgian municipalities, however, preference votes can and do matter quite significantly. Voters have the option of casting a ballot for the party list, thereby endorsing the list order of candidates as set by the party, or they can choose to vote for a number of preferred candidates within one party list (voters have as many votes as there are candidates within a party; they cannot vote for multiple parties; each ballot, whether it indicates a list vote or one or several preference votes, counts as one vote for a party).

To give an example: In a system without preference votes, if a party wins three seats, the candidates on the first, second and third list position each obtain a seat. However, if voters have the option of casting preference votes, and if the candidate who is on the fourth list position receives more preference votes than does the candidate on the third list position, the former may be able to move up one spot and secure a seat, while the latter is moved down the list and does not get elected. This so-called flexible list system approximates open-list PR. It is meant to personalize what are typically party-centered elections and to stimulate closer links between candidates and voters.[38] As I will show in greater detail below and in Chapter 6, this system has also greatly facilitated the cultivation of the ethnoreligious vote, especially among voters and candidates originating from Morocco and Turkey.

Local elections in Britain have also fostered tight linkages between candidates and voters of ethnic minority background.[39] Here, elections are held at the level of wards within municipalities. When groups are spatially concentrated within localities—as tends to be the case with the Muslim electorate— ward-level contests enhance groups' relative electoral leverage.[40] Candidates are elected by plurality vote in single- or multi-member elections.[41]

38. Wauters et al. (2012).

39. Dancygier (2010) and Garbaye (2005).

40. Dancygier (2014) and Trounstine and Valdini (2008).

41. In metropolitan areas the typical district magnitude is three. In some localities, elections are held in three consecutive years, with each contest electing one councilor per ward (no election takes place in the fourth year). In others, elections occur every four years, with three councilors being elected at once. Chapter 5 provides more details.

If parties pursue vote-based inclusion strategies, these combinations of citizenship laws and local electoral systems should—all else equal—be associated with higher Muslim parity ratios in Britain and Belgium than in Austria and Germany. Alternatively, these institutional differences may have little traction and ideological differences across party families, and voters could instead prove critical. If so, then the Left should have a better record of inclusion across countries.

Party Principles, Electoral Incentives, and Inclusion Outcomes

Table 4.2 includes information on the number and percentage of elected local Muslim politicians, covering approximately 70 municipalities in each country. I calculated parity ratios by dividing the percentage of councilors who are Muslim by the percentage of Muslims living in these municipalities. Parity ratios above one indicate that Muslims are overrepresented relative to their share in the population, while ratios below one indicate the opposite. Appendix A provides details about the sample of municipalities, and it explains the methods I used for collecting data on Muslim candidates and for estimating the size of the local Muslim population where official census figures are absent. In Austria and Germany, where I expect few Muslim candidates to run and to be elected, I restrict the data collection efforts to the most recent election outcomes (at the time of data collection, which was completed in February 2014). In Britain and Belgium, where I conduct more detailed analyses (see Chapters 5 and 6), I go back further in time, and I average parity ratios across years. Local elections in Britain take place in different years across municipalities, while in Belgium they occur on the same date across the country. As the number of Muslim politicians in Britain and Belgium has increased over the course of the covered time period, presenting mean statistics slightly underestimates the differences in parity ratios we observe across the two sets of countries (and therefore represents a conservative test). Further, because 98 percent of British Muslims live in England (according to the 2011 census) and because the electoral laws and parties diverge when comparing England with Scotland and Wales, the British sample consists of English municipalities only.

Table 4.2 illustrates that Muslim representation rises along with the potential for Muslim electoral clout, but no clear cross-national pattern emerges with respect to party principles or voter preferences. Though the salience of the equality and nondiscrimination category as well as voter preferences on these issues are similar in Austria, Germany, and Britain, Muslim parity ratios differ widely. Only Belgium seems to fit the pattern: Both parity ratios and commitments to equal treatment and nondiscrimination are highest here (though voters are somewhat less supportive of antidiscrimination measures).

TABLE 4.2. Muslim Political Representation in Municipalities across Countries

| | Importance of the Muslim Vote | | | |
| | Lower | | Higher | |
	Austria 2014	Germany 2014	Great Britain 2002–2013	Belgium 2006 & 2012
1. % Elected Muslims	1.43	3.22	6.26	8.47
2. Number of Elected Muslims	41	138	809	429
3. Muslim Parity Ratio	0.13	0.39	0.74	0.83
4. Correlation between % Muslim Population and % Muslim Councilors	0.56	0.41	0.85	0.96
5. Salience of Equal Treatment & Nondiscrimination	4.1	4.6	4.0	12.1
6. Citizenship Policy Index	0	2	5	5.5

Note: Country-level scores on "Equal Treatment and Nondiscrimination" represent the average salience of this dimension across center-left and center-right parties in each country.

The Citizenship Policy Index is based on Howard's (2009) coding of citizenship regimes (0 is the most restrictive, 6 is the most permissive).

Electoral incentives correlate more clearly with inclusion outcomes. Estimated Muslim parity ratios are lowest in Austria (.13), which also has the most restrictive citizenship regime as well as local electoral institutions that make it difficult for collective mobilization by minority groups to pay off at the polls. Parity ratios rise, but remain well below one, in Germany (.39) whose citizenship laws are a bit more liberal than Austria's. Descriptive representation jumps considerably once we move to Britain (a parity ratio of .74), where large shares of Muslims have obtained British citizenship and where ward-level elections can turn spatially clustered minorities into pivotal groups. Parity ratios are highest in Belgium (.83), the country with the most open citizenship regime and with a preference vote system that encourages electoral coordination along ethnoreligious lines.

In addition, the correlations between the size of the Muslim population and the percentage of Muslim councilors are lower in Austria and Germany than they are in Britain and Belgium (.56 and .41 vs. .85 and .96, respectively), indicating that only where large shares of Muslims are voting citizens and where electoral rules work in their favor does their presence ensure descriptive representation. Though in all four countries Muslims are more likely to enter city halls as their numbers rise, this link is much tighter in countries where the local Muslim population is more likely to have electoral leverage.

These cross-national figures are necessarily crude, but they are consistent with the idea that electoral incentives are more likely to sway local parties than are the principled commitments announced by national party leaderships in manifestos. Table 4.3 breaks down the number and percentage of Muslim

TABLE 4.3. Presence of Muslim Elected Politicians in Municipalities across Parties and Countries

	Presence of Muslim Politicians in Parties		Parties among Muslim Politicians	Party Parity Ratios
	%	N	%	
AUSTRIA (2014)				
Greens	5.4	17	41.5	0.50
Social Democrats (SPÖ)	1.5	16	39.0	0.14
Other	1.1	2	4.9	0.10
People's Party (ÖVP)	0.6	5	12.2	0.06
Far-Right (FPÖ and BZÖ)	0.2	1	2.4	0.02
GERMANY (2014)				
Left Party (Linke)	5.7	19	13.8	0.68
Greens	4.5	31	22.5	0.55
Social Democrats (SPD)	4.1	57	41.3	0.50
Other	4.0	14	10.1	0.48
Christian Democrats (CDU/CSU)	1.2	15	10.9	0.14
Liberals (FDP)	0.8	2	1.5	0.10
Far-Right (various)	0	0	0	0.00
GREAT BRITAIN (2002–2013)				
Labour	9.7	704	73.0	1.14
Other	9.5	48	5.0	1.12
Liberal Democrats	4.9	124	12.9	0.57
Conservatives	2.0	89	9.2	0.24
Far-Right (BNP & UKIP)	0.0	0	0.0	0.00
BELGIUM (2006–2012)				
Center-Left	17.4	312	73.7	1.71
Other	4.6	11	2.6	0.47
Center-Right	4.0	106	24.7	0.39
Far-Right (various)	0	0	0	0.00

Note: Party labels are not included for Belgium because party lists are often coalition of parties, and many municipalities feature a "Mayor's List" which is generally composed of politicians belonging to more than one party. The largest center-left parties are the Francophone and Flemish Socialist Parties (PS and SP.a, respectively). These two parties sometimes present joint lists with the Greens. Center-right lists include Christian Democratic Parties (CDH and CD&V) and Liberal Parties (FDF, MR, N-VA, and VLD). The largest far-right party is the Vlaams Belang. Note that the CDH holds conservative positions on social issues, but its stances on economic issues are more to the left. If the CDH were grouped under "Other," the percentage of Muslims in center-right parties would be 2.9 and the center-right parity ratio would be .29.

politicians across parties and provides parity ratios at the level of the party. Note that because in Belgium party lists are often coalition of parties, parties here are grouped together by family (see note in Table 4.3). For each country, parity ratios are displayed in descending order. This ordering also coincides with a left-right ideological scale: Within countries, parity ratios rise and fall along the left-right spectrum. The Left—especially the Greens and, in

Germany, the Left Party—features markedly higher shares of Muslim politicians than do parties on the Right. In English municipalities, 1 in 10 Labour councilors is Muslim, leading to a parity ratio of 1.14 (90 percent of Muslim councilors in the "Other" category belong to the Respect Party or are Independents). In localities in Belgium, over 17 percent of Left councilors have Muslim origins, producing a parity ratio of 1.71.

Within countries, center-left parties do have better inclusion records than do their counterparts on the Right, but their existing electorates are also less likely to oppose the incorporation of new ethnic minority groups, reducing the potential costs of inclusion. Furthermore, when comparing cross-nationally, it becomes clear that the Center-Left's outreach to Muslim candidates dwindles with Muslims' electoral clout. In Austria and Germany where Muslims have, on average, fewer possibilities to influence electoral outcomes, Muslims still have a difficult time winning on the social democratic ticket. Parity ratios for the SPÖ and the SPD are .14 and .50, respectively. These ratios are still higher than those observed among the ÖVP (.06) and the CDU (.14). However, when comparing parity ratios across countries, we see that center-right parties in Britain and Belgium are more likely to open their ranks to Muslim politicians than are social democrats in Austria. Germany's SPD has a lower parity ratio than do the British Liberal Democrats (.50 vs. .57), and its inclusion record is much closer to center-right parties in Belgium and Britain than it is to center-left parties in these countries.

These sizable cross-national differences—especially visible in Figure 4.4— are hard to square with accounts that are based purely on parties' and voters' expressed beliefs about nondiscrimination. Center-left parties are much more likely to act in accordance with these principles when these are properly aligned with electoral incentives, but they seem to ignore them when Muslim inclusion promises few electoral rewards. These results comport with the theoretical argument outlined in Chapter 2. Only vote-based inclusion will produce a substantial number of minority politicians, and only parties that confront a numerically sizable Muslim electorate will engage in this type of minority recruitment. Exclusion prevails, even among the Left, when the selection of Muslim candidates is expected to generate net vote losses.

On the flipside, among center-right parties, where commitments to equality and nondiscrimination are generally absent and where existing voters express less support for politics promoting these principles, rates of Muslim representation rise with Muslims' potential for electoral leverage. The cross-national results are suggestive here. Within countries, a closer look at municipal election results reveals that center-right parties do expend greater efforts to incorporate Muslim candidates when doing so is likely to be electorally beneficial. Figure 4.5 depicts the proportion of Muslim candidates (both winners and losers) who run on center-right and center-left lists, respectively, in Belgian municipalities in 2006 and 2012. Across lists, the

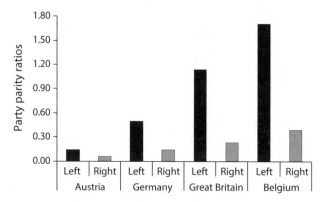

FIGURE 4.4. Muslim Parity Ratios by Party Type and Country
Note: Restricted to the main center-left and center-right parties, except for in Belgium where coalitions of parties often run on the same list (see note in Table 4.3 for further clarification).

percentage of Muslim candidates rises with the size of the Muslim electorate, but, as expected, center-right lists are less likely to contain Muslim candidates. However, once Muslims constitute more than 25 percent of the population, these partisan differences narrow considerably in both relative size and significance ($p < .001$ / $p = .193$ in municipalities where the Muslim population is smaller/larger than 25 percent).

In Belgium, then, center-right parties do feature Muslim candidates where such incorporation is critical for winning seats. The next chapter documents that similar dynamics are at work across municipalities in Britain. But even in German cities that contain large numbers of immigrant-origin citizens, the Christian Democrats (CDU) have made forays into this new voter group. For instance, reflecting on his party's defeat in the 2009 election in Cologne (home to sizable Turkish-origin communities), Peter Kurth, a leading CDU politician, reflected: "49 percent of Cologne's youth have a migration background. In five years [when the next elections will take place] they will all be over 16 years old and able to vote. . . . If the CDU does not take up the issue of integration it will have to come to terms with the fact that it simply won't make headway within certain cultural groups in urban milieus. Without these milieus elections cannot be won." When asked how the CDU would "walk the difficult tightrope" of "tapping new voting segments without scaring off traditional ones," Kurth suggested that the CDU could do more to recruit Turkish-origin candidates who care about family values and business.[42] The next election did indeed feature two such candidates.

42. Berger (2009).

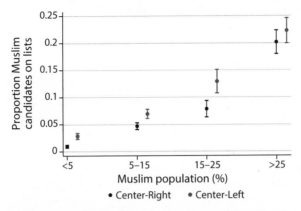

FIGURE 4.5. Muslim Candidates by Party Type and Size of Local Muslim Population (Belgium)

Note: Circles represent means, and capped bars represent 95 percent confidence intervals.

Alternative Explanations

This type of evidence casts doubt on an alternative explanation, namely that variation in the supply of Muslim candidates leads to variation in parity ratios across and within countries, but it is nevertheless conceivable that center-right parties have trouble recruiting a sufficient number of Muslim candidates.[43] Given their tepid, at times hostile, stances toward immigration and Islam, these parties may simply not be attractive choices for Muslims seeking to enter the world of politics, notwithstanding Muslims' greater degree of social conservatism. Likewise, it could be plausible that parties operating in countries where fewer Muslims are citizens face supply problems that help decrease descriptive representation. However, explanations focusing on supply cannot easily account for the observed differences. Figure 4.5 suggests that in Belgium, center-right parties apparently run very similar shares of Muslim candidates as do center-left parties—but only when the Muslim vote is potentially pivotal. Further, if center-right lists were truly constrained by supply in municipalities with smaller Muslim electorates they could compensate for such candidate shortages by placing Muslim candidates on high list positions, thereby boosting their election chances. Yet, in municipalities featuring small Muslim populations, the Right places Muslims on *less* favorable list positions than does the Left.[44] Examining all municipalities as a whole, center-right lists

43. On this point see Norris and Lovenduski (1995).

44. In municipalities with a low percentage of Muslims (less than 5 percent), the average list position of Muslim candidates is 17.8 among the Left and 21.9 among the Right ($p = .007$). In municipalities with a high percentage of Muslim residents (at least 25 percent), these figures are

do not put Muslim candidates on higher list positions than do center-left lists; there are no partisan differences. Finally, comparing Muslim with non-Muslim candidates at different sizes of the local Muslim population, I find that center-right parties place Muslim candidates on significantly worse list positions in localities containing few Muslim voters, but on significantly better list positions when the Muslim population stands at 25 percent or higher.[45] In sum, the Center-Right's stepped-up inclusion of Muslim candidates when the Muslim electorate is crucial, together with its reluctance to offer better list positions when Muslims are poorly represented on lists, indicates that candidate supply cannot easily explain inclusion outcomes.

Turning to differences across countries, it is also highly unlikely that a shortage of candidates drives Austria's and Germany's lower parity ratios. First, the sheer size of the representation gaps (e.g., 0.14 (SPÖ, Austria) vs. 1.71 (Center-Left, Belgium)) suggests that factors beyond supply are at work. Second, in many municipalities achieving representational parity would require only a few winning Muslim candidates out of a large pool of eligible Muslims. To illustrate using averages in German municipalities, a council composed of 62 members in a city where the Muslim population is 7 percent, or, approximately 23,000 members strong, would require just over 4 (4.34) Muslim councilors to achieve parity. Even if a minority (45 percent[46]) of Muslims had German citizenship, and, further, if only half of those were aged 18 or older[47] and therefore eligible to run, this leaves a pool of over 5,000 eligible candidates. Obviously, the majority of these would not be interested in running for office, even if parties were eager to recruit them. Many might not possess the socioeconomic resources conducive to running for office (though this would also be the case in Belgium and Britain).[48] Yet, it is not plausible

---

18.5 among the Left and 18.6 among the Right ($p = .939$) (but note that despite similar average list positions across municipalities, many more Muslim candidates compete in municipalities containing large numbers of Muslim voters). These differences in size and significance do not change when controlling for the number of candidates on party lists.

45. Specifically, in municipalities where the Muslim population is less than 5 percent, Muslim candidates are placed, on average, on spots that are 4 points lower ($p = .007$) than are non-Muslims, whereas in localities where at least 25 percent of the population consists of Muslims, Muslims occupy positions that are, on average, 2 points higher ($p = .019$). In all other municipalities, there are no significant differences in list positions across groups.

46. This estimate is based on data cited by the *Deutsche Islam Konferenz*; see http://www .deutsche-islam-konferenz.de/DIK/DE/Magazin/Lebenswelten/ZahlMLD/zahl-mld-node.html (accessed September 2, 2014).

47. It is easier for children born in Germany to obtain German citizenship than it is for adults born outside of Germany.

48. Examining the political underrepresentation of immigrants in Sweden, Dancygier et al. (2015) find that while immigrants' socioeconomic characteristics reduce their chances of winning local office when compared to those of natives, differences in these individual-level resources across groups can explain only a very small part of the representation gap.

to assume that parties are not able to find 4 qualified candidates out of a pool of 5,000 individuals. These figures—the relatively small number of winning candidates needed for parity and the large size of the eligible Muslim population—make it difficult to believe that shortages in Muslims willing to run for office are the driving force behind the cross-national differences in local-level parity ratios.

Further, research indicates that lack of interest on the part of the immigrant-origin, Muslim population is not to blame for their relative under-representation. In Germany, as well as in Austria, municipalities with even a small immigrant population often feature so-called immigrant or integration councils composed of immigrant-origin representatives (*Ausländer-* and *Integrationsbeiräte*). These bodies only have advisory functions, but they nevertheless include a large number of migrants (citizen and noncitizen) with whom party gatekeepers could connect if they chose to do so. As noted by Holtkamp and colleagues with respect to German municipalities, "the many members of the municipal integration and immigrant councils already suggests that, despite their, on average, more difficult socioeconomic position, a sufficient number of migrants is interested in political engagement. . . . Parties are likely not subject to strong demand or supply constraints when trying to ensure adequate representation on their lists."[49]

Moving on to national-level variables, can differences in countries' embrace of multiculturalism explain cross-national variation in descriptive representation? At first glance, this explanation appears plausible: Austria and Germany are at the low end of the multiculturalism scale whereas Britain and, more recently Belgium, have adopted a more multicultural stance.[50] Thinking about the mechanism connecting multiculturalism to increased descriptive representation, we would expect political parties operating in multicultural settings to encourage minority candidates to run campaigns based on their ethnoreligious heritage, or at least not to dissuade them from doing so. Inspired by a context that actively recognizes and appreciates minority cultures, minority candidates and voters should in turn feel free to coordinate on the basis of homeland, religion, ethnicity, or kinship. By contrast, where state-sponsored multiculturalism is weak or absent, these backgrounds should be immaterial or even harmful during elections. Parties should put much less emphasis on them, and candidates should be reluctant to employ their ethnoreligious origins for electoral purposes.

When investigating party behavior and election campaigns we do not see these behaviors materialize. Rather, candidates and voters adapt to electoral contexts, regardless of official state or party positions on multiculturalism. In

49. Holtkamp et al. (2013, 21), my translation.

50. For multiculturalism indices, see Multiculturalism Policy Index, http://www.queensu
.ca/mcp/, accessed September 2, 2014.

Belgium, for example, the Francophone Socialist Party explicitly denounces identity-based politics. In its 2003 manifesto, the party states that both the party and government as a whole "must refuse the temptation to seek 'community representatives' to resolve certain social tensions." In line with these statements, French-style republican assimilationism has been dominant in Brussels and in Wallonia.[51] Election campaigns on the ground belie these stated norms. As I will elaborate further in Chapter 6, campaigns by Muslim candidates in Belgian cities are marked by highly visible mobilization on ethnoreligious lines with election materials published in Turkish and Arabic. Mosques are key campaign venues.[52] One scholar of Muslim politics remarked about the 2012 Brussels local elections that "those who wished to cast a 'communitarian' vote had an embarrassment of riches"; a record number of Muslim candidates stood for office, and many of them campaigned in and around mosques, drawing support from their religious and ethnic networks.[53] These campaigns blatantly disregard official party stances on multiculturalism and instead respond to the incentives provided by a system that prizes preference votes. This disjuncture has produced a "process of cooptation of immigrant origin politicians and the targeting of immigrant voters . . . in a discursive context which still continued to condemn *communautarism* and depicted ethnic voting as phenomena to be avoided."[54]

Ethnic coordination in Brussels' municipalities has been pervasive because it makes electoral sense, regardless of officially declared state and party policy. Indeed, even in France, the poster child of ethnicity-blind republicanism, electoral recruitment has taken on communalist hues. A recent report notes, "Whereas French political leaders do not lose an opportunity to denounce the dangers of Muslim *communautarisme* (with a connotation of parochialism and tribalism), it seems that they are often the ones rushing to activate community networks in order to get elected or to keep people in check."[55] In fact, the report concludes that Muslims have been less politically powerful than their numbers may suggest because they have been less adept at playing the communitarian card than have other immigrant-origin groups. French politicians have begun to spur ethnic mobilization along, however, devising "Seductive strategies aimed at community leaders in order to attract ethnic votes."[56] For

---

51. Bousetta et al. (2005).

52. Many of these campaign materials can be found here: http://tractotheque.blogspot.com.

53. Torrekens (2012).

54. Teney et al. (2010, 275). Teney et al. further clarify (2010, 295) that "In French public discourse, *Communautarism* refers to the valorisation of cultural difference and the process of mobilisation around an ethnic identity. It is widely seen as something negative among French political elites."

55. Open Society Foundations (2011b, 249); emphasis in original. The report deals mainly with Marseille, but draws out implications for other French cities.

56. Ajala (2010, 85).

instance, when immigrant-origin candidates formed their own list that polled a respectable 14 percent in the first round of the 2008 municipal election in Goussainville (north of Paris), the Socialist Party criticized them "for being too focused on their ethnic origins." Nonetheless, eager to exploit these origins for electoral gain, the Socialists did not hesitate to include these candidates "in the second round of voting in order to win more seats . . . despite the supposedly abstract and non ethnically-specific values that the Socialists claimed to defend . . . politicians can easily adopt an ultrarepublican discourse while at the same time participating in ethnicized politics."[57] Finally, even in famously secular France, this type of mobilization has increasingly shifted from appealing to an "Arab" or a "Maghrebi" vote to targeting a "Muslim" vote.[58]

Austria, which typically ranks near the bottom of indices that measure the extent of multiculturalist policies, also features a low Muslim parity ratio. Yet, in the small—but growing—number of instances when electoral demography and institutions encourage coordination along ethnoreligious lines, candidates do not shy away from identity-based electioneering. In Salzburg, for instance, the Turkish-origin community is sizable enough (7 percent, or close to 10,000 residents, in 2001) to help bring about the election of Osman Günes on the SPÖ ticket. Campaigning in mosques, at Turkish weddings, and at kebab stands, often using Turkish-language materials, Günes admitted that "migrants have given me a big trust advance (*Vertrauensvorschuss*)."[59] His record number of preference votes—1,213 compared to the next-highest total of 393, obtained by the *mayor*—catapulted him from position 23 on the list to position 15 in an election where the SPÖ earned a total of 15 seats. The mobilization of coethnics secured Günes a seat on the city council and earned him the title of "Preference-Vote King" (*Vorzugsstimmen-König*).[60] This example illustrates that ethnoreligious campaigning can pay large electoral dividends even in a nominally monocultural setting and, moreover, that to be successful in a restrictive citizenship and local electoral context such mobilization must be extraordinarily impressive.[61]

Because of the slow but steady rise in Muslim citizenship acquisitions, Günes's campaign is not unique. Around the country, reports are emerging about the ability of Austro-Turkish candidates to drum up votes by drawing

57. Geisser and Soum (2012, 54).

58. On this point, see Ajala (2010).

59. Cited in *Der Kurier*, "Türke ist beliebtester Gemeinderat Salzburgs." March 11, 2014. Accessed September 2, 2014 (http://kurier.at/chronik/oesterreich/osman-guenes-tuerke-ist -beliebtester-gemeinderat-salzburgs/55.484.434).

60. See *Salzburg 24*, "Osman Günes (SPÖ) ist Vorzugsstimmen-König." March 10, 2014. Accessed September 2, 2014 (http://www.salzburg24.at/osman-guenes-spoe-ist-vorzugsstim men-koenig/3889086#forum).

61. Note that Bird et al. (2011a) also make the argument that national multiculturalism policies do not have a large impact on the political representation of immigrants.

on ethnoreligious networks and identities.[62] Similar campaign styles and tactics have long been in evidence among Muslims in British cities and have prompted the inference that British multiculturalism is responsible for this brand of identity politics. The fact that elections in officially monocultural Austria and republican-assimilationist France can be fought—and won—in the same way undercuts this interpretation.

Conclusion

This chapter has provided a macroperspective on the politics of Muslim electoral inclusion across countries. The first part of the chapter presented parties' commitments to principles of equal treatment and nondiscrimination. Drawing on an original text-analysis project of general election manifestos, I showed that, in keeping with its historical roots, the contemporary Left casts itself as being much more devoted to these principles than does the Right. In all four countries, center-left parties consistently emphasize equality and nondiscrimination in their platforms, but parity ratios vary dramatically across these parties. In a nutshell, cross-national variation in inclusion decisions show little trace of these partisan ideological differences that are so starkly visible in national party rhetoric. Though, within countries, the Left always features more Muslim politicians than does the Right, variation in cross-national electoral incentives appears to better account for differences in inclusion outcomes. The next chapter further probes the plausibility of this argument by examining the causes and consequences of Muslims' electoral inclusion in Britain.

62. See, e.g., Beig (2010), Pink (2013), and Schwaiger (2013).

5

Vote-Based Inclusion and the Transformation of Electoral Politics

The previous chapter has argued that parity ratios rise once the Muslim electorate is sizable and mobilized. In such contexts, more Muslims will enter city halls than where, due to citizenship regimes and local electoral institutions, Muslims do not constitute a sufficiently sizable voting bloc. Where Muslims cannot reward parties with substantial support, they stand lower chances of being nominated and elected. The fact that inclusion outcomes vary with the openness of citizenship and electoral laws suggests that parties are much more responsive to the Muslim vote than they are to their stated positions about equality and inclusiveness. Whereas parties' official stances on minority inclusiveness vary little by party type across countries, inclusion outcomes very much do.

The purpose of the present chapter is twofold: First, I furnish additional, more fine-grained subnational evidence that supports the notion that the electoral importance of the local Muslim population can best explain parties' inclusion strategies. Second, I draw out some of the consequences of this electoral logic—specifically of parties' eagerness to rely on ethnoreligious kinship networks when the Muslim vote is crucial—for the nature of party politics. In a national political context where class has traditionally had a strong impact on partisan cleavages, I show that this reliance has increased electoral volatility and decreased the electoral salience of class in Muslim enclaves. Though others have shown that ethnicity can supersede class, most focus on the idea that low-income natives abandon the Left to vote for parties on the Right. Others point out that middle-class ethnic minorities whose economic interests should align with the Right end up supporting center-left parties.[1] I instead highlight the conditions under which low-income minority electorates come to cast ballots *against* the Left.

Most of this chapter is devoted to examining inclusion dynamics within Britain. The cross-national divergence in parity ratios strongly suggests that electoral incentives play a critical role, but we may be concerned that other, country-level factors (e.g., party systems, migration histories, or group characteristics) drive the relationships between citizenship and electoral institutions on the one hand and candidate inclusion outcomes on the other. I therefore turn to an in-depth investigation of candidate selection outcomes in thousands of local electoral contests in English municipalities. By studying elections at the level of the ward, we can see how contextual factors that influence the anticipated net vote gains of inclusion shape parties' selection decisions while holding constant country-level variables.

Specifically, the ways in which Muslim and non-Muslim voters sort into small electoral wards (the median ward population in my sample is approximately 11,800) means that parties will encounter relatively fewer pressures for symbolic inclusion: Electoral wards that have a significant Muslim presence are home to fewer middle-class voters (who might favor minority inclusion) and instead comprise disproportionate shares of low-income voters (who are less likely to do so). Table 5.1 shows that as the share of the Muslim population increases in a ward, the education and employment rates of non-Muslim residents drop off (the census does not measure income, but these two variables are good proxies). Recall from Chapter 4 that Britons' support for laws banning ethnic discrimination declines as their incomes fall (irrespective of their ideological leanings) as does their support for Muslim religious accommodation (see below). Yet, thanks to ward-level elections and settlement dynamics Muslim voters are more likely to share the same electoral space with such low-income voters than they are with higher-income, cosmopolitan voters. This electoral geography increases the odds that the selection of Muslim candidates will produce an electoral backlash, and it lowers the chances that parties face pressures to include symbolically: Cosmopolitans and minorities are less often grouped together than are ethnocentrists and minorities.

This chapter shows that candidate selection outcomes are consistent with the notion that parties are primarily concerned about winning seats when making inclusion decisions. Parties balance their inclusion efforts carefully, incorporating Muslim candidates where they expect the smallest non-Muslim backlash (relative to the size of the Muslim vote), and excluding them where catering to the non-Muslim electorate is more sensible. Parties hesitate to

1. See, e.g., Bird et al. (2011a), Dancygier and Saunders (2006), and Heath et al. (2011).

TABLE 5.1. Skill and Employment Status of Non-Muslims, by Muslim Ward Population Size (%)

Muslim Population in Ward (%)	Non-Muslim Population:	
	Without Qualifications	Unemployed
<5	22.6	5.9
5–20	19.9	8.8
20–35	23.8	11.5
>35	29.4	14.0

Note: Figures are from the 2011 census (available at www.nomisweb.co.uk) and cover England and Wales.

include Muslim candidates in wards where preference divergence and the expected backlash of non-Muslims voters are greatest, urban areas of Muslim concentration that feature a relatively low-skilled, economically deprived electorate. But once the size of the Muslim electorate reaches a critical threshold, these effects reverse, and parties actually include Muslim candidates at higher rates. When Muslims become pivotal voters and party members, inclusion predominates—even if such inclusion provokes resentment in neighboring wards and potentially undermines the party brand as a whole. Comparing these results to the dynamics structuring the inclusion of Hindu candidates, I further argue that it is plausible to assume that party behavior is indeed related to the specific inclusion dilemmas produced by the Muslim presence, rather than to ethnic and religious difference per se.

Turning to the second goal of this chapter, I next consider some of the political consequences that arise when parties predominantly follow electoral incentives. Since in areas of Muslim concentration—and hence potential voting strength—Muslim communalism, traditionalism, and religiosity are more widespread, vote-based minority electoral inclusion will affect the nature of party politics. Parties' pursuit of the Muslim vote, I argue, has made election outcomes more volatile and less class-based. Enclave communalism is thus double-edged: On the one hand it allows for the cheap and efficient delivery of votes, a feature that parties value. On the other, voting on the basis of kin and clan is associated with personalistic, candidate-centered rather than with programmatic, party-centered campaigns. The kinship politics of the enclave are therefore associated with more volatile election outcomes and with election results that are less strongly related to the socioeconomic characteristics of the electorate. Muslim neighborhoods that should be leftist strongholds on the basis of their class and immigrant composition instead are *less* likely to deliver consistent victories for Labour. Among Muslim voters living in enclaves, having low incomes—typically a strong predictor of Labour Party identification—is much *less* likely to lead to alignment with the Party. Together, these results show that parties' inclusion strategies have helped transform the nature of electoral politics. In wards where the Muslim vote is critical, ethnoreligiously based kinship cleavages structure electoral contests.

Muslim Inclusion and the Electoral Logic in Britain

If parties primarily follow electoral incentives, we should observe that the incorporation of minority candidates rises and falls with its expected *net* vote gain across municipalities within countries. Thus, even in districts where Muslims are numerous but where parties are concerned that inclusion generates a backlash, parties will tread carefully. Conversely, if parties mainly want to ensure representational equality, they will be less worried about the potential backlash that arises in such districts.

Parties will be more reluctant to include Muslims when preference divergence, competition over resources, and antipathy towards Muslims are highest—relative to the votes that Muslim voters can supply. Based on evidence presented in the previous chapters, inclusion should therefore be more fitful in urban centers of Muslim concentration, especially where the population is disproportionately poorer and less educated. Poverty exacerbates resource competition, complicating parties' inclusion strategies. Moreover, among non-Muslims low rates of education and income are associated with anti-Muslim sentiment. For example, when the 2008 British Social Attitudes Survey asked about the construction of a mosque in one's neighborhood, low-income and low-skilled Britons expressed the most intense opposition. Such respondents were also significantly less likely to state that they felt favorably toward Muslims.[2] Survey responses of this kind have to be treated with a bit of caution, as the more educated may answer in more socially acceptable ways. Yet, at a minimum, they reveal that those of lower socioeconomic status express hostile attitudes toward Muslims and the accommodation of Islam, a pattern that others have documented as well.[3] The fact that Muslim elected

---

2. Of those with below-median incomes, 39/24 percent stated that the construction of a mosque would bother them a lot/a little compared to 36/2 percent who said that this would not bother them/be something they would welcome. Among respondents with above-median incomes, 28 and 27 percent were extremely and moderately opposed, respectively, while 42 and 3 percent where indifferent or welcoming, respectively. This distribution of preferences was similar when broken down by whether or not respondents had educational qualifications and when the dependent variable was a feeling thermometer towards Muslims. Further, income and skill generally remained significant predictors when additional controls (age, gender, union member, and white ethnicity) were included (see National Centre for Social Research (NatCen) 2010; my calculations).

3. E.g., Field (2012) and Ford (2016).

representatives often successfully campaign for the provision of religious goods, such as halal meat in schools, Islamic burial grounds, and the building of mosques[4] further raises the stakes of Muslim electoral inclusion.

These issues will likely be on the minds of party selectors when considering the slate of candidates they will run in local contests. Across the main parties—Labour, the Conservatives, and the Liberal Democrats—candidate selection tends to be a local affair. Local party institutions above the level of the ward (covering the authority or parliamentary constituency, for example) usually approve a panel of potential candidates, but the local party (typically at the ward level) is charged with selecting council candidates. The national party leaderships are generally not consulted in this process. Though local party leaderships can vet and veto candidates, local residents who join the ward party are involved in the final selection of candidates.[5] Local party elites thus act as initial gatekeepers, but party members also have a say about who stands in elections. In the Labour Party, for example, a local party committee first decides whether potential candidates are "suitable" to compete for selection, a decision that the party's rule book considers a "matter of judgment."[6] However, once nominations are approved, ward party members, rather than party elites, vote on the selection of candidates who run in ward elections.[7]

If parties weigh the benefits of Muslim electoral inclusion against the costs of a non-Muslim backlash, the selection of Muslim candidates should drop off in highly urbanized wards where Muslims are sizable (and hence represent economic and cultural threats) and where voters are comparatively poorer and less educated. In these wards, parties don't expect strong cosmopolitan preferences that would persuade them to select minority candidates, even if only on a symbolic basis. In the empirical models that follow, the independent variable of interest is therefore a ward's level of socioeconomic deprivation at different levels of the Muslim population. Inclusion should decrease as wards with a significant Muslim population become increasingly poorer and less educated, and these trends should be especially visible in densely populated urban areas where poorer and pious Muslims tend to settle. Yet, once the Muslim population becomes very large, these effects should reverse as parties calculate that enclave communalism is a net benefit to them. Although parties

---

4. Gale (2005), Lewis (1994), and Tatari (2010).

5. Copus (2004) and Leach (2006).

6. The Labour Party (2008, 89).

7. Liberal Democrat and Conservative candidates are also selected by local party members (Ali and O'Cinneide 2002; Copus 2004). Copus (2004, 74) considers the differences in selection procedures across parties to be "slight." The main difference, he notes, is that while Conservative and Liberal Democratic practice may at times depart somewhat from party guidelines this is less likely to be the case for Labour. (The below analyses at the ward-party level include party fixed effects.)

may generally be wary of the trappings of communalism and traditionalism, they welcome these social characteristics when they can be usefully deployed at the ballot box.

ELECTION DATA AND POLITICAL COMPETITION

I test these hypotheses at the level of the ward-party. My dataset covers English municipal elections held between 2002 and 2010, yielding 6,784 ward-level elections and 42,650 candidates. It includes the 32 local authorities that make up Greater London, as well as 36 metropolitan authorities located throughout the country (in the Northeast, the Northwest, the West Midlands, and in Yorkshire and the Humber; see Appendix A for a list of municipalities). In Greater London, elections are held every four years (my data cover 2002, 2006, and 2010), and in nearly all wards three seats are up for election. In metropolitan districts, almost all wards also contain three seats, but here elections are held in three consecutive years, with one seat being contested each year, and no election taking place in the fourth year (my sample comprises 2002, 2003, 2004, 2006, 2007, and 2008). Metropolitan wards underwent boundary changes prior to the 2004 election, and a full slate of candidates was therefore elected in multimember elections in 2004 (as in London); wards returned to single-seat elections in subsequent years. In all municipalities, the number of candidates that parties can put up cannot exceed the number of open seats, and elections are held according to plurality rule. When three seats are being contested, voters can cast votes for one, two, or three candidates (across and within parties), but they cannot award candidates with more than one vote (this system is known as the bloc vote). As I will discuss later, this type of ticket-splitting allows voters to single out candidates on the basis of ethnoreligious ties, rather than party. In single-seat races, voters have one vote and pick one candidate.

Before delving into the analysis, let's first have a look at how selection patterns vary across parties and wards. If the electoral calculus is paramount, the main reason why parties would include newcomers who are disliked by existing voters is if these new electorates are sizable *and* if they can take their candidates and votes elsewhere (or if the new group can withhold turnout altogether, which could be damaging depending on group size and vote margins). I have assumed that once it is sufficiently large, there is some degree of competition over the minority vote, and Chapter 4 showed that Muslim candidates win seats for parties other than the Center-Left. But we also want to know whether this outcome is actually driven by parties' competitive recruitment strategies within the same electoral arena. By contrast, if different parties pursue inclusion across different districts, this would be more difficult to square

TABLE 5.2. Nomination of Muslim Candidates by Major Parties across English Wards (2002–2010)

Number of Major Parties Running a Muslim Candidate	Number/Percent of Ward Elections by Muslim Population Size:							
	<5%		5–20%		20–35%		>35%	
	Number	Percent	Number	Percent	Number	Percent	Number	Percent
Zero	4,542	93	866	57	38	17	7	4
One	322	7	473	31	80	36	26	15
Two	19	0	147	10	80	36	71	42
Three	1	0	23	2	24	11	65	38

Note: "Major Parties" refers to the Labour Party, the Liberal Democrats, and the Conservatives.

with the notion that electoral competition *between* parties prompts elites to place Muslims on the ticket.

Overall, 84 percent of Muslim candidates run for one of the three major parties, with 35, 26, and 23 percent campaigning for Labour, Lib Dems, and Tories, respectively. Table 5.2 presents statistics on the number of ward-elections in which none, one, two, or all of the three major parties select a Muslim candidate, disaggregated by the size of a ward's Muslim population. The number of parties that select Muslims to run for office should increase along with the Muslim population, and this is what we observe: In 93 percent of ward-elections where Muslims constitute less than 5 percent of the population, no major party competes with a Muslim candidate. This figure decreases steadily as Muslims' potential electoral clout rises. Once Muslims make up between 20 and 35 percent of the population, only 17 percent of ward-elections do not feature Muslim candidates running for a major party, and this number plummets to 4 percent in wards where Muslims are a considerable electoral force (over 35 percent of the population).

Furthermore, an increasing number of parties selects Muslim candidates as the Muslim electorate grows: When the Muslim population is moderate in size (between 5 and 20 percent) 10 percent of ward-elections are fought with Muslim candidates running for two of the three major parties. This number rises to 36 percent when the Muslim population is large (20 to 35 percent) and to 42 percent when it is very large (over 35 percent). In other words, when the Muslim electorate is very sizable, more than one major party—and often all three—vie for the Muslim vote and recruit Muslim candidates. In wards where winning without Muslim support becomes exceedingly difficult, it is rarely the case that only one of the major parties puts forth a Muslim candidate. Moreover, in these rare instances (15 percent of elections), it turns out that half of the time (13 out of 26 ward-elections) Muslim candidates run as Independents or for smaller parties, such as the People's Justice Party or Respect. Both of these parties, and particularly Respect, have drawn strong Muslim support by combining local appeals (e.g., relating to religious accommodation or economic issues) with international ones (e.g., pertaining to Kashmiri self-determination or the Iraq war).

Far from being captured by one party, the Muslim electorate is thus usually in a position to cast ballots and run candidates across a number of parties, and this is especially so where it constitutes a substantial portion of the electorate. The preponderance of Muslim candidates in such areas is not only a result of non-Muslim party elites calculating that their party can only win with a Muslim on the ticket. In wards of Muslim concentration, Muslims tend to become party members; they constitute substantial portions of the selectorate in charge of making nomination decisions; and they often favor candidates with similar religious and kinship backgrounds.[8]

Table 5.3 presents similar information by party. It shows the percentage of ward-elections in which each party selects Muslim candidates, broken down by whether or not one or both of the competing parties also select Muslim candidates, and by the share of the Muslim population. In all instances, parties are more likely to select a Muslim candidate if one or both of the other major parties do so as well. For example, examining all ward-elections, the Labour Party runs Muslim candidates in 12 percent of contests; this share goes down to 7 percent when Lib Dems or Tories do not jump in, and it increases to 36 and 71 percent, respectively, when restricted to wards where one or both of the other two parties also select Muslim candidates. Similar trends are visible for the Liberal Democrats and the Conservatives: Each party is more likely to nominate Muslims in wards where one of the other two parties does the same.

Further, across parties, selection becomes significantly more likely as the share of the Muslim population rises. Across wards, the Labour Party tends to be most active in recruiting Muslim candidates, followed by the Lib Dems, with Tories not too far behind. These results are similar to those observed in the Belgian case (see previous chapter), where right-of-center lists begin to include substantial number of Muslim candidates once electoral demography compels them to do so.

Nevertheless, it is perhaps somewhat surprising that the Conservatives field Muslim candidates when other parties continue to run non-Muslims. For instance, in 41 percent of ward-elections in which 20 to 35 percent of the population is Muslim but where neither Labour nor Lib Dems runs a Muslim candidate, a Muslim Conservative candidate is seeking office. Why would the Tories risk an ethnocentrist backlash when other parties are not overtly jockeying for the Muslim vote? This might seem counterintuitive. But note, first,

---

8. Garbaye (2005), Purdam (1998), and Solomos and Back (1995).

TABLE 5.3. Nomination of Muslim Candidates by Major Parties across English Wards, by Selection Decisions of Other Parties (2002–2010)

		Ward-Elections in which Parties Select Muslim Candidates (%)		
Muslim Population		Labour	Lib Dems	Conservatives
All		12	9	7
< 5%		3	2	2
5–20%		24	17	14
20–35%		54	44	43
> 35%		85	75	56
By Number Of Other Major Parties Running Muslim Candidates				
All	Zero	7	5	4
	One	36	24	19
	Both	71	48	43
< 5%	Zero	3	2	2
	One	7	5	5
	Both	14	11	17
5–20%	Zero	20	15	11
	One	32	21	19
	Both	48	28	27
20–35%	Zero	41	41	42
	One	56	45	46
	Both	71	41	41
> 35%	Zero	65	50	46
	One	83	74	53
	Both	92	79	58

Note: "Major Parties" refers to the Labour Party, the Liberal Democrats, and the Conservatives.

that there are only 28 ward-elections of this type in the dataset; in the remaining 69 ward-elections in which a Muslim Conservative runs (keeping the Muslim population between 20 and 35 percent), at least one Muslim contender stands for one of the two other major parties.

Second, an inspection of some of these cases illustrates that this phenomenon tends to represent short-term miscalculations by Labour and the Liberal Democrats, not by the Conservatives. Examples are instructive: In Great

Lever ward in Bolton (a former mill town in Greater Manchester) where three seats were up for election in 2004, neither Labour nor the Lib Dems nominated Muslim candidates, while the Tories nominated two. The two Muslim Tory candidates, Mohammad Idrees and Ansar Hussain, won the largest vote shares, followed by Labour's candidate, Prentice Howarth (implying, in turn, that Idrees and Hussain outperformed the non-Muslim Tory candidate who failed to win a seat). Labour switched course in the following elections: In two out of the three subsequent single-seat contests, Labour ran Muslim candidates who each won handily. By 2008, all three parties were nominating Muslims. In another example, Thornhill ward in the northern town of Kirklees, a strong showing by the British National Party (BNP) likely scared Labour and Lib Dems away from including Muslim candidates. In the 2002 and 2003 Thornhill single-seat contests, BNP candidates scored 17 and 28 percent of the vote, respectively, and came in two points ahead of Labour in 2003. Nonetheless, the Conservative Muslim candidates emerged victorious in both years. Labour took note, and in each of the following elections the party ran Muslim candidates.[9] These examples suggest that parties do make selection mistakes, but also that they recalibrate quickly, picking the inclusion strategy that maximizes their chance of winning the next time around.

CANDIDATE SELECTION OUTCOMES
AND THEIR DETERMINANTS

These data and examples illustrate that there is both hesitancy to incorporate Muslims when the electoral rewards are uncertain and competition when Muslims become a pivotal part of the electorate. Party leaders will take into account whether Muslims' electoral leverage will suffice to counterbalance the electorate's hostility towards this group and their representation in politics. Because this hostility rises with the extent of economic disadvantage in a ward (as discussed above), in the following analysis local socioeconomic deprivation stands in as a proxy for the ethnocentrist backlash. I measure this variable with the Index of Multiple Deprivation. This index, assessed every three years, is commonly used to describe the extent of material deprivation in small local areas and to identify disadvantaged localities. It quantifies several dimensions of deprivation (including in the areas of education, income, employment, housing, and services) and takes into account the demand and the supply side, incorporating population characteristics (such as income, employment, and education) as well as area-based scarcity (such as availability and condition of housing and education). The sample represents the wide variation in depriva-

---

9. Though there were boundary changes in 2004, the boundaries of Thornhill ward remained the same (but the ward was renamed to Dewsbury South).

tion experienced in the country as a whole (see Appendix B for summary statistics and sources). Further, as area-based socioeconomic deprivation rises, so do Muslim and overall economic disadvantage and, by implication, resource competition as well as cultural distance. It is not the case, however, that areas that are economically deprived generally have high Muslim population shares; deprivation is also high in some all-white, non-Muslim areas and is not a proxy for Muslim concentration.[10]

The dependent variable measures whether a party selects (1) or does not select (0) a Muslim candidate, and I control for the number of seats that are being contested in the ward. I also include non-Muslim incumbency, which can lower the odds of Muslim inclusion. Party leaders are usually hesitant to replace sitting candidates, and this effect is likely compounded when the aspiring candidate belongs to a minority group.[11] Controlling for incumbency also serves another purpose: Economically deprived wards tend to be the type of working-class wards where Labour is particularly entrenched. Without accounting for incumbency, a connection between economic conditions and selection could therefore simply reflect Labour strongholds with machines that any candidate, including those of Muslim faith, would find difficult to penetrate (there are no term limits). I measure incumbency with a dummy, indicating whether parties ran a non-Muslim incumbent in the previous election. Since selection calculations may not be constant across regions and elections, region and year fixed effects are included, as are party dummies.[12] Finally, I limit the regressions to the three major parties (Labour, Conservatives, and Liberal Democrats), as smaller parties may only compete once candidates come forward (results are similar when examining all parties).

Parties are indeed more reluctant to select Muslim candidates when they expect a significant electoral backlash. The interaction between economic deprivation and the share of the Muslim population is negative (see Table 5.4 and Figure 5.1); as wards become more economically disadvantaged, the strong effect of the size of the Muslim electorate diminishes. Put differently, when an ethnocentrist backlash is expected, it takes a larger Muslim electorate to secure nomination.[13] Figure 5.1 presents this effect graphically. It depicts the change in the probability of parties selecting a Muslim candidate when the

10. The correlation between the overall (Muslim) unemployment rate and deprivation is .90 (.67) (p = .000). To calculate the latter, I restrict the sample to wards where at least 100 Muslims reside. The correlation between economic deprivation and the percentage of Muslims is .31 (p = .000). Many economically disadvantaged wards contain predominantly white, non-Muslim residents.

11. Norris and Lovenduski (1995).

12. On the Muslim vote in the aftermath of the Iraqi invasion, see Curtice et al. (2010).

13. Note that the positive coefficient of *Economic Deprivation* in Table 5.4 denotes the effect when *Muslim Population* is set to zero, and is hence not substantively meaningful.

TABLE 5.4. Selection of Muslim Candidates across Wards in
English Municipalities

Muslim Population (%)	.118***	.119***
	(.00843)	(.00865)
Economic Deprivation	.00649***	.00801***
	(.00176)	(.00202)
Muslim Population (%) ×	−.00111***	−.00118***
Economic Deprivation	(.000165)	(.000168)
Number of Seats		.309*
		(.152)
Non-Muslim Incumbent in		−.369***
Previous Election		(.0481)
Conservatives	−.376***	−.485***
	(.0457)	(.0526)
Liberal Democrats	−.165***	−.236***
	(.0434)	(.0509)
Constant	−2.521***	−2.755***
	(.131)	(.233)
Region Fixed Effects	Yes	Yes
Year Fixed Effects	Yes	Yes
Peudo-R²	.321	.337
N	19,110	12,767

Note: The dependent variable is whether a party selects (1) or does not select
(0) a Muslim candidate. The unit of analysis is the ward party during a given
election.
Coefficients are from a probit model. Robust standard errors (clustered on
the ward) are in parentheses.
* p<0.05; ** p<0.01; *** p<.001

percentage of Muslims in a ward rises from 1 to 15 percent (upper panel), at
different levels of economic disadvantage.[14] As the Muslim population grows
in size, so do nomination chances, but this effect is much weaker when wards
are economically disadvantaged, and where a good portion of the electorate
therefore likely harbors ethnocentrist views. An increase in the Muslim population from 1 to 15 percent at minimum levels of economic deprivation is associated with a 36 point rise in the probability of Muslim candidate selection,
but this rise drops to 7 points in the most deprived wards.

The lower panel of Figure 5.1 in turn shows the effect of economic deprivation on selection chances at different levels of the Muslim population. It can
be interpreted as the effect of the anticipated ethnocentrist backlash when the
perceived threats associated with Muslim representation vary. When deprivation rises from one standard deviation below to one standard deviation above

14. This change roughly corresponds to a change from one standard deviation above to one
standard deviation below the mean; the standard deviation is 9.2, the mean is 5.3.

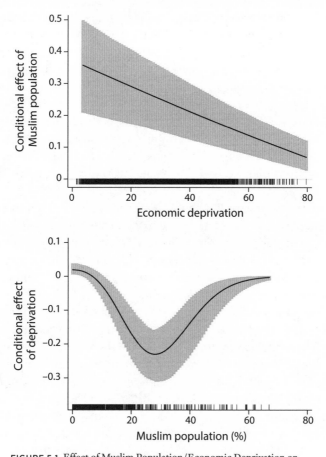

FIGURE 5.1. Effect of Muslim Population/Economic Deprivation on the Probability of Selecting a Muslim Candidate at Different Levels of Economic Deprivation/Muslim Population

Note: The results are based on Model 2 in Table 5.4. The dependent variable is whether or not a ward party runs a Muslim candidate. The solid lines trace the conditional effects, and the shaded areas cover the 95 percent confidence intervals. In the upper panel, the conditional effect is that of the *Muslim Population* changing from one to 15 percent. In the lower panel, the conditional effect is that of *Economic Deprivation* changing from 14.8 to 43.1 (one standard deviation below/above the mean). The rug plots (the vertical lines along the *x*-axes) depict the distribution of *Economic Deprivation/Muslim Population* across wards.

the mean, the probability of selecting a Muslim candidate decreases by up to 23 points (or about three-quarters of a standard deviation of the dependent variable). This occurs when a ward's Muslim population is approximately 30 percent. In such high-deprivation, high-concentration wards, parties expect that the nomination of a Muslim candidate will cause some of their non-Muslim constituents to jump ship, and their reservations about slotting such a candidate deepen as a result. When the Muslim population is smaller, parties expect anti-Muslim hostility, proxied by deprivation, to be less widespread. Economic deprivation consequently has a weaker, though still negative, effect on Muslim candidate selection when the Muslim population is less sizable. Finally, the net gains from inclusion will rise once the expected size of the Muslim vote begins to surpass the size of the backlash. In Muslim enclaves, where Muslims are decisive in determining selection and election outcomes as both selectors and as voters, effects reverse. Here, the mobilizational strength of the Muslim electorate wins out, and Muslim descriptive representation increases.

These results mesh well with this book's main theoretical propositions. Another implication of these propositions is that trade-offs should be particularly stark in very urbanized wards. Based on the social geography of migration that was sketched in Chapter 3, inclusion trade-offs in deprived areas should be especially salient in urban centers where Muslims' degree of religiosity, social conservatism, and economic disadvantage are highest. Here Muslim preferences clash with those of the majority electorate. I therefore broke down the analyses, dividing the sample based on whether a ward's population density was above or below the sample median (not shown). In low-density wards, effects are quite muted. Going from minimum to maximum levels of deprivation, the difference in the effect of the Muslim population on the probability of inclusion is 10 points. In more urbanized, high-density wards, this difference stands at 26 points. Turning to the effect of economic deprivation, I find that increases in this variable are associated with at most a 7-point drop in low-density wards (though this effect is not statistically significant at conventional levels). By contrast, in highly urbanized, densely populated wards (found in East London, Birmingham, and Bradford, for example), the likelihood that parties will select a Muslim candidate declines by as much as 27 points as the socioeconomic status of the electorate and material conditions decline.[15]

ALTERNATIVE EXPLANATIONS

That parties are reluctant to nominate Muslim candidates in areas of high concentration, deprivation, and urbanization is, I have argued, partly driven by the distribution of Muslim preferences. Dense urban Muslim settlements are characterized by Muslim communities that are disproportionately religious,

---

15. The difference in the interaction terms across models is significant at $p = .053$. Note also that wards whose Muslim population is at the very high end—45 percent or higher—are all densely populated, a settlement feature that is common across England and in much of Western Europe (see Chapter 3).

socially conservative, and poor—characteristics that provoke hostility among segments of the non-Muslim electorate, especially in economically deprived areas. Yet, several alternative mechanisms may be at work. For example, the negative effect of economic deprivation may be due to reasons of candidate supply, with fewer candidates coming forward where income and education levels are low. Existing evidence, however, suggests that supply factors are not at work. For instance, based on a survey of local candidates across parties (fielded from 2007 through 2009), only a small number (between 10 and 20 percent across parties) thought that ethnic minorities were underrepresented in local councils because they were not interested in politics or because they lacked the confidence for being involved in politics. Instead, a plurality of respondents agreed with the statement that "Political parties don't do enough to recruit" ethnic minority candidates.[16]

Moreover, even if it were true that few potential Muslim candidates emerged in deprived wards, parties cast a much wider net as candidates have to reside in the municipality, but not in the ward, where they compete for election. Only slightly more than half (55 percent) of all candidates actually reside in the wards where they run for election, and this number tends to be lower in urban areas and among the major parties.[17]

Could it be that Muslims who decide to come forward in low-income, high-concentration areas have fewer political skills, and that more politically competent Muslims decide not to compete in these wards for fear of losing? To answer this question systematically, information would be needed on all Muslims who consider entering local races as well as those who end up running; such data are not available. However, local cases generally do not fit this pattern. Tower Hamlets, for example, is home to a large, economically disadvantaged Muslim population, and it is one of the country's most deprived authorities. Bangladeshis sought entry into the local Labour Party early on, but party leaders resisted these advances in the face of native opposition. It was only once Bangladeshis ran successful campaigns as independents and became ward party members that Labour opened its ranks to Muslim candidates. The candidate pool remained the same, but selection outcomes changed.[18] Analogous events unfolded in other cities with sizable Muslim populations of relatively lower socioeconomic status, including Bradford and Birmingham.[19] Case studies are more likely to mention the competition for representation within Muslim communities among several aspiring politicians than to suggest that too few qualified Muslims were available to run.

16. For detailed results, see Rallings et al. (2010, 373).
17. Rallings et al. (2010, 367).
18. Eade (1989) and Glynn (2008).
19. Regarding Bradford, see Le Lohé (1975). On Birmingham, see Solomos and Back (1995).

If supply side explanations are inadequate, perhaps the answer lies in the behavior of the Muslim electorate. Muslims living in deprived wards may be less likely to vote. Facing a politically disengaged electorate, selectors could then surmise that a Muslim candidate will not boost the co-ethnic vote here. Qualitative and quantitative evidence rules out this mechanism. Muslim electorates, including those living in deprived areas, often display high turnout rates, buttressed by the mobilizational capacity of ethnic networks.[20] Survey data also confirms that Muslim voters with low incomes are no less likely to vote in local elections than are their high-income counterparts.[21] In short, it is doubtful that explanations stressing supply or turnout can account for the dampening effect of economic deprivation (and the associated ethnocentrist backlash) on Muslim electoral inclusion in areas of Muslim concentration.

Lastly, it is possible that in poorer areas selectorates resist the entry of *any* minority group, regardless of the groups' economic standing, religious demands, or social values. To test for this possibility, I replicated the analysis focusing on the selection of Hindus.[22] Hindus are a good comparison group because they share many potentially relevant traits with Muslims, but they differ in their religiosity, social conservatism, and socioeconomic status in ways that should significantly reduce the electoral backlash associated with inclusion. The majority of Muslims and Hindus in England (in 2001, 68 and 85 percent, respectively) trace their origins to the subcontinent. They thus have similar skin colors and ethnic backgrounds as do Muslims, making it less likely that such features cause differences in electoral inclusion. Both groups began to arrive in large numbers in the 1960s, with male workers arriving first, to be joined by families later. Additional inflows arrived via East Africa after being expelled by leaders of newly independent African nations. Politically, both groups lean towards Labour and report above-average turnout rates in local elections.[23]

The two groups do vary considerably in the features that shape parties' selection strategies: social and religious values and economic standing. The religious presence of Hindus has not given rise to the same degree of opposition as has that of Muslims.[24] This is in part due to the fact that the salience of Hindus' religious practice is less pronounced, even in enclaves. Mosques far outnumber Hindu temples, and there are about twice as many Hindus per temple as there are Muslims per mosque.[25] This aligns with varying degrees of

20. Fieldhouse and Cutts (2008) and Garbaye (2005).
21. EMBES (2010).
22. To identify Hindu candidates I used the same name-based procedure that I employed for Muslim candidates (see Appendix A).
23. EMBES (2010).
24. Bleich (2009).
25. Peach and Gale (2003, 479).

religiosity: When asked "How important is your religion to you?" 51 percent of Muslims, but only 17 percent of Hindus, stated that religion was "extremely important" to them.[26] Furthermore, religious radicalism and violence are not politically salient issues when it comes to European Hindus.

Additionally, Muslim electorates may present a greater threat in the fight over public resources and therefore provoke a more substantial backlash and, hence, a steeper vote loss at the polls. Muslims are almost three times more likely than Hindus to be unemployed; their labor market participation rate is close to 20 points lower than that of Hindus; and Muslim men's hourly wages are about two-thirds those of Hindu males.[27] Even in wards where economic deprivation is high (above the sample average) Muslim economic need exceeds that of Hindus. In such wards, the mean Muslim unemployment rate is 16.6 percent compared to that of Hindus, which registers 5.7 percent. In other words, where resource competition is likely to be high, Hindus do not pose a significant economic threat to non-Muslim voters. The allocation of goods to Hindus has thus not been politicized in recent years. Indeed, a BNP publication in Oldham specifically asked white residents to target Muslims with harassment, but to spare Hindus.[28]

Given these group characteristics, party gatekeepers are not likely to conjecture that Hindu candidates will alienate voters as economic deprivation rises. When I repeat the above analyses on a sample of Hindu candidates, this implication is borne out (see Appendix B). Regardless of the size of the Hindu population, economic deprivation does not influence selection. At the same time, results indicate that local parties still respond to electoral and institutional constraints. A higher number of seats bodes well for Hindu candidates while non-Hindu Labour incumbency does not. Thus it is not the case that Hindus encounter no hurdles when seeking to gain entry into electoral politics. Rather, variation in the threat potential of groups generates variation in the kind of barriers local parties put up when selecting candidates.

Summing up this section, we can conclude that selection outcomes are consistent with parties seeking to maximize their chances of capturing seats. Muslims are less likely to cross the selection hurdle where parties expect to reap net losses from inclusion, namely in economically challenged wards where anti-Muslim sentiment and conflicts over material goods are at their peak. However, such wards become attractive as the Muslim population grows sufficiently sizable to neutralize a non-Muslim backlash at the polls. Here, candidates can tap into tight, ethnoreligious social networks, and they can

26. See EMBES (2010). Overall, 94 percent of Muslims and 73 percent of Hindus said that religion was very or extremely important to them ($p = .000$).

27. See Hills et al. (2010) and data from the 2001 census.

28. Allen (2005, 55).

campaign on a communal basis. Party elites incorporate Muslims in these set-tings even though, as Chapter 3 illustrates, it is precisely in these wards that Muslim voters are especially likely to espouse preferences and behavioral norms that deviate most sharply from those of the broader majority popula-tion. The rest of this chapter elaborates on the role of ethnoreligious cleavages in elections and demonstrates their effects on the nature of party politics.

Implications of Vote-Based Inclusion for the Nature of Party Politics

If electoral inclusion is most common in vote-rich enclaves, how does this incorporation affect the nature of party politics? Case studies of individual localities have highlighted the significance of communal, clan-based cam-paigning in Muslim neighborhoods. Descriptions of local mobilization drives typically mention the candidate-centered character of Muslim election cam-paigns—partisanship is said to take a back seat, as the kinship ties that fostered chain migration and concentrated settlement are today being employed for electoral purposes.[29] According to a survey of Muslim councilors conducted in the mid-1990s, three quarters of these politicians have called upon loyalties based on caste and *biraderi* (patrilineal kinship ties) when seeking to rally fellow Muslims to the polls. In the same survey, Muslim councilors stated that local parties had tried to manipulate the salience of the *biraderi* cleavage for political gain and indicated that the Conservative Party had sought to "divide the Muslim Labour vote by highlighting the *biraderi* identities of Muslim La-bour candidates and selecting rival *biraderi* Conservative candidates."[30] Fi-nally, these kinship ties are also used to recruit new party members and to urge fellow Muslims to vote en bloc to ensure the selection and election of a favored candidate. Aggregate election data lend support to the mobilizational role of these networks: Muslims' electoral registration rises to 96 percent in neigh-borhoods whose Muslim population share is 15 percent or higher, compared to 58 percent in areas where this share is below 5 percent.[31]

The 2004 election in Manningham ward, Bradford, illustrates how the sa-lience of the *biraderi* can upend election outcomes. Manningham's population was over two-thirds Muslim in 2001 (the highest in the sample), and commu-nal politics in this inner-city ward has had a long history. The "essential style of politics" some have argued, has been "clan-based, clientelistic and non-ideological" with party labels being mere "flags of convenience."[32] With many

29. See, e.g., Akhtar (2013), Eade (1989), Glynn (2008), Purdam (1998, 2001), Scott (1972/73), and Solomos and Back (1995).

30. Purdam (2001, 151).

31. Fieldhouse and Cutts (2008).

32. Baston (2013, 44).

voters casting ballots on the basis of ethnoreligious, kinship ties, the 2004 election resulted in a highly unusual outcome: The three seats that were open went to three different parties, with Labour, the Tories, and the Liberal Democrats each capturing a spot. Since each party ran three candidates (all Muslim), this result implies that many voters either only made use of one of their votes or that they distributed their votes (up to three) across parties based on religion and kinship. Either way, many voters did not endorse the full slate of candidates put forth by each of the major parties.

In the great majority of multimember ward elections, by contrast, voters do support candidates on the basis of party, and the same party wins all seats. To put the Manningham result in perspective, among the 2,657 ward elections in my dataset where three seats were in play, only 15 percent produced councilors that were of two different parties, but less than 1 percent—a total of 9—yielded winners belonging to three different parties. Furthermore, with economic deprivation above the 95th percentile, Manningham should have been safe territory for Labour. In wards with similar economic profiles, Conservative candidates simply do not win.[33]

ETHNORELIGIOUS SUPPORT

It is possible that this unusual election outcome reflects idiosyncrasies of Mannigham's Mirpuri community. Alternatively, ethnoreligious voting and the partisan volatility that ensues may characterize enclave politics more broadly. Though local descriptions of communal voting exist, we do not have a good sense of how typical this behavior is or what its electoral repercussions are. To shed some light on these questions, let's take a look at how Muslim candidates perform with respect to their co-partisans running in the same ward in multimember ward elections. Figure 5.2 displays the *Muslim Vote Proportion*, which divides the number of votes attained by a party's Muslim top vote getter by the number of votes that the same party's non-Muslim top vote getter receives in elections where parties field more than one candidate. Ratios above one indicate that Muslims outperform their non-Muslim co-partisans, while ratios below one mean they do worse. The *Muslim Vote Proportion* ranges widely, from a minimum of zero to a maximum of 3.4; the mean/median is .97/.93. On average, then, voters award fewer votes to Muslim candidates within the same party. As Figure 5.2 (top-left) clearly shows, this penalty is largely a feature of wards whose Muslim electorate is small. However, when Muslims constitute between 20–35 percent of the population, Muslim

---

33. I define wards with similar economic profiles as those that are within 5 points of Manningham's multiple deprivation score. Within that range, Manningham is the only ward to produce a Conservative councilor.

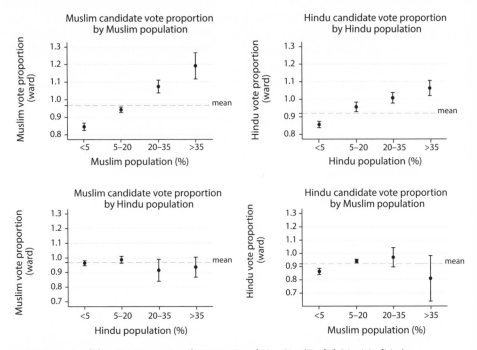

FIGURE 5.2. Candidate Vote Proportions by Group Population Size (English Municipalities)
Note: The circles display means, and the bars represent 95 percent confidence intervals. The dashed lines reflect the sample means.

candidates actually do better at the polls, outperforming non-Muslims running on the same ticket by about 7 percentage points. And in wards with very high Muslim population shares (above 35 percent), Muslim candidates receive, on average, 20 percent more votes than do their non-Muslim co-partisans. Though intraparty vote differences are common, as factors such as incumbency, personal knowledge of the candidate, or gender enter into voters' decisions, the size of the vote gap between candidates of different faiths observed in Muslim enclaves is high.[34]

These dynamics are consistent with vote choices that are at least in part divorced from partisanship and instead motivated by ethnoreligious attachments among Muslims—as well as among the non-Muslim electorate. Yet, it is conceivable that these election outcomes reflect minorities supporting minorities irrespective of faith or ethnicity, rather than being a product of one-sided ethnoreligious mobilization. The bottom-left panel of Figure 5.2 calls this interpretation into question. It shows that increases in the size of Britain's third-largest religious group—Hindus—are not associated with a rise in Mus-

34. Among non-Muslims, the mean/median vote proportion between a party's top ranked candidate and the runner-up is 1.10/1.06.

lim candidates' fortunes. By the same token, Hindu candidates do not outperform non-Hindu candidates of the same party as the Muslim population expands (bottom-right). The *Hindu Vote Proportion* remains consistently below 1, and it drops off significantly when moving to wards whose Muslim populations range from 20 to 35 percent to those wards where this figure surpasses 35 percent ($p =.04$; bottom-right panel). Lastly, we have suggestive evidence that Muslim enclaves also differ in the *extent* to which ethnicity, religion, and kinship influence election campaigns. The top-right panel of Figure 5.2 reveals that Hindu candidates competing in Hindu enclaves also obtain higher vote shares than do non-Hindu contenders running on the same party ticket. However, these gains are considerably more modest when compared to those attained by Muslim candidates standing in Muslim enclaves.

Comparisons with Hindu electoral inclusion illuminate the significance of ethnoreligious kinship networks in structuring electoral inclusion. But to what extent is co-ethnic and co-religious favoritism unique to Muslims living in Britain? Ward-level electoral institutions could be exceptionally well-suited to this type of communal campaigning. Additionally, British Muslims may be especially adept at rounding up the community vote. A brief look at evidence from Belgium demonstrates that these behaviors travel. Though Belgium features at-large contests using PR rather than ward-level, plurality elections, Muslim candidates in Belgium also engage in ethnoreligious electioneering (see Chapter 6). As mentioned in Chapter 4, Belgian voters have the option of casting ballots for individual candidates, and voters of Moroccan and Turkish origin are said to make disproportionate use of this practice to support co-ethnics. Individual-level survey evidence has further shown that voters of Moroccan and Turkish descent in Brussels' municipalities are significantly more likely to cast preference ballots for ethnic minority candidates than are those of Belgian descent. According to exit polls in three municipalities in Brussels taken during the 2006 local elections, only 24 percent of respondents with a Belgian mother, but 79 and 58 percent of respondents with a Turkish or Moroccan mother, respectively, said they gave preference votes to ethnic minority candidates.[35]

These portrayals of candidate and voter behavior are based on analyses and rich descriptions of electoral campaigns in a few municipalities. The election data that I have collected, which cover 69 municipalities, 2 election cycles, 984 party lists, and over 28,000 candidates, offers a glimpse of the prevalence of such phenomena. Figure 5.3 presents the percentage of preference votes Muslim and non-Muslim candidates obtain within a party, respectively, at different levels of the local Muslim population (note that the population breakdown differs from the figures pertaining to English wards because it refers to

---

35. Teney et al. (2010, 291).

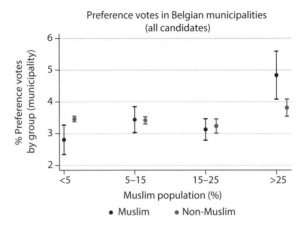

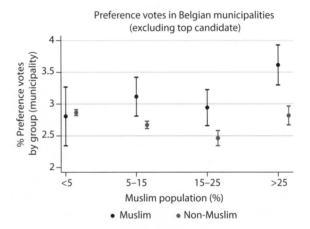

FIGURE 5.3. Preference Votes in Belgian Municipalities for Muslim and non-Muslim Candidates
Note: The circles display means, and the bars represent 95 percent confidence intervals

municipalities that are larger in size). Whereas the top panel includes candidates running on all list positions, the bottom panel excludes candidates that are placed on the top spot. The latter candidates usually garner by far the most preference votes as voters tend to endorse their parties' top candidate, but list leaders are rarely Muslim. Similar developments unfold in either scenario: In municipalities where Muslims form only a small part of the electorate, non-Muslim candidates tend to collect a higher percentage of preference votes. Once the Muslim population rises, so do votes cast for Muslim contenders, but non-Muslim candidates see their fortunes fall in these locations. All too aware of these dynamics, party gatekeepers have opened up their lists to Muslim candidates, especially in areas of Muslim concentration. The next chapter

will explore some of the consequences that these inclusion decisions and support patterns have for the representation of women. For now, these aggregate
results are in line with the notion that voting on the basis of ethnoreligious ties
is not limited to English municipalities.

ETHNO-RELIGIOUS CLEAVAGES AND THE TRANSFORMATION OF ELECTORAL POLITICS

Religion, ethnicity, and kinship are salient features of electoral politics in areas
of high Muslim concentration. How, then, do nominally nonethnic parties fare
in contexts where ethnoreligious ties and kinship networks shape electoral
participation? In Manningham, parties appear to simply be organizational
conduits that allow candidates from different kinship groups to compete for
office. But, as noted above, Manningham is at the end of the distribution, both
in terms of the size of its Muslim population and of the socioeconomic composition of its electorate. Nevertheless, if faith and kinship guide voter behavior in settings where these cleavages are not connected to party labels, we
should expect more electoral volatility. Voters may switch their support to
candidates based on kinship and clan from one election to another. In past
years, such behavior existed largely *within* the Labour Party. As a result, religiously diverse working-class wards delivered large and steady majorities for
Labour, making it seem like Muslim voters were safely captured by the party
when, instead, substantial parts of the Muslim electorate supplied clan-based
bloc votes.

Having caught on to these mobilization tactics, other parties, including the
Liberal Democrats and the Tories, have sought to strengthen their presence
in Muslim enclaves. The fact that local Labour parties relied on the efficiency
of kinship networks to secure council seats, thereby legitimizing clan-based
politics and the representatives it produced, has generated higher degrees of
electoral uncertainty for the Left once these kinship ties are deployed elsewhere. As a result, electoral volatility rises in Muslim enclaves. We can most
easily get a sense of this volatility by looking at the average net change of Labour's vote share from one election to the next (between 2002 and 2010).[36]
This measure can take on values between 0 and 1; in the sample it ranges from
0 to .46, with a mean of .06 and a standard deviation of .05. Figure 5.4 makes
clear that as the Muslim electorate grows so does variation in a ward's Labour
vote share across elections. The Labour Party's election results are most unstable in Muslim enclaves, where the average net change is .13. This score puts

---

36. I take the average since not all wards have the same number of elections across years. This
measure is an adaptation of the electoral volatility index as calculated by Nooruddin and Chhibber
(2008).

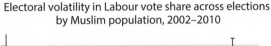

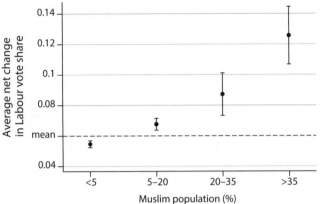

Electoral volatility in Labour vote share across elections
by Muslim population, 2002–2010

FIGURE 5.4. Volatility of Labour Vote Share in English Ward Elections
(2002-2010), by Ward Muslim Population Size
Note: The circles display means, and the bars represent 95 percent confidence intervals. The dashed line reflects the sample mean.

Muslim enclaves, on average, between the 90th and 95th percentile in terms of electoral volatility.

One may wonder whether these high levels of electoral volatility are indeed brought about by the electoral behaviors of religious minority groups or whether it is instead something intrinsic to these wards that generates high degrees of partisan instability. Perhaps Muslims have settled in areas that are marked by chronic political problems or poor governance, resulting in fickle partisan attachments and a weak party presence no matter who the residents may be. To adjudicate between these two scenarios, I look at past levels of electoral volatility, focusing on just over half of the municipalities in my sample—the 36 metropolitan boroughs—whose ward boundaries did not change between the early 1980s and the early 2000s.[37] I next examine levels of electoral volatility between 1982 and 1990, broken down by wards' Muslim population share as recorded in 2001, to see whether Labour's vote shares were highly volatile in wards that would only later become areas of Muslim concentration.[38]

37. I am grateful to Carlos Velasco Rivera for this idea. In London boroughs, ward boundaries changed in 1998, making it impossible to compare election results from the 1980s with results in the 2000s. In metropolitan boroughs, ward boundaries underwent some changes before the 1980s (and again in 2004), and I therefore choose the eight-year period between 1982 and 1990.

38. Though it is possible that some of these wards, for instance in Bradford, already had a sizable Muslim population in the 1980s (the census did not include a religion category until 2001), the demographic development of the Muslim population in Britain makes this highly unlikely.

The top panel of Figure 5.5 shows how electoral volatility changes as we move from wards with low to high levels of Muslim concentration in metropolitan boroughs between 2002 and 2003 (boundary changes went into effect in 2004), while the bottom panel depicts the same measure for the same wards, but between 1982 and 1990. In earlier decades, before Muslims became a sizable political force in what are present-day Muslim enclaves, levels of electoral volatility were nearly identical across wards. When Muslims were, for the most part, not yet in a position to swing elections, Labour's vote shares were similarly variable across locations. The top panel, by contrast, shows that in later decades there is a significant uptick in volatility in areas of Muslim concentration.[39] In short, wards became electorally more volatile for Labour once Muslim voters and politicians gained extensive electoral influence.

Moreover, it is not the case that this greater variability centers around a very high average vote share for Labour. The proportion of Labour winners across elections[40] does increase with the size of the Muslim population, but it falls off sharply in Muslim enclaves (see Figure 5.6). In wards where Muslims constitute between 20 and 35 percent of the population, 73 percent of winners belong to the Labour Party, but in wards whose Muslim population exceeds 35 percent, this share declines to 64 percent.[41] This drop-off is even more remarkable considering that electorates in Muslim enclaves are, on average, less educated and have much lower incomes than elsewhere.

Despite facing significant economic disadvantages, wards in which Muslims comprise a high share of the electorate are not captured by the Left. Though left parties have been shown to sustain losses to far-right parties in the face of ethnic diversity, Labour's underperformance in areas with a large Muslim presence is driven by the voting behavior of *minorities* who do not vote according to class lines—not (only) ethnocentrist voters belonging to the majority electorate.[42] A considerable portion of these vote losses can be attributed to gains made by the Liberal Democrats among Muslims. It is doubtful, however, that the majority of Muslim voters living in enclaves are drawn to the Liberal Democrats for purely ideological reasons. The party did benefit from Muslims' deep frustration with Blair's decision to participate in the Iraq

39. The difference in volatility in wards with a Muslim population between 20–35 percent and 35 percent or more is significant at $p = .047$.

40. For example, if a ward elects 8 councilors between 2002 and 2010 and 4 belong to the Labour Party, this results in a proportion of Labour winners of .5.

41. This 9-point difference is significant at $p = .109$ (two-tailed). Because election results are aggregated across years, the number of observations is lower than in previous analyses (56 wards feature Muslim populations above 35 percent).

42. In a regression where the Proportion Labour Winners is the dependent variable, Muslim enclaves are consistently associated with negative effects while variables measuring the strength of the nativist BNP are insignificant. See Appendix B for more detail.

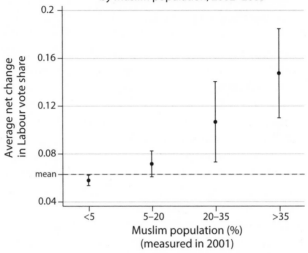

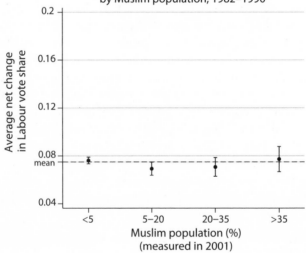

FIGURE 5.5. Changes in Volatility of Labour Vote Shares in English Ward Elections over Time

Note: The circles display means, and the bars represent 95 percent confidence intervals. The dashed line reflects the sample mean. In both graphs the *% Muslim Population* refers to 2001 levels.

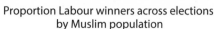

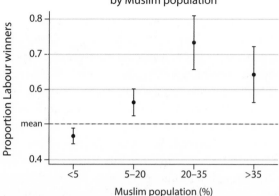

FIGURE 5.6. Labour Winners in English Ward Elections, by Ward Muslim Population Size
Note: The circles display means, and the bars represent 95 percent confidence intervals. The dashed line reflects the sample mean.

war,[43] but Muslim voters, especially those living in predominantly Muslim neighborhoods, were significantly more likely to support Muslim than they were non-Muslim Liberal Democrats: The *Muslim Vote Proportion* among Liberal Democrats in areas where Muslims constitute at least 35 percent of the population is 1.12, and it rises to 1.16 in the years *following* Britain's participation in the Iraq war.[44] Labour's support of the Iraqi invasion gave the Lib Dems an opportune opening, but we should not observe this preference for co-religionists if it were only party platforms that caused Muslims to shift their support from Labour to the Lib Dems.

Rather, kinship-based campaigns also unfold within the Liberal Democratic camp. In fact, well before the 2003 Iraqi invasion clan politics influenced election outcomes, even during general elections. In 1983, Bradford West's Labour MP, Edward Lyons, defected to the Social Democratic Party (the party later joined with the Liberal Party to form the Liberal Democrats). Approximately one-third of the parliamentary constituency's electorate was Muslim, and Lyons, having "formed good relations with clan leaders . . . was able to take a number of them with him." While Muslim support meant that Lyons was able to secure an unusually high turnout for Labour in the previous election, in 1983 this support was transferred to the Social Democratic Party,

43. See Curtice et al. (2010).

44. Furthermore, the difference in the *Muslim Vote Proportion* attained in Muslim enclaves by Labour vs. the Liberal Democrats is not statistically significant ($p = .46$).

resulting in a much reduced Labour vote and, ultimately, in a victory for the Tories.[45]

Far from being a purely local affair, limited to one party, the electoral politics of the enclave can thus have repercussions for national politics as well. To cite another example, in 1997, when the Conservatives lost 11 percentage points nationwide, they managed to gain 5 points in Bethnal Green and Bow (East London). The constituency features a large Muslim population of Bangladeshi origin, and the Tory Muslim candidate competed against Oona King, a non-Muslim Labour candidate.[46]

In other constituencies the Labour Party also cannot count on the Muslim vote. In his memoirs, former Labour MP Roy Hattersley, who represented the Birmingham Sparkbrook constituency for more than three decades, described how the "well-organised and invariably loyal Kashmiris [who] had cast their disciplined vote early in the day" helped him win reelection.[47] But when Hattersley returned to his old constituency in 2005, he noted that circumstances had changed: "For more than 30 years, I took the votes of Birmingham Muslims for granted . . . if, at any time between 1964 and 1997 I heard of a Khan, Saleem or Iqbal who did not support Labour I was both outraged and astonished. . . . Anxious immigrants who throw themselves on the mercy of their members of parliament are now a minority. Their children and grandchildren will only vote for politicians who explicitly meet their demands."[48] Some of these demands relate to policy, while others have more to do with personalized constituency service (for example, helping voters fill out government forms or assisting them in obtaining visas for relatives from abroad). Expecting political representatives to actually represent the interests of voters is a healthy development. Where this shift has occurred, Muslims are no longer electorally captured, and parties won't be able to ignore their interests. Increases in electoral volatility can therefore signal progress. However, the severed link between Labour and Muslims can also reflect the continued salience of communal networks whose leaders are not necessarily elected on the basis of their policy stances, competence, or responsiveness.

Furthermore, the fact that the Labour Party does worse in areas of Muslim concentration implies that class politics is on the wane in these areas. After all, Muslim enclaves tend to be more economically deprived than other areas. Beyond the aggregate voting results I have presented thus far, narratives of electoral politics in the enclave also indicate that religion and kinship networks trump class in structuring campaigns and voting behavior. Akhtar's

45. Samad (1996, 94).
46. Fisher et al. (2015).
47. Cited in Sobolewska et al. (2015, 33).
48. Hattersley (2005).

participant observations of electoral campaigns in several Birmingham wards are particularly insightful:

> Biraderi-politicking is important in Pakistani community politics . . . substantive, policy-related issues were not typically discussed on canvassing campaigns by the main parties. . . . What appears to have been of utmost importance was the chain of familial or social networks, and more specifically, the difference between biraderis, which dictated how constituents were contacted. So, for example, which house doors were knocked on and by whom depended on which candidate/campaigner had links to or knowledge of the residents. Furthermore, if candidates encountered women or young people, they were told to tell their husbands and fathers, respectively, that such-and-such a candidate from such-and-such a region in Pakistan had called by.[49]

Criticisms of this style of politics have emerged from within the Pakistani community. In 2003, Shahid Malik, then a member of Labour's National Executive and later MP for Dewsbury, told the BBC "that the Party has unwittingly allowed the clans to infiltrate British politics by influencing who is chosen from within Pakistani communities to go forward for candidate selection. . . . 'The Labour Party and other parties got used to dealing with those [clan] people and there seems to be an unwitting collusion there between the parties and first generation British Pakistanis.'" Nazir Ahmed, a member of the House of Lords, stated that patrilineal clans were paramount in electoral politics: In "Peterborough, Bradford, in Birmingham, when they put up candidates, from the Jatt Biraderi or the Rajput Biraderi, it does not matter what their politics is, when it comes to voting they will vote for their own. And this is what happened during my Parliamentary selections. People said 'Well he's a Jatt so we won't vote for him.'"[50]

In Bradford, clan politics have shaken up partisan alignments, as illustrated by the 2004 election results in Manningham cited earlier. But even a decade earlier, ethnoreligious clan linkages had taken the place of partisan attachments in this northern city. Recognizing the ensuing electoral volatility, the National Executive Committee of the Labour Party suspended several local ward parties in heavily Pakistani areas for a time in the mid-1990s. The reason: Their members, mostly of Kashmiri origin, had supported the Conservative candidate because he was from the "right" clan.

> For the first time in Toller Ward . . . candidates were fielded by the two main political Parties, who both emphasised and concentrated on loyalties within the community. The Conservative candidate was a Muslim for the

49. Akhtar (2013, 97).
50. Both quotes are cited in Akhtar (2003).

Jat Clan, which had a very large association in the area, and the Labour candidate was a Muslim from the Bains Clan, which had a much smaller presence in Toller Ward. Two of the existing Labour councillors were from the Jat Clan, which led to divided loyalties and conflict. During the local election campaign many Asian community divisions and loyalties were highlighted, and many young men roamed the streets for several weeks with the enthusiastic support of their elders. "*Jat or Bains*" was the frequent cry on the streets. The whole election came to be seen as between warring clans. . . . Both political parties had released forces which the party hierarchies did not understand, and could not control.[51]

Philip Lewis, an expert on Muslim politics in Bradford, further explains how these dynamics work: "a Kashmiri politician mobilises his kinship network to gain control of a local ward party. When he wins the seat as a Labour councillor, his Kashmiri rival decides to offer himself to the Tories. Clan and caste rivalries are then played out on the streets and bewildered voters wake up to discover this or that party's safe seat has fallen to the opposition."[52]

Once in a while the vulnerabilities of the clan-based machines are exposed, with repercussions for national politics. In Bradford West (the parliamentary constituency covering Manningham and several other wards), George Galloway, running for the Respect Party, beat out Labour's Imran Hussain in a 2012 by-election. Hussain had been approved by Kashmiri elders and local power brokers in what critics denounced as a discussion-free "coronation," rather than a democratic selection meeting.[53] Local religious leaders (*pirs*) added their endorsement and pronounced that support for Hussain was a religious duty. Galloway managed to cleverly exploit the liabilities of the *biraderi* political machine while at the same time appealing to traditional Muslim sensibilities. He credibly argued that the expedient bargain struck between clan elders and the major parties had failed large portions of the local electorate— smaller clans, non-Kashmiri voters as well as young people and women—and that even though he was competing on the Respect ticket he was in fact the true leftist in the campaign, the "real" Labour candidate. He also sent leaflets to Muslim addresses championing his supposed Muslim credentials: "God KNOWS who is a Muslim. And he KNOWS who is not. . . . Let me point out to all the Muslim brothers and sisters what I stand for. I, George Galloway, do not drink alcohol and never have. Ask yourself if the other candidate [Labour's Imran Hussain] in this election can say that truthfully."[54] Though Galloway defeated Hussain handily, he could not sustain his momentum. Despite La-

---

51. Bradford Congress (1996, 88–89).

52. Lewis (2002, 138–39).

53. Peace and Akhtar (2015, 235).

54. See Baston (2013) and Gilligan (2012) for further details on the by-election.

bour's disastrous 2015 general election results, the party retook Bradford West with Naz Shah (of Pakistani descent), while Imran Hussain emerged victorious in neighboring Bradford East.[55]

The *biraderi* is especially significant among Pakistani Muslims, but similar forces are at work among other groups. In London's East End, for instance, the prevalence of Bangladeshi councilors has produced a political culture and election campaigns in which homeland politics, religion, and factional divides dominate politics. These cleavages have split the Labour Party. In 2012, five Bangladeshi councilors were expelled from the party for actively campaigning for an opposition candidate who had been endorsed by the mayor, Lutfur Rahman. Rahman had initially been nominated to run as a mayoral candidate for Labour, but was deselected by the Party's National Executive Committee amidst allegations that he had links to fundamentalist Islamist organizations and engaged in voter fraud to secure his selection.[56] Ousted by Labour, Rahman ran and won as an Independent, but a number of Labour councilors of Bangladeshi origin appeared to be more loyal to the mayor than to their party.

Reacting to these episodes, one former Labour Party manager stated that, "Labour is struggling to retain control over its local party in the east end. It's as if a small corner of the party had mutated, like in some bad sci-fi flick, and taken on a life of its own outside Labour. . . . This is a monster we [the Labour Party] created."[57] Once outside Labour, Rahman also found support among far-left forces looking for votes. "In this respect," a journalist remarked, "Rahman was merely the latest footnote in a sorry tale of the pro-Islamist Left—the Hitler/Stalin pact of the twenty-first century."[58]

Rahman was eventually removed from his mayoral post after a high court judge declared him guilty of corruption, voter fraud, and bribery. Moreover, the mayor was found to have engaged in "undue spiritual influence." Remarkably, this judgment relied on a nineteenth-century law that sought to limit the influence of Roman Catholic clergy on Irish Catholic immigrant voters, who were deemed more susceptible to the political pronouncements of bishops than to those of the secular political establishment. The judge found that Rahman had exploited voters' religious beliefs to pressure them into voting for

55. The election of Shah was not without controversy. Labour's National Executive Committee imposed an all-female shortlist in Bradford West, perhaps in an effort to break with the area's patriarchal clan politics. Amina Ali, a London-based female politician of Somali descent, was initially selected, but she pulled out. A selection panel then picked Shah, also a woman but a Bradford local and newcomer to politics. Among some members of Bradford's Kashmiri political establishment the selection of Shah was a source of deep resentment (Kuenssberg 2015). In 2016, Shah was suspended from the Labour Party for making anti-Semitic remarks, but the Party lifted her suspension after a few months.

56. See, e.g., Eaton (2010) and Hill (2010).

57. Marchant (2012).

58. Bloodworth (2015).

him. Evidence of unlawful spiritual influence came in the form of a public letter written by 101 imams and Madrassah teachers instructing Muslims to vote for Rahman as well as statements allegedly made by Rahman's campaign that competing candidates would shut down mosques and that supporting Rahman was a "religious duty."[59]

Rahman had at this point left the Labour Party, but fraudulent voting practices and religious bloc voting were nourished by segments of the party long before the well-publicized Rahman affair, and they have unfolded in local authorities elsewhere.[60] Critics therefore refer to Labour's inclusion strategies in Pakistani-Muslim enclaves as a "Faustian pact with community elders . . . [whereby the] bloc vote has reinforced a lazy form of multiculturalism on the left, which saw someone as Kashmiri Muslim first with certain views and policies derived from that ethno-religious identity."[61]

Though rooted in ethnoreligious networks and identity, linkages between politicians and voters in Muslim enclaves are not only about religion or community politics. They are also about access, which can range from ordinary constituency service to patron-client relationships. The latter are quite common among immigrant electorates more generally, whose unfamiliarity with the new environment, coupled with language barriers, creates the need for intermediaries. However, insofar as clientelistic linkages are based on reciprocity—services are only rendered if it is clear that clients cast ballots for the patron—they are susceptible to electoral malpractice. As Sobolewska and colleagues note in their report about voter fraud in Pakistani and Bangladeshi-origin communities,

> we have heard many first-hand accounts of this phenomenon whereby the services of the councillor were understood to be exclusively "earned" by those local residents who have cast a vote for this candidate. Thus, by contrast, voters who supported the opposition were understood to have no claim on the elected councillor's time and help. . . . This is a very extreme expression of patronage politics, which is common in Pakistan and Bangladesh . . . where these kinship networks originate. . . . As a result, many of our interviewees explained that the voters wanted the candidates to see them vote for them so that their claim to the future councillor's services can be clear and beyond doubt.[62]

The report continues with a quote from an "Asian activist":

59. Barnett (2014). For a discussion about the parallels between Muslim and Irish Catholic voters with respect to the legislation on religious influence during elections, see Fraser (2015).
60. See, e.g., Akhtar (2013), Sobolewska et al. (2015), and Solomos and Back (1995).
61. Goodhart (2012).
62. Sobolewska et al. (2015, 28).

In my election, people brought me their postal vote forms. They would sign them and then say 'you can vote whichever way you like.'. . . Saying 'look, these are my household's and they have all signed them, they have all filled it in, I haven't ticked them, here you tick them and you can post them.[63]

These fraudulent activities do not represent the norm, but they show how tight ethnoreligious networks can be grafted onto electoral politics, even in the context of a long-established, economically developed democracy where programmatic class-based cleavages have long been thought to dominate electoral politics.[64] Yet, where religious clan politics are salient, class politics appear to be absent.

To what extent do these campaign and voter narratives match up with the voting behavior of individual Muslims? It is possible that egregious cases of voter fraud and *biraderi* politics make the headlines, but that the voting behavior of the majority of Muslims living in enclaves does not look any different from those living elsewhere. We can gain further insights into this question by probing how class and local sociodemographic contexts interact to shape partisan identification. If ethnic politics of the enclave indeed leads to a decline in the salience of class in electoral politics, we should observe that Muslims' economic backgrounds fare worse in predicting identification with the Labour Party in wards that contain a very high number of Muslims compared to those that do not.

In Table 5.5 we see that living in Muslim enclaves attenuates the effect of income on Labour Party identification among Muslims. The dependent variable is whether the respondent thinks of herself as Labour (coded 1) or as belonging to some other party (coded 0).[65] Of particular interest is the interaction term, *Muslim Population > 35% × Low Income*. The negative coefficient denotes that having low incomes is not as strongly related to identifying with the Labour Party if Muslims live in wards where the Muslim population share exceeds 35 percent. In these wards, having few means is not necessarily

63. Ibid.

64. Cross-nationally, the incidence of clientelism in the electoral process declines with economic development (Stokes et al. 2013); but see also Kitschelt (2000).

65. These results are based on the EMBES (2010); the question reads: "Generally speaking, do you think of yourself as Labour, Liberal Democrat, [Scottish National/Plaid Cymru,] or what?" I define wards with a high share of Muslims as those whose population is at least 35 percent Muslim; this operationalization coincides with the categorization used previously, and it also represents the 75th percentile among Muslim respondents. To measure income, I rely on a 14-point scale denoting household income. Respondents who fall below the median are classified as having low incomes. A substantial number of respondents declined to answer questions about income. I therefore ran additional models using multiple imputation. The results are very similar to the ones presented in Table 5.5.

TABLE 5.5. Effect of Class on Muslims' Labour Identification in Enclaves

		Population Density	
		High	Low
Muslim Population >35 %	.206	.181	.129
	(.250)	(.301)	(.389)
Low Income	.259	.244	.231
	(.151)	(.223)	(.214)
Muslim Population >35 %	−.593**	−.742*	.235
× Low Income	(.227)	(.317)	(.410)
Male	−.0140	−.168	.108
	(.123)	(.182)	(.178)
Age	.00636	.00907	.00239
	(.00508)	(.00660)	(.00862)
Constant	.337	−.107	.176
	(.416)	(.847)	(.496)
Region Fixed Effects	Yes	Yes	Yes
Pseudo-R²	.022	.027	.024
N	565	313	241

Note: The dependent variable is whether a respondent thinks of herself as Labour (1) or not (0). High/low population density wards are defined as those wards whose population densities are above/below the median (when the sample is restricted to Muslim respondents).

The sample is composed of respondents who think of themselves as belonging to the Muslim religion.

Coefficients are from a probit model (weighted). Robust standard errors (clustered on the ward) are in parentheses.

* $p<0.05$; ** $p<0.01$; *** $p<.001$

associated with thinking of oneself as Labour. This weakened class effect goes hand in hand with the high salience of ethnoreligious and kinship cleavages in the enclave, and it helps explain why we observe Labour Party losses in areas of Muslim concentration. Moreover, these effects are largely a product of densely populated wards. The middle and right columns break down the results by a ward's population density.[66] In densely populated enclaves where, I have argued, we are most likely to observe strong links bound by kinship, tradition and religion, low household incomes are not associated with identifying with the Left. Figure 5.7, which depicts the predicted probabilities of Labour identification at different levels of income and a ward's Muslim population, reveals the size of these effects. Outside of the enclave, having low incomes is associated with a 71 percent chance of thinking of oneself as Labour. However, this proportion drops by over 20 points for Muslims who have

66. High/low population-density wards are defined as those wards whose population densities are above/below the median (when the sample is restricted to Muslim respondents).

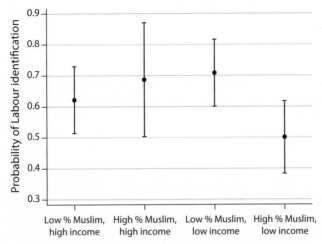

FIGURE 5.7. Labour Party Identification among Muslims, by Respondents' Income and Ward Muslim Population Size
Note: Circles are predicted probabilities, bars are 95 percent confidence intervals. These results are based on Table 5.5 (high population density wards).

low incomes and who reside in wards that are home to a sizable Muslim population. In dense enclaves, class does not map onto partisanship among the Muslim electorate. Aggregated to the ward and parliamentary constituency level, these political behaviors undergird the politics of the enclave, where election results are increasingly volatile, and the Left's fortunes decline.

Conclusion

Parties are cautious when selecting Muslims in settings where such inclusion could cost them precious votes, but they readily recruit Muslim candidates when failure to do so spells electoral defeat. These dynamics were already visible in the cross-national comparison, which revealed that Muslims stand a much better chance of gaining entry into local politics in countries where their votes are more likely to be coveted in local elections. In this chapter, I build on these findings while holding constant variables at the country level that may otherwise influence the incorporation of minority candidates and varying local factors that affect the net vote gain that parties anticipate inclusion to generate.

I further explored the repercussions of parties' vote-driven inclusion strategies for the nature of party politics. Parties' keen interest in recruiting the Muslim vote in Muslim enclaves has prompted them to cultivate links with clan elders who promise to deliver bloc votes to their favored candidates. Although this type of politics served the Labour Party well in the past, in more recent years the increased salience of ethnoreligious and kinship ties that local Labour Parties helped foster has contributed to vote losses for these parties and to a political climate where class is much less relevant in shaping partisan attachments.

In these ways, the vote-based incorporation of Muslim candidates and voters has promoted a style of politics in the enclave that is distinct from areas where parties consider Muslims to be less crucial electorally. In doing so, this inclusion has transformed electoral cleavages and altered the social identity of parties in the process. Campaigns based on religion and kinship not only bring in candidates who place greater value on these social markers; they are also mainly a male affair. The next chapter therefore investigates the implications of vote-based inclusion for gender parity. It will demonstrate that when pursuing inclusion in the hopes of attracting Muslim votes, parties systematically privilege male over female candidates and thereby contribute to a decrease in women's representation.

6

Religious Parity
versus Gender Parity

The assessment of short-term net vote gains governs parties' selection decisions. Chapter 5 highlighted the long-run repercussions of this strategy for the party system and political cleavages. This chapter considers the consequences of minority inclusion for the identity of parties: How and when does Muslim inclusion affect the gender balance among candidates?

The prominence of male-dominated ethnoreligious kinship ties in the recruitment of the enclave vote suggests that men will have an edge. It therefore seems logical that Muslim electoral inclusion would be an entirely male affair, altering parties' gender composition in the process and presenting a profound dilemma to parties—especially those on the Left—that advocate for both gender equality and minority inclusion. Yet, as I have argued throughout this book, we cannot assume that the characteristics and preferences of the minority population are neatly reflected in the minority candidate pool. Parties' inclusion objectives critically mediate this relationship. Though traditional kinship networks and patriarchal social orders are salient in Muslim enclaves throughout Western Europe (see Chapter 3), parties' inclusion goals vary within and across countries. This difference in turn generates differences in candidate types. The predictions developed in Chapter 2 state that some parties will be eager to benefit from the mobilizational advantages that minority candidates enmeshed in the world of the enclave can offer, while others will choose to forego these and opt for candidates who are more palatable to voters of the majority population, even if such candidates cannot boost minority turnout in the same way.

One implication of this logic is that variation in inclusion goals leads to variation in gender parity. In the case of symbolic inclusion, party gatekeepers will disproportionately pick female candidates, who, I elaborate below, can more easily signal assimilation on a salient dimension. By contrast, when parties pursue vote-based inclusion, they are more likely to select male candidates, since men are better equipped to deliver the enclave vote.

There is, then, a stark trade-off between religious parity and gender parity: When parties select only a few symbolic candidates, gender parity will improve slightly, but Muslim parity ratios will be low; when parties incorporate a large number of Muslim candidates, religious parity will rise, but the gender balance will be skewed further towards men. In addition to a simple compositional logic driving this latter effect, this decrease in overall gender parity is exacerbated when parties do not balance the entry of a new, mostly male, group with measures that put women on an equal footing. As I will show below, this scenario plays out in the Belgian case, where the presence of Muslim candidates crowds out female winners, in part because parties fail to treat women fairly in the allocation of list positions.

These dynamics speak to one of the central issues raised by the Muslim Question: the concern that Muslim immigration presents a challenge to progressive achievements in the area of gender equality.[1] But they also reveal that majority institutions and actors—in this case parties and party gatekeepers—are not as gender egalitarian as debates about Muslim integration would have it. The mobilizational advantages of male Muslim candidates and parties' keen reliance on them, combined with parties' continued unfavorable treatment of female candidates, means that parties that include a large number of Muslim candidates will see their share of female politicians decline.

This chapter first expands on the theoretical predictions, focusing on how the two inclusion types lead to different gender preferences and, further, how uncertainty about candidate types means that parties—and voters—need to rely on shortcuts to assess a prospective candidate's belief system. Next, I look at religious parity and gender parity outcomes in local elections across countries. Muslim women are relatively overrepresented in Austria and Germany, where symbolic inclusion is more common and religious parity is low, but they are relatively underrepresented in Great Britain and Belgium where vote-based inclusion occurs more frequently, and religious parity is higher. I then probe the underlying voter and party mechanisms by investigating election and selection outcomes at the municipality, party, and candidate level in one country, Belgium. Belgium is a very useful—and hard—case. The PR list system allows us to observe parties' list placement of candidates by religion and

1. Cesari (2013) and Norton (2013).

gender, while the distribution of preference votes provides clues about voter behavior. Belgium is a hard case because of its relatively strong and binding gender parity laws: The two top spots have to be filled by one man and one woman, and lists have to include an equal number of men and women. In spite of these rules, I find that when parties hope to recruit the Muslim vote, gender parity suffers. Muslim men outperform Muslim women at the polls, and parties further advance Muslim men's election chances by placing them on more favorable list positions than women. Together, these developments reduce the share of elected women, both Muslim and non-Muslim, and they hold in highly urbanized municipalities where Muslim attitudes toward gender roles are especially conservative.

Inclusion Types and Candidate Types

Variation in the importance of the Muslim vote leads to differences in inclusion goals. What unites parties operating in these different environments, however, is the need to pick not just *any* candidate, but a candidate who can fulfill particular inclusion objectives: namely, vote mobilization or symbolic representation. Failure to pick a vote mobilizer when the Muslim vote is significant, especially in the context of a majority population who is suspicious of inclusion efforts, can cost parties precious votes. Here, parties miss their chance to make electoral headway within the minority community, and they may still manage to alienate a portion of the majority electorate. Conversely, when symbolic inclusion is the goal, picking a candidate who is later revealed to deviate significantly from majority norms and values similarly risks the loss of majority votes that cannot be counterbalanced by a sufficiently large minority electorate.

Minority candidates are often scrutinized, in part because opposing parties hope to inflict damage on parties that are diversifying their lists. The Austrian Social Democrats (SPÖ), for instance, had to defend their choice of candidates when the far-right Freedom Party (FPÖ) charged the former had become an "Islamistenpartei" (Islamist Party). Though the FPÖ's accusations can generally be dismissed as nativist rhetoric (their campaign slogan encouraged voters to support "Viennese blood"), the SPÖ nonetheless found itself having to defend candidates who had ties to Islamist organizations. Specifically, SPÖ candidate Resul Ekrem Gönültaş who ran for a seat in the national parliament in 2013, is a member of the Islamic Federation (*Islamische Föderation*), an offshoot of Milli Görüs. The latter is a large Turkish Islamic diaspora organization that is under state surveillance in Germany and Austria. According to Germany's office for the protection of the constitution (*Verfassungsschutz*), it rejects Western democracy and envisions an Islamic social order. Austro-Turkish

Green politician Efgani Dönmez blamed the SPÖ for making candidates like Gönültaş politically and socially acceptable (*salonfähig*), a move he said would prompt social democratic voters to opt for the far-right.[2]

In Sweden, a minor scandal broke out when Omar Mustafa, head of the Islamic Association, was elected to the Social Democrats' Board, an important national party institution. Though many Social Democrats seek to diversify the party's ranks to include Muslims, Mustafa's views on gays, women, and Israel came under public attack, leading the party leader, Stefan Löfven, to conclude that Mustafa "cannot be a member of the party if he does not stand up for equal rights and gender equality."[3] Mustafa resigned, and a slew of editorials followed, calling the incident "one of the formative moments in the modern Swedish multiculturalism debate."[4] Years earlier a foreign-born candidate running in Swedish local elections could have predicted this outcome. He noted that as "an immigrant from the Middle East" to be viable within party politics "you have to prove that you are not hostile to women. . . . The burden of proof is on you."[5]

This quote underscores the fact that irrespective of their past activities or true beliefs, immigrant-origin candidates can make for easy targets. With respect to Muslim candidates, political opponents will highlight matters that arouse concern among the majority population. The Belgian populist party *La Droite*, for example, accused Abdurrahman Kaya, a Socialist councilor of Turkish origin in Anderlecht (a Brussels municipality with a large Muslim population, where I expect vote-based inclusion to dominate), of submitting a "discriminatory and sexist" proposal: The kitchen in a new municipal building, Kaya supposedly suggested, should be walled off, so that women preparing meals could be hidden from male eyes. Kaya, a teacher of Islamic religious studies, disputed the allegations vehemently and planned on filing a complaint against his detractors.[6] In Evere, another Brussels municipality, Kébir Bencheikh won a seat on the ticket of the Christian Democratic CDH; he soon had to defend his involvement with Islamist militias, dating back to the 1970s when he was a student in Casablanca.[7]

2. Pink (2013).

3. "Omar Mustafa to leave role as head of Islamic group?", Radio Sweden, April 13, 2013 (http://sverigesradio.se/sida/artikel.aspx?programid=2054&artikel=5504206, accessed April 23, 2013). Allegations of anti-Semitism were also made.

4. This is the assessment of political scientist Andreas Johansson Heinö; see "Mustafa-affären är här för att stanna", April 18, 2013 (http://andreasjohanssonheino.blogspot.se/2013/04/mustafa-affaren-ar-har-for-att-stanna.html, accessed April 23, 2013).

5. Blomqvist (2005, 91).

6. La Dernière Heure (2013).

7. Voogt and Dorzee (2006).

Summarizing Belgian parties' inclusion strategies, Eelbode and colleagues note that both the Socialists and the Christian Democrats "were so eager to attract ethnic votes . . . [in local elections, that they] were not careful when selecting ethnic minority candidates." As a result, both parties "faced scandals over unsuitable candidates on their lists (for instance, members of the Grey Wolves, an ultranationalist, neofascist Turkish organization)."[8] In Germany, Turkish-origin candidates and party members are also often said to have connections with, for instance, the Grey Wolves, the transnational religious Gülen movement, or Milli Görüs. Such linkages—real or fabricated—can give rise to attacks from political opponents within and outside parties and can produce unwanted headlines such as "NRW [North Rhine Westphalia] CDU tolerates radical Turks within its ranks."[9]

These examples substantiate the notion that selecting the "wrong" type of candidate can have adverse consequences. But how do parties pick the "right" type of candidate? Much of the literature on candidate evaluation relates to *voters'* assessments at the ballot box. Lacking sufficient knowledge about all the potentially relevant background characteristics of competing candidates, voters will use information shortcuts—such as partisanship, gender, ethnicity, or local roots—to guide their decisions.[10] Parties anticipate this behavior and select candidates accordingly.

However, voters are not the only actors with inadequate information. Party selectorates also confront a high degree of uncertainty when presented with office-seekers, especially when they do not personally know the applicant. As Norris and Lovenduski note, "Party selectors . . . often have minimal information on which to make their decisions . . . [and] may therefore rely on background characteristics as a proxy measure. . . . As a result, individuals are judged by their group characteristics."[11] When prospective candidates are members of ethnoreligious minority groups, especially groups with a recent migration background, this uncertainty and resulting reliance on information shortcuts is likely exacerbated. Due to a host of factors—such as language barriers, cultural and religious differences, segmented labor markets and residential segregation—intergroup contact between minority and majority populations tends to be limited.[12] As a result, party selectors, who are generally

---

8. Eelbode et al. (2013, 459).

9. See "NRW-CDU duldet radikale Türken in ihren Reihen," *Der Westen,* May 31, 2014 (available at http://www.derwesten.de/politik/nrw-cdu-duldet-radikale-tuerken-in-ihren-reihen-id9410209.html, accessed June 18, 2015).

10. Chandra (2004), McDermott (1998), Popkin (1991), Posner (2005), and Shugart et al. (2005).

11. Norris and Lovenduski (1995, 14).

12. Koopmans (2010) and Musterd (2005). Studies about Muslims in the Netherlands suggest

members of the local majority population, have little knowledge about minority groups' sociopolitical landscape, especially in the early years of inclusion. After several election cycles in which minority groups play an active part, party members become more knowledgeable, and the selection of specific community leaders—as is the case in some English city wards, for instance— becomes a conscious choice. However, in the initial years, party selectors are typically uncertain about which individuals are best suited to fulfill their parties' inclusion objectives.

In Kreuzberg (Berlin), for example, a district with a very large Turkish population whose members are gradually acquiring German citizenship, all major parties for the first time nominated candidates with Turkish roots to stand in the 2011 local elections. Yet, parties apparently chose candidates that were neither in step with parties' own platforms and values nor with those of the German-Turkish electorate. According to one local observer, "The parties apparently believe that Turkish voters will vote for a Turk ... [but] none of the selected Turks can speak for the Turks in Kreuzberg. The mainstream-Kreuzberger is a rather pious Muslim who values family and tradition," and the selected candidates do not fit this profile; "How is it, furthermore, that even 50 years after the [guestworker] recruitment treaties, the major parties [*Volksparteien*] still do not know how to deal with their Turkish citizens?"[13]

In Brussels, similar developments have transpired. Here, "political parties still do not have a clear understanding of the Muslim religious landscape which often remains *terra incognita*."[14] Though Muslims have had a long presence in the capital region, large-scale citizenship acquisitions did not occur until the 1990s, and parties therefore had little incentive to learn about Muslims' electoral behavior. Once confronted with a sizable Muslim electorate, this ignorance has complicated recruitment efforts. Parties realize that selecting a candidate whose appearance is "too Muslim" ("islamiquement connoté") is risky, while failure to do so may also cost votes among the Muslim electorate.[15] Likewise, writing about the inclusion of ethnic minority (mostly Moroccan and Turkish) candidates in Ghent and Antwerp, Eelbode finds that parties on

---

that less religious Muslims have more regular contact with the majority population than those who are more religious, whose contacts are mostly within their own group (cf. Voas and Fleischmann 2012, 530). These dynamics should make it more difficult for parties to gain knowledge about candidate types in Muslim religious enclaves.

13. This is the assessment of Ercan Karakoyun (2011), a German writer of Turkish descent. Karakoyun further notes that the SPD nominated a Turkish nationalist, the Left Party (*Die Linke*) opted for a Kurdish nationalist, and the Greens picked a candidate far removed from the party's program. Only the CDU's candidate shared the Turkish electorates' belief in faith and family values.

14. Dasetto (2011, 128); emphasis in original.

15. Dasetto (2011, 128).

the Left and the Right (excluding the Far-Right) were eager to recruit minorities, but were wholly uninformed about who would make a good candidate. Recruitment efforts were geared towards finding candidates who could best mobilize their communities' vote. This was not lost on ethnic minority representatives. As one complained, the parties "just hope that you manage to attract as many votes as possible. You are a vote machine and nothing more than that."[16] Whether a candidate's ideology was consistent with that of the party was much less relevant. One consequence of this emphasis on vote mobilization "irrespective of . . . ideology" was that "conservative, Islamic groups [were] now closely linked to the social democratic party,"[17] a development that created some unease.

Party selectors thus face a tall order. Depending on their inclusion goals, they will have to assess whether candidates are adept at mobilizing the minority vote—or whether they genuinely espouse party platforms and values. When parties are after symbolic inclusion, they will also want to ensure that candidates can signal adherence to party ideology to the majority electorate. If parties had unlimited time and resources, they would poll voters to see which candidates are best at attracting the minority vote or least likely to turn off majority voters. To evaluate whether prospective candidates are sufficiently assimilated, follow the relevant behavioral norms, and subscribe to shared values, they would have to conduct thorough interviews. But talk is cheap. In fact, Muslims who are prominent in the European public sphere have often been accused of "double talk," changing their message about the role and meaning of Islam or their interpretation of controversial political events depending on the audience they are addressing.[18] Parties would therefore also have to examine current and past behaviors. When vetting candidates for positions at the national level, this may be an option (though the Austrian and Swedish examples cited above suggest that even here the vetting process is far from perfect), but these tools are likely unavailable to local parties. Just as voters have to rely on cues, the relative lack of information about minority communities will lead local party elites to use information shortcuts when assessing Muslim candidates, at least in the early years of electoral inclusion.

What, then, are the cues that party gatekeepers come to rely on? Two types of information will be especially relevant: positions in religious organizations and gender. These two cues operate differently depending on parties' inclusion objectives. When parties hope to capture the Muslim vote, they will consider both the mobilizational capacity of candidates and the preferences of Muslim voters. First, parties will presume that individuals who

---

16. Eelbode (2013, 141).
17. Eelbode (2013, 132).
18. Bowen (2007, 189–193), Dasetto (2011, 133), and Lindekilde (2013).

hold prominent posts in religious institutions will be well positioned to mobilize their co-religionists' vote. Second, when office-seekers do not have official links to religious bodies, party selectors will use gender as an information shortcut. They will assume that men are better able to liaise with religious institutions and tap into ethnic networks for electoral purposes and, further, that Muslim voters will prefer men over women.

By contrast, when parties do not need to secure large portions of the Muslim vote, parties favor women over men. More concerned with a vote backlash from the majority population and hoping to reach out to cosmopolitan voters, these parties are more likely to select candidates who, simply by seeking to run for office, demonstrate that they are not bound by traditional gender roles or the strictures of purdah in ways that men cannot. This signal may be reinforced if they do not wear a headscarf. Even if majority voters cannot tell whether a Muslim candidate is male or female (because they are unfamiliar with Muslim candidates' names), parties interested in symbolic inclusion figure that women who step into the world of politics are less likely to be associated with compromising views and statements than men are. The next section elaborates these logics.

Selecting the Right Type of Candidate

Vote-based inclusion steers parties towards candidates who can liaise with mosques and other religious institutions. Being a leading member in a religious organization; a board member of a prominent mosque; or employed in religious schools are attributes that aspiring candidates can use to signal their involvement with local Muslim communities. Such positions often either require deep pre-existing ties with sizable segments of the Muslim community, or they engender such ties once individuals come to occupy them. Though these links are generally not political in nature, they can nevertheless be harnessed successfully to get out the vote.

In Brussels, for instance, a number of local councilors are also elected to posts on the country's Islam Council (L'Organe Représentatif du Culte Musulman de Belgique, ORCMB). Others have been presidents of mosques before assuming elected office. These councilors' investment in the religious lives of their communities can be a significant source of votes.[19] In British cities, it is quite common for Muslim councilors to be on committees of local mosques. These individuals are also often prominent community leaders who have acted as interlocutors between local government and Muslim communities before being elected to local councils themselves. In Pakistani enclaves, for instance, *biraderi* elders commonly used to serve as vote brokers for non-Muslim, ma-

19. Dasetto (2011, 135) and Koksal (2007, 15).

jority politicians, striking out on their own in later years.[20] Reliance on the *biraderi* system for electoral purposes (see Chapter 5) has led to the exclusion of female politicians. "Women in particular have been disenfranchised . . . [by the] *biraderi* . . . networks," noted Salma Yaqoob, one of the few female Muslim politicians to capture a seat, winning for the Respect Party in Sparkbrook, Birmingham. Yaqoob further stated that Respect "came under considerable pressure when [the party] . . . selected a candidate whose family were originally from the same village in Pakistan as the sitting Lib Dem councillor. It was alleged we were splitting the biraderi vote."[21]

As this last statement suggests, larger kinship communities and religion interact in interesting ways when it comes to local party politics. Not all Muslim politicians who are fixtures in their communities are necessarily pious. In fact, many associate with religious institutions because this raises their own standing within the community. As Werbner, drawing on her ethnographic work about Manchester Pakistanis, notes, "the mosque is the central forum in which the elite competes to legitimise its status."[22] These individuals' embeddedness in ethnoreligious networks together with their elevated status in the community can matter decisively for capturing significant portions of the Muslim electorate.

One consequence of using visible links with religious institutions as an information shortcut to assess the popularity and mobilizational capacity of prospective candidates is that male candidates will come to outnumber female candidates. Islamic representative bodies, mosque leaderships, and other religious organizations tend to be overwhelmingly led by men. Thus, even though parties who hope to attract Muslim voters do not have to favor male Muslim over female Muslim candidates per se, their relative lack of knowledge about the social organization of the Muslim electorate combined with their prioritization of candidates' mobilizational capacity will lead them to count on cues that end up favoring men.

Additionally, party elites eager to cater to the Muslim electorate may, in fact, *deliberately* favor Muslim men over women. Gender is arguably the most easily observed feature of an aspiring candidate. If gender provides useful information, this information is essentially costless for party leaders to obtain.[23] The less knowledgeable party elites are about which candidates will have the most electoral appeal among Muslim voters, the more likely they are to select

20. Akhtar (2013) and Solomos and Back (1995).

21. Cited in Peace (2013, 308). In other campaigns (notably in Bradford West), Respect was happy to attack female Muslim candidates who challenged the local Muslim establishment. The party's support of Yaqoob must therefore be seen as a strategic move, not an endorsement of gender equality.

22. Werbner (1990, 310).

23. See also Chandra (2004, 37ff.) on the relative cost of cues at the candidate level.

male candidates. An organizational and a preference mechanism underlies this proposition. First, Muslim men are more likely to have the organizational links with mosques and other ethnoreligious bodies than women are. Thus, even if office-seekers are not members of these institutions themselves, party elites may still conjecture that men can better establish ties with such organizations than women can. Indeed, when identifying Muslim politicians in Brussels who do not hold religious positions but who are very engaged in Muslim religious activities, Dasetto, an expert on Islam in Belgium, only mentions men. These men do not always display their connection to religious networks overtly, but they are happy to lean on their support during electoral campaigns. Zibouh estimates that close to two-thirds of Maghrebi candidates for the Brussels regional parliament have direct or indirect links to mosques.[24] Beyond the mosque, Zibouh also notes that women candidates find it very difficult to visit popular campaign spots such as cafés and tearooms where Muslim men gather and where male candidates routinely distribute election materials.[25]

Second, an explicit preference mechanism can also be at work. Even if party leaders do not have deep knowledge about the Muslim electorate, they will be aware of Muslims' comparatively less egalitarian conception of gender roles. In keeping with their views on the division of labor, Muslim voters may simply prefer male over female candidates. Anticipating this preference, party gatekeepers will select men over women when the goal is vote-based inclusion. Finally, over time, uncertainty should decrease as parties learn more about Muslim candidates and their performance at the polls. If Muslim men indeed obtain more votes than do Muslim women (net of a backlash), parties who want to capture the Muslim vote will prefer to nominate men.

The story flips when we consider scenarios in which Muslims are not pivotal voters. In this case, the nomination of Muslim candidates (when it occurs at all) is expected to bring in a comparatively smaller number of Muslim votes, and is therefore also geared towards another audience, cosmopolitan majority voters. Inclusion is supposed to send a message to cosmopolitan voters that the party is inclusive and tolerant of the "right" type of Muslim. When this type of symbolic inclusion is the objective, party leaders will want to make sure that the selected candidate indeed abides by the norms and values of the party and of society writ-large. Once again, gender can function as a useful cue. Specifically, the mere fact that a Muslim woman is attempting to run for office implies that she is not supportive of patriarchal structures and belief systems that constrain women's activities outside the home. Entering the male-dominated (non-Muslim) world of politics, a female candidate will have to engage with men well beyond her kin group. It is therefore implausible to

---

24. Zibouh (2010, 80–84) and Dasetto (2011, 135).
25. Zibouh (2010, 77).

assume that she supports the physical seclusion of women, a practice often associated with strong Muslim religious faith. A male office-seeker—even one holding identical beliefs about the status of women and about the role of religion in the private and public sphere—cannot use his gender (or an information shortcut that is similarly costless) in the same way.

Another signal of religiosity and tradition available to women but not to men is veiling. While the wearing of a headscarf or a burqa can send several messages,[26] not all of them religious in nature, the *absence* of veiling is more indicative of relatively weaker commitments to traditional ideology and religious faith. Party selectors who hope to nominate a progressive, secular Muslim candidate but who have very little insight about "who-is-who" in the Muslim community, can play it safe by choosing a female candidate of Muslim origin, especially if she chooses not to veil. As Geisser and Soum note in the French context, female politicians with Muslims roots "are portrayed as emblematic figures of successful integration and the fight against patriarchal traditions from their country of origin."[27] In Belgium, an ethnic minority representative put it this way: "The image of the ethnic minority woman is that of an oppressed woman, in need of help, deserving a voice. . . . Voters prefer to cast their vote for ethnic minority women [rather than men] . . . often as a sympathy vote: we support women's emancipation . . . in the case of ethnic minority men, one thought: they want to keep their wives at home."[28]

Once parties become more knowledgeable about the Muslim communities in their districts, their reliance on shortcuts will decline. Moreover, at times they can use other cues such as organizational memberships in secular organizations. For instance, when the Frankfurt CDU placed a Turkish-born woman, Ezhar Cezairli, on an attractive list position in 2011, the party also knew that Cezairli was a founding member of the "Frankfurt Initiative of Progressive Women" that advocated for headscarf bans in schools.[29] However, parties will still be constrained by the majority electorate's general lack of information about Muslim candidates. To the extent that party selectors believe that non-Muslim voters prefer (nonveiled) women over men, symbolic inclusion will still be associated with a relative over-representation of women.

The observable implications that emerge from the discussion thus far is the following: When parties do not need to rally a large Muslim vote, we should observe a higher share of female Muslim candidates than when parties hope to attract a big slice of the Muslim vote. As a result, when the Muslim vote is sizable and electorally significant, the inclusion of Muslim candidates should

---

26. Blaydes and Linzer (2008) and Patel (2012).

27. Geisser and Soum (2012, 60).

28. Celis et al. (2014, 49).

29. *Die Tageszeitung*, "Reine Kopfsache", March 5, 2010.

not only lead to an overrepresentation of men among Muslim elected councilors; given a finite number of list positions and council seats, it may also
decrease gender parity *overall*. In this way, electoral inclusion of religious minorities may undermine gender parity, especially in urban contexts where
Muslim gender norms are, on average, conservative.

Religious Parity and Gender Parity across Countries

I first test cross-national patterns before turning to within-country evidence.
Muslim parity ratios are higher in Belgium and Britain, where citizenship laws
are relatively liberal and local electoral laws tend to empower immigrant-
origin minorities, than they are in Austria and Germany, two countries with
an institutional environment that is less permissive. However, religious parity,
I have argued, will come at the expense of gender parity. We should therefore
expect a relative underrepresentation of female Muslim councilors in Britain
and Belgium when compared to Austria and Germany.

Though the institutional configurations generate clear predictions, it is
plausible that other differences across countries confound the hypothesized
relationships. For instance, if Muslims in Austria and Germany were more
supportive of egalitarian gender roles, we would predict similar outcomes
with respect to gender parity. In this scenario, there would be a higher supply
of female Muslim candidates because Muslims in Germany and Austria would
be more open to the idea of women engaging in activities outside the home,
including seeking elected office, resulting in a higher share of females among
Muslim politicians than in Britain and Belgium.

Survey responses collected by the European Social Survey indicate that
gender attitudes do not vary in these ways. When asked whether women
should be prepared to cut down on paid work for the sake of the family, a
majority of Muslims in all four countries agreed. In Austria and Germany, 64
and 61 percent of Muslims held this view, respectively, whereas in Belgium
and Britain the comparable figures are 63 and 54 percent.[30]

A majority of Muslims in all four countries supports a traditional division
of labor, but we may still be concerned that expressed survey attitudes do not

30. This refers to the same question as in Chapter 3; see Appendix B for the question wording.
When using the 5-point ordinal variable (with answers ranging from "agree strongly" to "disagree
strongly"), ordered probit results indicate that Muslims in Austria and in Germany are significantly *more* conservative than Muslims in Britain (and not significantly different from those in
Belgium). However, the Austrian results have to be treated with caution. Austria only participated
in one of the ESS rounds in which the relevant question was asked, and only 29 Muslims were
surveyed. I therefore consulted surveys conducted in Austria of Muslim respondents only. A 2012
survey (polling Turkish and Bosnian Muslims) confirms that Muslims have quite traditional views
about gender roles. For instance, 75 percent of Muslims believe that in order to lead a happy and
fulfilled life, a woman has to have children (Ulram and Tributsch 2013).

correlate with behavioral outcomes (though it is less obvious why the correlation between attitudes and behaviors would vary across these countries, in all of which the status of Muslim women has been highly politicized). Other confounding factors may relate to differences in the national origins of Muslims. In Austria and Germany Turkish-origin residents comprise the largest share of Muslims, followed by those from Bosnia and Herzegovina. In Belgium, most Muslims trace their roots to Morocco, followed by Turkey. In Britain, by contrast, the majority of Muslims are of Pakistani and Bangladeshi origin. It is conceivable that groups differ in their views about engaging in electoral politics or that majority electorates harbor more resentment towards certain ethnonational groups than others.[31] These factors would in turn influence selection strategies at the elite level. In light of these constraints, let's look at the trade-off between gender parity and religious parity across municipalities within one country, Belgium.

Religious Parity and Gender Parity in Belgium

The Belgian case is well-suited for this analysis. First, because elections in Belgium combine party lists and preference votes, we can assess the consequences of both elite and voter behavior. By examining party lists, we can observe the presence of Muslim candidates, their gender as well as their list position. This allows me to investigate not only whether or not Muslim men and women compete, but also whether parties place Muslim men in more electable positions than they do Muslim women. By examining election results, we can next test whether Muslim men indeed mobilize more votes than do Muslim women *within the same party*. Second, voting is compulsory in Belgium, and nonvoters are fined. As a result, turnout is typically very high.[32] It is therefore unlikely that uneven turnout rates across groups (by gender, religion, degree of conservatism, partisanship, etc.) will affect outcomes. By implication, parties worry less about getting voters to the polls and more about voters choosing their lists over plausible alternatives. When they want to recruit significant portions of the Muslim vote, they will have to nominate candidates who they think can attract a large co-ethnic following.

Additionally, the distribution of Muslim preferences in Belgium reflects the social geography of migration that, I have argued, is typical of European Muslims: The most traditional and religious Muslims live in highly urbanized environments, where they encounter relatively liberal, progressive natives.

31. On differences in political behavior across immigrant-origin groups, see Dancygier (2010) and Michon and Vermeulen (2013). On majority reactions based on size and national origin, see Hainmueller and Hangartner (2013).

32. In the sample of municipalities used here (see below), the mean and median turnout rate is 90 percent.

Moreover, unlike in Britain, elections are held at the municipality (not the ward) level, ensuring that liberal cosmopolitans and conservative minority voters actually tend to occupy the same electoral arena. Continuing with the survey question about gender attitudes cited earlier (see Chapter 3), 71 percent of Muslims living in big cities hold conservative gender attitudes, compared to 56 percent of those living outside these cities ($p = .033$). The most inegalitarian views can be found in Brussels, where 81 percent of Muslims believe that women should cut down on paid work for the sake of family, leading to a massive 44-point opinion gap with non-Muslims in Belgium's—and Europe's—capital region ($p = .000$). These conservative gender views match up with employment patterns: In 2008, only one-quarter of women of North African (mainly Moroccan) origin were employed.[33] We should therefore expect that voters and parties prefer Muslim male over Muslim female candidates, and that this preference should be particularly pronounced in highly urbanized settings, such as in Brussels.

Returning to the problem of candidate supply that arose in the context of the cross-national comparisons, when we examine patterns *within* a country it is plausible to assume that districts that feature a large, conservative Muslim electorate will produce higher shares of male than female office-seekers, regardless of parties' inclusion goals. We may thus worry that within the Belgian case, we simply observe a lower share of female Muslim candidates in Muslim enclaves because they do not consider running for office.[34]

Though supply may be a factor, parties in Belgium still have tools at their disposal to compensate for this problem. In Belgian municipalities, local party leaders—not local party members or supralocal party organs—are decisive in determining selection. A recent survey of local parties in Belgian municipalities found that retiring candidates, mayors, party chairmen, and party board members exercise the greatest degree of influence in composing party lists. Though party members often get the opportunity to share their views about the list before the election, they cannot actually vote on the nomination or ranking of candidates. As a result, members are found to rarely matter in the selection process.[35]

Thus, if parties are concerned about gender parity among Muslim candidates, party gatekeepers can systematically favor Muslim women. Second,

33. More precisely, the employment rate of women of North African origin with/without Belgian citizenship was 26.9/20.2 percent. Analogous figures for men of North African origin were 62.9/47.5 percent; see Corluy et al. (2011, 360).

34. In general, women's lower likelihood to compete in elections—rather than their failures at the polls—is a major reason for women's underrepresentation in politics (Lawless and Fox 2010).

35. De Winter et al. (2013).

even if party elites have trouble recruiting female Muslim candidates in Muslim enclaves, they can place Muslim women on safer list positions than Muslim men, thereby raising the chances that Muslim women make it into office. While we cannot observe whether or not party gatekeepers discriminate in favor of selecting female Muslim candidates, we *can* observe list placement. As I will show in more detail later, it is not the case that Muslim female candidates occupy more desirable spots, a finding that is consistent with a vote-mobilization logic and inconsistent with the idea that inadequate supply is the crucial constraint.

Lastly, Belgium is an interesting case because of its strong gender parity laws. In Belgian local, regional, and national elections, lists have to feature an equal number of men and women. In 2006, at least one woman and at least one man had to occupy the top three list positions, and by 2012 this was true for the first two positions. We therefore do not have to *assume* that parties support gender parity (though many of them do)[36] and consequently face a potential trade-off when including Muslim candidates. Lists that do not comply with gender parity laws are not permitted. As a result, Belgium is a hard test for my theory as parties face strong incentives to include female candidates. As gender parity rules are becoming increasingly common across Europe and beyond,[37] the lessons from the Belgian case should be especially relevant.

Religious Parity vs. Gender Parity: Cross-National Results

Table 6.1 presents Muslim and female representation across countries. We see stark differences with respect to gender: Nearly half of Muslim councilors in Austria are women (46.3 percent), but this is only true for 14.4 percent of councilors in British municipalities. These gaps are especially striking considering that the share of non-Muslim women politicians is identical. This share is also quite low, belying simplistic portrayals of a progressive Europe encountering a reactionary Islam. In countries without strong gender parity rules (Austria, Germany, and Britain), women constitute only one-third of councilors. As hypothesized, the percentage of women among Muslim councilors is also comparatively higher in Germany, reaching 40.6 percent. Comparing across religious groups in Austria and Germany, Muslim women are overrepresented, while in Britain they are severely underrepresented (see sixth row). The extreme underrepresentation of Muslim women in English local councils comports with the prediction that ward-level elections, and the ways they aggregate voter types, rarely compel parties to include symbolically. When

36. See Meier (2004).
37. Krook (2013).

TABLE 6.1. Religious Parity and Gender Parity across Countries

| | Importance of the Muslim Vote | | | |
| | Lower | | Higher | |
	Austria 2014	Germany 2014	Great Britain 2002–2013	Belgium 2006–2012
1. % Elected Muslims	1.43	3.22	6.26	8.47
2. Number of Elected Muslims	41	138	809	429
3. Muslim Parity Ratio	0.13	0.39	0.74	0.83
4. % of Elected Muslims who are Women	46.3	40.6	14.4	36.4
5. % of Elected Non-Muslims Who Are Women	33.8	33.8	33.6	38.9
6. Muslim/Non-Muslim Female Representation Ratio (4./5.)	1.37	1.20	0.43	0.94
7. T-test (difference of means in 4. and 5.):	1-tailed: $p = .047$ 2-tailed: $p = .093$	1-tailed: $p = .049$ 2-tailed: $p = .097$	1-tailed: $p = .000$ 2-tailed: $p = .000$	1-tailed: $p = .147$ 2-tailed: $p = .293$

Muslim candidates are placed on the ballot, it is generally because the Muslim vote is both pivotal and substantial.

Turning to Belgium, where gender parity laws are in effect, the share of women among Muslim councilors is lower (as expected) than it is in Austria and Germany, but higher than in Britain. In the Belgian municipal councils sampled here, 36 percent of Muslim councilors are female. Yet, this share is not significantly lower when compared to the percentage of women among non-Muslim Belgian councilors, which stands at 39 percent, perhaps an indication that gender parity laws also have a positive impact on the recruitment of Muslim women.[38] However, as I will show shortly, this picture masks substantial cross-municipality variation.

Summing up, different inclusion goals are indeed associated with different candidate types: In Austria and Germany, where parties are, on average, less concerned with capturing the Muslim vote, the share of Muslim councilors is rather low. However, when parties do include Muslim candidates, they most often hope to run secular and assimilated Muslim candidates, leading them to seek out women. In Britain and Belgium, where parties are more likely to court the Muslim electorate, Muslim parity ratios are signifi-

38. Some have suggested that parties who are eager (or required) to include women *and* ethnic minorities may select ethnic minority women, thereby fulfilling two criteria with only one slot (Donavan 2012; Hughes 2011).

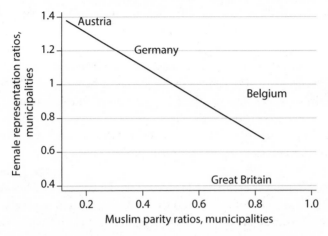

FIGURE 6.1. Religious Parity and Female Represenation across Countries

cantly higher, but female representation ratios (the percentage of women councilors among Muslims divided by the percentage of women councilors among non-Muslims) are substantially lower. These findings suggest that there is a steep trade-off between including Muslims and including women, as illustrated by Figure 6.1.

Religious Parity vs. Gender Parity: Within-Country Results

Does this logic also hold within one national context? To answer this question, I begin by illustrating the trade-offs between religious parity and gender parity at the municipality level, distinguishing between highly urbanized and less highly urbanized municipalities.[39] Highly urbanized areas should generate the most severe trade-offs, because it is here that Muslim views are most socially conservative. It is worth emphasizing that these data are not meant to test for the effect of urbanity, net of Muslim electoral leverage, and vice versa. As can be seen in the scatterplots below, municipalities that are less densely populated also feature lower shares of Muslims. The social geography of migration has produced these settlement outcomes, whereby Muslim enclaves are predominantly found in inner cities. It has led to urban areas of Muslim concentration that are relatively more conservative and traditional, and it is electorates in these neighborhoods whose votes are often coveted by political parties. Though it would be very interesting to investigate whether the dense

---

39. I define a highly urbanized municipality as one whose population density is above the sample median's population density.

infrastructures of cities have an independent or reinforcing effect on the beliefs and values of communities—perhaps because they facilitate the monitoring of norm violations, as suggested in Chapter 3—the empirical correlations between inner-city residence and social conservatism that chain migration has produced make it very difficult to disentangle urbanity from other enclave characteristics. When distinguishing between more and less urbanized areas I therefore do not intend to make any causal statements about the effects of urbanity. Rather, the degree of urbanization together with the size of the Muslim population serves as a proxy for the degree of Muslim traditionalism and religiosity.

The scatterplots presented in Figure 6.2 depict correlations between the percentage of Muslim councilors and female representation ratios at the level of the municipality.[40] In highly urbanized municipalities and in Brussels' municipalities this relationship is negative (and statistically significant at $p < .05$): As the percentage of councilors who are Muslim rises, we observe a relative underrepresentation of Muslim women councilors. On the other hand, in municipalities where relatively fewer Muslims are elected, Muslim women are relatively overrepresented compared to non-Muslim female politicians. In less urbanized municipalities and in Flanders and Wallonia—where Muslims exhibit less conservative views about gender roles—female representation ratios and Muslim inclusion do not co-vary. It is not the case, however, that in highly urbanized municipalities relationships are driven solely by municipalities with very large Muslim population shares. Specifically, when I restrict the sample to municipalities whose Muslim population is less than 20 percent, correlations in highly urbanized/Brussels municipalities are $-.31$ ($p = .053$) and $-.46$ ($p = .096$). Figure 6.3 breaks down these data slightly differently. It shows that in Brussels' 19 municipalities, less than a third of Muslim councilors are women, but this share is 12 points higher among non-Muslim councilors. Outside of Brussels, by contrast, the percentage of women is 6 points higher among Muslim councilors than it is among non-Muslim councilors. Inclusion outcomes among left lists exhibit identical gender gaps (though the overall share of women is higher), in part because the majority of Muslim councilors are elected on left lists.

These bivariate relationships are in line with the trade-offs between gender and religious parity that emerged in the cross-national comparison. Moreover, selection and election outcomes at the party-list level map onto the story told here. To clarify, parties put together ordered candidate lists that they present on the ballot. Voters then have the choice of either endorsing this ranked list by casting a list vote, or they can cast a preference ballot, whereby they vote

40. Special thanks go to Tom Doesselaere (manager of elections, Flemish government) for helping me understand Belgian local elections and for providing me with data.

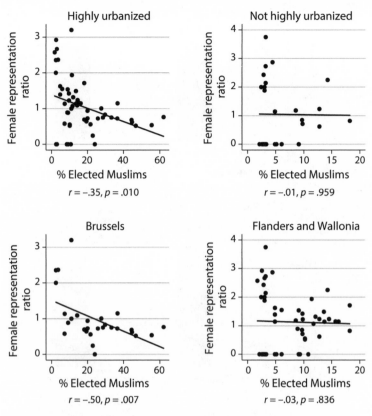

FIGURE 6.2. Female Representation and Muslim Inclusion (Belgium, 2006–2012)
Note: The "Female Representation Ratio" divides the percentage of Muslim councilors who are female by the percentage of non-Muslim councilors who are female. Observations are at the level of the municipality and are based on 2006 and 2012 local
election results in Belgian municipalities. In the graph entitled "Brussels" one outlier
is removed (when the outlier is included $r = -.37$, $p = .047$). Results are not driven by
higher Muslim population shares in urban municipalties: When restricting the sample to municipalities whose Muslim population is less than 20 percent, correlations
in highly urbanized/Brussels municipalities are $-.31$ ($p = .053$) and $-.46$ ($p = .096$).

for one or several candidates within the same party (voters can indicate as
many preferences as there are candidates; either type of ballot counts as *one*
vote for the party). When allocating seats to candidates within parties, the
most highly ranked candidates benefit from list votes and from preference
votes. Other, lower-ranked candidates can get elected on the basis of preference ballots only when their votes surpass an eligibility threshold, which is in
turn based on the total number of votes won by the party.[41] The candidate who
is placed first on the list typically receives the most preference votes and

41. André et al. (2012).

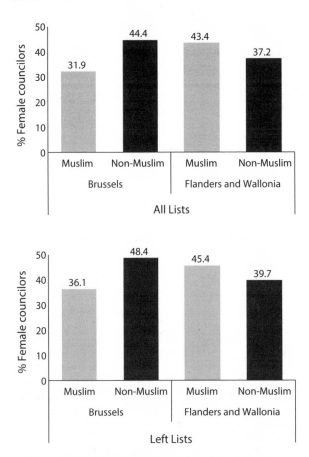

FIGURE 6.3. Percentage of Female Councilors by Religion, Region, and Partisanship (Belgium, 2006–2012)

thereby benefits from both types of ballots, but lower-ranked candidates can also amass significant preference votes that lead to a re-ordering of candidate ranks when compared to the original list.

One way of capturing the importance of preference votes is to investigate whether candidates "jumped" the list. For example, if a candidate's assigned list position was 10, but thanks to preference votes her final ranking was a 7, she jumped 3 spots. If the party wins a total of seven spots, this candidate makes it into the council on the basis of preference votes. Are Muslim men more likely to jump the list? Table 6.2 certainly suggests this to be the case (this table and the analyses that follow are restricted to highly urbanized municipalities where Muslim preferences are more conservative; effects elsewhere are either weaker or insignificant). The table excludes candidates on the top spot who garner by far the most preference votes as well as those who

TABLE 6.2. Average List Jumping and Preference Votes by Candidate Religion and Gender (Belgium 2006–2012)

Candidate Religion & Gender	Average Jump	Preference Votes (%)
Muslim Male	3.28	3.24
Muslim Female	1.14	2.67
Non-Muslim Male	−2.11	2.40
Non-Muslim Female	−0.29	2.55

Note: Candidates occupying the highest and the lowest list positions, respectively, are excluded. The sample is restricted to highly urbanized municipalities.

occupy the lowest list position.[42] It shows that Muslim male candidates register by far the highest jumps: on average, they improve on their initial positions by 3.28 points. Muslim women follow with a jump of 1.14. Non-Muslim candidates show the least improvement over their assigned list position: women register a drop of .29 spots, and men's position decreases by an average of 2.11. The distribution of preference votes (i.e., the percentage of a party's preference votes a specific candidate receives) shows analogous trends: Muslim men once again are at the top, followed by Muslim women. On the basis of preference votes, then, it appears that Muslims—men and women—have the electoral edge, but that Muslim men are by far the best vote mobilizers.

These dynamics are not driven by Muslims' placement on the list and hold when we control for candidates' initial placement. Table 6.3 presents regressions with two dependent variables, list jumping and the share of preference votes.[43] I control for list position (as well as list position squared) and for a host of other variables at the party-list and municipality level.[44] Figure 6.4 (based on Model 3 in Table 6.3) is a visual representation of the list-jumping results.

42. Parties will sometimes place popular candidates on the lowest list position because this position is highly visible. These candidates, so-called list-pushers, often attract a large number of votes; in some cases they are local celebrities who run but intend to resign their seat once elected. I therefore exclude candidates who occupy the lowest list position.

43. Note that jumps within (though not across) lists are, by definition, correlated with one another—jumps by one candidate have to be matched with drops by another. This is not the case for preference votes as voters can cast preference votes for as many candidates as are on a list.

44. I include the following variables at the party-list level: the number of candidates, the percentage of preference ballots (vs. ballots that endorse the existing list ranking), and dummies for left and far-right parties. At the municipality level, I control for population density and population size (logged): all else equal, we may observe fewer preference votes in urban areas where voters and candidates are less likely to know one another. Moreover, similar results obtain when substituting list quartile dummies for list position. The regressions also account for region and year; standard errors are clustered on the municipality-list.

TABLE 6.3. List-Jumping and Preference Votes at the Candidate Level (Belgium 2006–2012)

	List Jumping			Preference Votes (%)		
Muslim	6.277***	6.642***	6.712***	.986***	.871***	.897***
	(.519)	(.537)	(.544)	(.101)	(.112)	(.112)
Female	1.514***	1.535***	1.537***	.193***	.186***	.186***
	(.263)	(.262)	(.262)	(.0343)	(.0336)	(.0336)
Muslim × Female	−3.864***	−3.830***	−3.824***	−.756***	−.793***	−.791***
	(.520)	(.525)	(.525)	(.111)	(.113)	(.113)
List Position	−.374***	−.441***	−.442***	−.331***	−.296***	−.296***
	(.0335)	(.0357)	(.0357)	(.00958)	(.00861)	(.00860)
List Position Squared	.0180***	.0195***	.0195***	.00597***	.00517***	.00518***
	(.00081)	(.000863)	(.000863)	(.000228)	(.000201)	(.000201)
Number of Candidates	−.232***	−.168***	−.162***	−.112***	−.145***	−.143***
	(.00728)	(.00792)	(.00777)	(.00536)	(.00883)	(.00892)
Left List		−.0278	−.104		−.0163	−.0443
		(.0649)	(.0644)		(.0491)	(.0511)
Far-Right List		.617***	.318		−.309	−.418**
		(.165)	(.164)		(.159)	(.159)
Population Density		−.0000591***	−.0000531***		.00000183	.00000402
		(.0000109)	(.0000100)		(.00000641)	(.00000639)
Population (Log)		−1.519***	−1.587***		.798***	.773***
		(.100)	(.100)		(.0979)	(.0989)
% Preference Ballots			−.0168***			−.00615*
			(.00370)			(.00251)
Wallonia	.137	.139	.147	.140*	−.0817	−.0789
	(.114)	(.0905)	(.0894)	(.0699)	(.0811)	(.0810)
Flanders	−.249	−.0857	.0220	.304***	−.0123	.0272
	(.145)	(.0998)	(.101)	(.0767)	(.0814)	(.0812)
Year 2006	.0635	.148*	.195**	−.0983	−.143**	−.126*
	(.0951)	(.0608)	(.0594)	(.0545)	(.0501)	(.0490)
Constant	4.651***	20.00***	21.70***	9.858***	2.074**	2.698**
	(.393)	(1.172)	(1.231)	(.251)	(.798)	(.847)
N	13,887	13,887	13,887	13,887	13,887	13,887
R²	.299	.306	.307	.512	.542	.542

Note: OLS coefficients are shown, with robust standard errors (clustered on the municipality list) in parentheses (*$p < .05$; **$p < .01$; ***$p < .001$). The dependent variable "List Jumping" is the difference between the rank as originally assigned (i.e., the list position) and the rank the candidate attained once preference votes are taken into account. The dependent variable "Preference Votes" measures the percentage of preference votes a candidate obtains within a list. Candidates occupying the highest and the lowest list positions, respectively, are excluded. The sample is restricted to highly urbanized municipalities.

The advantage of Muslim men emerges even more strongly in these analyses, and overall results reflect the simple descriptive statistics. Muslim men jump an average of 6–7 spots (the coefficient of the variable *Muslim* is the effect of being a male Muslim candidate). To be sure, Muslim women candidates also draw in additional voters; compared to non-Muslim candidates, both Muslim men and Muslim women are able to amass disproportionately large

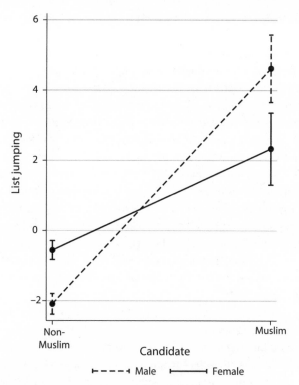

FIGURE 6.4. List Jumping by Religion and Gender (Belgium, 2006–2012; Highly Urbanized Municipalities)
Note: The circles display the marginal effects of religion and gender on list jumping, and the bars repesent 95 percent confidence intervals. Based on the results presented in Table 6.3 (third column).

preference votes that allow them to jump the list. But according to the negative interaction term (*Muslim × Female*), Muslim men move up considerably more spots than do Muslim women (see Figure 6.4).

These aggregate effects are consistent with Muslim gender attitudes and electoral campaigns described above. Further, recall from Chapter 5 that individual-level surveys have documented that Brussels voters of Moroccan and Turkish descent are significantly more likely to cast preference ballots for ethnic minority candidates than are those of Belgian descent,[45] and that these preference votes rise in areas of Muslim concentration. It is therefore unlikely that non-Muslim voters are responsible for these results. Moreover, non-Muslim female candidates actually tend to improve on their initial list position (see the *Female* coefficient and the position of non-Muslim females in Figure 6.4), a result we would not expect if there was strong general male bias in

45. Teney et al. (2010).

these municipalities. Very similar dynamics shape the distribution of preference votes.

These results lend some credibility to those who claim that parties vie for the Muslim vote, and that Muslim voters take individual candidates into account when deciding which list to vote for.[46] At the voter level, it appears that Muslim men can mobilize votes more effectively than can Muslim women and, in fact, more so than non-Muslims. We can easily see, then, why parties would want to be especially proactive in recruiting male Muslim candidates. When doing so, however, they face institutional constraints in the form of gender parity laws.[47] Nevertheless, parties that want to capture a slice of the Muslim vote can distinguish themselves by placing Muslim men on relatively high list positions. List positions are very visible: Not only are they clearly marked on the ballot, they are also printed on campaign posters of individual candidates. These posters are prominently displayed on shop windows and buildings during the election campaign. Shop owners will often hang up posters of candidates running for different party lists, but who share the same Moroccan or Turkish background.[48]

Conversely, if parties are more invested in ensuring gender parity among Muslim and non-Muslim councilors, they will assign better spots to females. In the sampled municipalities, 32 percent of parties on the Left, and only 22 percent of all other parties place women in the coveted top spot. Based on this metric, the commitment to gender equality is actually quite low overall, but higher among parties whose platforms are generally more progressive on gender issues.

Do parties compensate for the mobilizational potential of Muslim men by boosting the list positions of women? To answer this question, I compare average list quartiles across groups. Candidates in the first quartile occupy the top quarter of positions; candidates placed in the fourth, bottom quartile are on the least competitive positions. Table 6.4 breaks down list placements by candidate religion, gender, year, and list size. Based on these measures, party placement strategies further *exacerbate* the female disadvantage: Focusing first

46. See Celis et al. (2014) and Eelbode (2013).

47. Notwithstanding these laws, in highly urbanized areas we observe that the share of women among Muslim candidates is higher in municipalities where relatively few Muslims reside (56 percent) compared to municipalities where more Muslims reside (42 percent; municipalities with few/many Muslims are those with Muslim population shares below or at/above the sample median). This difference is statistically significant at $p = .032$. However, the total number of female Muslim candidates is much higher in municipalities of high Muslim concentration compared to those where relatively fewer Muslims live (1291 vs. 59 candidates).

48. For pictures of these posters, see, for example: http://tractotheque.blogspot.be/2012/10/molenbeek-2012-mobilite-plurielle-liste.html (accessed April 9, 2014). See also Teney et al. (2010, 275) and Zibouh (2010, 38 and 52).

TABLE 6.4. Average List Quartile (Belgium 2006–2012)

Candidate Religion & Gender	All Lists			
	Both years	2006	2012	Change
Muslim Male	2.35	2.37	2.33	−0.05
Muslim Female	2.41	2.47	2.36	−0.11
Non-Muslim Male	2.43	2.42	2.44	0.01
Non-Muslim Female	2.58	2.58	2.58	0.00
N	14,399	6,808	7,591	
	Large Lists Only			
Muslim Male	2.32	2.37	2.29	−0.09
Muslim Female	2.35	2.37	2.33	−0.03
Non-Muslim Male	2.44	2.44	2.45	0.01
Non-Muslim Female	2.59	2.58	2.59	0.01
N	10,923	4,998	5,925	

Note: Candidates occupying the lowest list positions and lists with only one candidate are excluded. The sample is restricted to highly urbanized municipalities. Large lists feature at least 33 candidates, the sample median.

on placement across elections (all lists), we see that Muslim men feature an average list quartile position of 2.35, the lowest value across groups. Muslim women are placed in better positions, on average, than are non-Muslims while non-Muslim women tend to end up with the least favorable placement. Muslims (both men and women) are hardly ever placed on the top spot (not shown), so the relative advantage of Muslim candidates is smaller than it appears in this simple analysis. At the very least, however, these figures do not suggest that parties compensate for Muslim men's extraordinary ability to attract preference votes by raising the relative position of women. Non-Muslim women fare especially poorly: they occupy the least competitive spots.

Examining trends over time, we see that Muslim men's placement has become even more favorable between elections, dropping from 2.37 in 2006 to 2.33 in 2012. As parties gain more knowledge about the vote potential of Muslim male candidates, they are more—not less—likely to allocate better spots to them. Though the list position of Muslim women also shows signs of improvement, Muslim women do not catch up to their male counterparts. Additionally, when we only look at larger, more successful lists—that is, lists that can attract many candidates and that are much more likely to win seats[49]—it emerges that Muslim women and men started out in similar positions in 2006,

49. The mean/median number of seats that a party with at least (less than) 33 candidates (the sample median) obtains is 8/6 (2/0).

TABLE 6.5. Percent Female Winners, Party Level (Belgium 2006–2012)

% Muslim Candidates	−.386**	−.522**	−.512**
	(.124)	(.159)	(.187)
Number of Candidates	.343	.510*	.506*
	(.199)	(.234)	(.237)
Left List		5.962*	5.926*
		(2.348)	(2.390)
Far-Right List		11.42*	11.49*
		(5.050)	(5.100)
Top Female		26.45***	26.46***
		(2.696)	(2.706)
Population Density		.000313	.000344
		(.000344)	(.000402)
Population (Log)		−1.209	−1.054
		(2.668)	(2.860)
% Muslim Population			−.0270
			(.206)
Wallonia	−8.571*	−3.648	−3.642
	(3.689)	(3.633)	(3.639)
Flanders	−3.278	1.593	1.570
	(3.622)	(3.638)	(3.638)
Year 2006	1.422	−0.907	−0.895
	(2.578)	(2.240)	(2.237)
Constant	32.86***	27.49	26.06
	(7.194)	(23.43)	(25.05)
N	350	350	350
R^2	0.036	0.297	0.297

Note: OLS coefficients are shown, with robust standard errors, clustered on the municipality-list, in parentheses (*$p < .05$; **$p < .01$; ***$p < .001$). The dependent variable is the percentage of winners on a list who are female. The sample is restricted to highly urbanized municipalities.

but that Muslim women fell behind Muslim men by 2012. Having gained a better understanding of Muslims' performance, these parties do not counterbalance the mobilizational capacities of Muslim men by placing Muslim women on higher spots. Rather, they privilege Muslim men. Last, the fact that non-Muslim women are found at the bottom remains a constant feature. Though gender parity rules are in place, equal numbers do not translate into equal treatment on the list.

We can conclude that party strategies do not compensate for Muslim men's ability to get out the preference vote. Even if it is the case that Muslim men are more likely than Muslim women to come forward as potential candidates, parties do not counteract this supply problem by placing Muslim women on more winnable spots. Rather, male Muslim candidates occupy more auspicious list positions than do other candidates, including Muslim females.

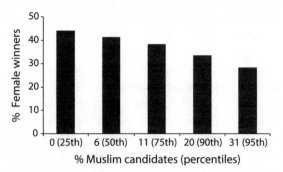

FIGURE 6.5. Female Winners and Muslim Candidates across Local Party Lists (Belgium, 2006–2012; Highly Urbanized Municipalities)
Note: Based on the results presented in Table 6.5 (third column).

These selection mechanisms should combine with voter behavior outlined above to reduce the number of women councilors on lists that include Muslims. Parties who want to capture the Muslim vote by featuring a large number of Muslim candidates should see their share of female winners decline. Results in Table 6.5 support this prediction. The dependent variable is the percentage of female winners in a party (the sample is thus restricted to parties that win at least one seat). The effects are sizable: A 10-point rise in the percentage of Muslim candidates (the sample mean is 8.2; the standard deviation is 9.6) is associated with a 4–5 percentage point decrease in the share of female winners. Expressed differently, when the share of Muslim candidates is at the 25th percentile, on average 44 percent of winners are women, but this percentage declines to 39 percent when a party's share of Muslim candidates is at the 75th percentile, and it drops to 28 percent when this share is at the 95th percentile (see Figure 6.5). Looking at other results, we see that lists that feature women in the first position witness, on average, a 26 percentage point rise in the share of female winners. We also see that left lists (and even far-right lists) produce more female winners than do other lists (mainly those of the Center-Right). However, parties that include Muslim candidates, which are also mostly found on the Left, will elect fewer women.

Parties that want to counterbalance the notable male bias that arises when Muslim candidates are on the ballot should thus nominate women for the top post. Interestingly, left parties seem to do just that: 37 percent of left lists that feature a high share[50] of Muslim candidates are headed by women, but this is only true for 18 percent of left lists that include fewer Muslims.[51] This

50. Defined here as those parties with a percentage of Muslim candidates above the sample median (far-right parties are excluded from the calculation).

51. This difference is significant at $p = .010$ and holds for highly urbanized municipalities.

phenomenon only holds among left lists. Among other lists, the probability of a woman occupying the top spot does not vary by the share of Muslim candidates they feature. This balancing among the Left may be based on deliberate strategy. Aware that the inclusion of Muslim candidates drives down women's chances of being elected, these parties pick a woman to lead the list. But it may also simply reflect the principles and political realities guiding left parties that seek to marry gender parity with religious parity: Those parties that prioritize gender equality also put a premium on the electoral inclusion of Muslims—even if this inclusion threatens to undermine gender parity.

Conclusion

This chapter sheds light on a further consequence of Muslim political inclusion: its impact on the presence of another underrepresented group, women. In doing so, the chapter underscores the importance of understanding the inclusion objectives that parties pursue.

Whether if forced to by law or because of ideological commitments, European parties are increasingly seeking to add women to their candidate rosters. Many of them also would like to add immigrant-origin candidates to the mix. Yet, when it comes to the incorporation of Muslims, achieving both of these goals can prove elusive for vote-seeking parties operating in vote-rich enclaves. The pursuit of gender equality perfectly complements symbolic inclusion, for it is women of Muslim origin that can most easily signal their embrace of gender egalitarianism—a highly divisive and salient issue in European debates about Muslim integration. It is on this issue dimension that symbolic candidates need to credibly communicate their integration credentials, and women are better able to accomplish this task than are men. However, women are *not* better at rallying the enclave vote. If parties want to aggressively court the Muslim vote, the goal of gender parity will suffer. The only way around this dilemma is for parties to systematically disadvantage non-Muslim men, but the evidence presented here demonstrates that they are instead mostly disadvantaging non-Muslim women.

These findings produce several implications. One of the key questions that has dominated public and scholarly debates about the Muslim Question is whether the normative beliefs and cultural practices of Europe's Muslims are compatible with those of non-Muslim majority societies.[52] The role and treatment of women has been singled out as one of the most frequently discussed issues in this regard. Additionally, questions about gender equality go to the

---

Among less urbanized municipalities, the difference is smaller and statistically insignificant (5 points, $p = .510$).

52. Triandafyllidou et al. (2012) and Vertovec and Wessendorf (2010).

core of the multicultural dilemma. One often-voiced concern is that multicultural policies that actively recognize the cultural traditions and religious beliefs of minorities might in fact end up threatening the autonomy and equality of women.[53]

Questions of multicultural recognition have long been discussed by political theorists.[54] Within this debate, one of the most contentious issues has revolved around how policies of recognition affect "internal minorities" such as women and children. Critics charge that multiculturalist policies can undermine the liberty and life chances of women with some going so far as to suggest that feminism and multiculturalism are incompatible.[55] It is therefore not surprising that attacks against multiculturalism are increasingly linked to concerns about gender equality.[56]

A common line of critique states that national multicultural regimes empower self-appointed community leaders who are typically male and conservative, and much attention has been paid to the supposed effects of national integration models. This chapter demonstrates that the electoral process can lead to similar outcomes, irrespective of a country's official stance on state-sponsored multiculturalism. Like their counterparts in France, Francophone parties in Belgium condemn *communautarisme* and promote assimilationsism in principle, but they readily play the communitarian card if it helps them get an edge in elections, no matter the consequences for gender parity.

This chapter has made plain that the electoral process—perhaps more so than national integration policies—sharpens multicultural dilemmas of recognition on the ground. It further prompts us to rethink the notion that political inclusion promotes or is at least correlated with integration in other realms; depending on partisan inclusion objectives, electoral incorporation may in fact slow down rather than facilitate the social acceptance and assimilation of minority groups. The concluding chapter fleshes out these and other implications.

53. Macey (2009) and Wikan (2002).
54. Barry (2001), Benhabib (2002), Kymlicka (1995), Okin (1999), and Song (2007).
55. Barry (2001); cf. Shachar (2001) and Song (2007).
56. Langvasbråten (2008), Roggeband and Verloo (2007), and Siim and Skjeie (2008).

7

Implications and Conclusions

As democracies diversify, so too do the candidates and groups that seek representation in government. In most democratic settings, political parties are the vehicles through which the political entry of new groups occurs, but parties adapt unevenly to demographic changes in the electorate. In some cases they diversify their ranks swiftly, while in others existing elites and core voters successfully resist the entry of newcomers. Political parties are, in part, coalitions of un-likeminded constituents who nonetheless join forces in support of candidates and legislation. Understanding *who* constitutes these coalitions allows us to understand which members of our societies gain access to representation and which do not.

Drawing on evidence from several hundred municipalities in four countries, this book has demonstrated that whether or not inclusion unfolds is less a product of lofty ideological conviction and has much more to do with sober electoral calculations. When considering inclusion, parties assess the vote gains they expect the nomination of minority candidates to generate. If the selection of minority candidates triggers sufficient ethnocentrist vote losses to make it a net vote loser, exclusion prevails, no matter a party's rhetoric on inclusiveness and nondiscrimination. Parties move to symbolic inclusion once the minority electorate, together with cosmopolitan majority voters, is sufficiently large to yield electoral rewards. Symbolic candidates are meant to shape a party's image. They raise minority parity ratios only somewhat and tend to please majority voters more than they do minority voters; the critical feature of symbolic candidates is their assimilation to majority norms and preferences. This alignment becomes irrelevant, however, when the minority electorate is so sizable that elections cannot be won without it. Here, parties opt for vote-based inclusion and pick minority candidates who are best equipped to rally the minority vote. If these candidates and the minority vot-ers that elect them follow politically relevant norms and practices that are difficult to square with those of core voters, vote-based inclusion can under-mine a party's reputation and coherence.

These inclusion paths and the motivations that guide them are general and can be applied to different minority groups and parties in advanced democra-cies. When thinking through the trade-offs inherent in different incorporation types and the consequences that flow from them, the content and spatial dis-tribution of minority preferences begins to matter. Having focused on Euro-pean Muslims, this book has shown that inclusion dilemmas are most severe where the Muslim vote is most critical. It is in areas of Muslim concentration that minority norms and behaviors deviate sharply and visibly from those of their neighbors. When electoral rules and citizenship laws make it possible for such areas to become electorally pivotal, minority political incorporation can transform the character of parties, compromise their ideological integrity, strain coalitions and eventually alter the fault lines along which elections are fought.

Though inclusion decisions are made with short-run electoral fortunes in mind, parties' records of minority inclusion have enduring repercussions that go well beyond specific parties or elections. The incorporation of previously excluded minorities into the arena of electoral politics likely influences minor-ity social integration and majority-minority relations. It also alters the trajec-tory and social bases of electoral coalitions. As a result, minority electoral incorporation can change the identity of parties and transform the party brand in the long run. Minority inclusion—even if undertaken on the basis of short-term strategic considerations—can therefore have broad, meaningful and long-lasting impacts on society and democracy.

In this conclusion, I speculate on what conditions make such transforma-tive changes more or less likely, and, in doing so, I lay out questions that future research can address. I begin with a discussion about how variation in inclu-sion types may lead to differences in the quality of intergroup relations and hypothesize how exclusion, symbolic inclusion, and vote-based inclusion each affect majority perceptions of the minority as well as minority sociopolitical integration. Even though these inclusion types likely have important effects on the nature of intergroup relations, they are an unintended consequence; parties' recruitment decisions are not driven by attention to these relations. Rather, the evidence presented in this book has shown that they are based on the mobilizational heft of the minority group relative to the majority popula-tion. I therefore next consider how changes in the mobilizational structures that parties confront—most notably the weakening labor movement—changes the attractiveness of ethnic and religious networks in which minorities are embedded. The comparative organizational edge of minority enclaves can in turn make it more difficult to incorporate minorities within existing cleavage structures.

Building on this insight, the final section conjectures how and under what conditions the entry of minorities into electoral politics can set in motion a fundamental reordering of existing party systems. Such a transformation has occurred in other advanced democracies, most notably in the United States. Transformative restructuring may also be on the horizon in Europe, and I consider how features of European party systems and minority electorates could influence the nature of this change.

Inclusion Types and Minority Integration: The Perspective of the Majority

It had long been assumed that when it comes to minority assimilation, especially as it pertains to immigrants, incorporation in one area propels incorporation in others. For instance, as minorities become more economically integrated, they will also be more likely to advance politically and socially. This assumption has been challenged by more recent accounts, and this book suggests that the process can even be reversed.[1] Depending on the inclusion type, electoral incorporation can in fact *hurt* minority social integration.

VOTE-BASED INCLUSION AND MAJORITY PERCEPTIONS OF THE MINORITY

Electoral inclusion can be damaging to social integration if the type of minority candidates and voters to whom parties are seeking to appeal differ significantly on a set of salient dimensions from the majority society. In the case of European Muslims, the foregoing chapters demonstrated that the type of minority voter who is coveted by parties engaged in vote-based recruitment is substantially more culturally distinct, religious, socially conservative, and economically deprived than the average majority voter. What is more, he is also quite a bit less integrated on these dimensions than is the average Muslim voter.

The fact that parties go after the least assimilated group members, who tend to evoke the greatest suspicion and resentment among majority voters, makes sense in contexts where electoral geography rewards spatial concentration *and* where spatial concentration coincides with less assimilation and greater adherence to in-group cultural norms and practices. As electoral districts shrink in size, a spatially concentrated group's potential for electoral

---

1. See Dahl (1964) for the conventional view; see Hochschild et al. (2013), Maxwell (2012), and Ramakrishnan (2005) for more recent research.

leverage rises. Conversely, in geographically large districts such power is diluted. Turning to the relationship between concentration and assimilation, the preceding pages highlighted that religious minorities often cluster together in dense spaces because this concentration makes it easier to carry out the daily duties required of their faith. It also helps to sustain ethnoreligious behavioral norms, which are more easily monitored in tightly woven neighborhoods than in sprawling suburban or rural areas.

This feature of spatial concentration pertains to many minority groups. Among immigrants in the United States, the move out of the ethnic enclave into more mixed areas has historically coincided with higher levels of assimilation. Individuals who seek greater acculturation and socioeconomic success hope to leave the enclave, at least in settings where enclaves are associated with limited upward mobility. By contrast, those who stay behind may lack the linguistic, cultural, or economic resources to move or may simply prefer living in culturally familiar surroundings.[2]

As a result of these sorting processes, the political incorporation of minorities can actually foster negative attitudes toward the group. This unfolds when vote-maximizing parties operate in an institutional context that grants political power to spatially concentrated groups. Insofar as a minority group's traits become more distinct from those of the majority in areas where the group is densely clustered, this proposition should travel to other settings.

Moreover, to the extent that minority concentration also brings with it increased segregation from the majority population, electoral politics will be one of only a few arenas in which members of the majority encounter members of the minority. Taking vote-based candidates whose purpose is to rally the votes of the least assimilated group members as representatives of the group as a whole, majority voters may adopt a skewed view of the minority population and will deduce that minority residents are much less assimilated than they in fact are. They will also fault minority voters for rallying behind candidates the majority finds unacceptable, even though a substantial number of minority voters, especially outside the enclave, does not relate to vote-based candidates.

The controversial tenure of corrupt Tower Hamlets mayor Lutfur Rahman—eventually expelled by Labour for his connections with Islamic extremist groups—and the media coverage it spawned exemplify this dynamic. Rahman mobilized Muslim voters by engineering massive amounts of bloc votes, some obtained fraudulently, and he used the moral clout of clerics to admonish Muslim voters to cast ballots for him (see Chapter 5). Though most British Muslims probably condemn Rahman's behavior, the majority public is much more likely to be exposed to news about Muslim politicians who

2. Massey (1985).

employ similar tactics than it is to read about how British Muslims feel about their representatives. They may therefore draw the conclusion that Muslim voters on the whole endorse candidates like Rahman.

Yet, minority residents are often deeply dissatisfied with the selection process and fault parties for nominating flawed candidates. Commenting on the selection of minority candidates by local parties, an ethnic minority member of the Green Party in a Belgian city complained that the choice of candidates "really was an insult to the ethnic community. If these people have to represent you, that is just embarrassing."[3]

Vote-based inclusion can thus be counterproductive to minority integration overall. It can lead to the empowerment of candidates who cause the majority public to become more circumspect and resentful of the minority population while leaving large sections of the minority population frustrated with the political process.

One important question to ask, however, is "compared to what?" That is, is symbolic inclusion or even exclusion from elected office more conducive to generating a favorable perception of the minority? And, if so, what are the trade-offs involved?

SYMBOLIC INCLUSION AND MAJORITY PERCEPTIONS OF THE MINORITY

One important function of symbolic minority candidates is to court those majority voters who value diversity and who do not feel comfortable in ethnically homogenous parties whose leaders readily surrender to or even stoke voters' xenophobic inclinations. Additionally, a potential consequence of symbolic inclusion might be that majority voters are more likely to deem the minority population as a whole as assimilated to mainstream norms. Just as is the case with vote-based candidates, symbolic candidates can function as barometers of collective assimilation.

If it were the case that parties' selection decisions were motivated not by the short-run desire to win elections but by bringing about favorable majority attitudes, one prescription would be for parties to systematically pursue symbolic inclusion rather than exclusion or vote-based inclusion; in other words, they would need to be patient. If parties practiced symbolic inclusion while minority assimilation occurred with the passage of time, the trade-offs that this book has explored might not be so stark: Once preferences of residents living in minority enclaves are more in line with those of the majority, parties that eventually shift to vote-based candidates will nominate individuals who are a better fit with existing constituencies and party principles.

3. Eelbode (2013, 132).

Quite aside from the paternalistic nature of such an approach, much of this book has established that parties are largely impatient. They mainly consider the immediate electoral pay-offs—not majority perceptions—when devising their positions towards minority candidates and electorates. Yet patience becomes more likely where strong regional or national party leaderships can impose candidates on local parties. For central party leaders, generating more positive opinions about minorities is not necessarily a purely philanthropic exercise. Good intergroup relations can have notable electoral benefits: As majority views of the minority become more favorable, appeals to minority voters will incur smaller ethnocentrist vote losses. This strategy can therefore bring significant electoral rewards in the long run and allow parties to widen their coalitions.

Though attractive, these circumstances are unlikely when party elites operate with shorter time horizons, as they typically do. As is often the case in politics, the strategies that produce the best outcomes for individual candidates may not offer the most desirable collective outcomes. Nevertheless, if central elites were in charge of nominations, they might still opt for symbolic candidates in districts where vote-based inclusion could have delivered victories. In the age of social media and round-the-clock news coverage, parties must anticipate that the statements and behaviors of vote-based politicians travel well beyond the enclave. The anecdote about sex-segregated Labour rallies that opened this book is but one example of this dynamic.[4]

Afraid that vote-based candidates could hurt the party brand and thereby alienate voters across the country, central party elites might be willing to sacrifice some contests and nominate symbolic candidates in districts where the nomination of a vote-based candidate would have generated more local votes. By writing off a few individual districts, strong party organizations would protect the collective good.

To summarize, symbolic inclusion may promote more positive majority views than does vote-based inclusion, but in the enclave it does not offer the same return in minority votes. Nonetheless, when vote-based inclusion makes the most electoral sense in a given race, symbolic candidates might still be nominated: (1) if party selectors adopt long time horizons over the course of which minority preferences and behaviors become more closely aligned with those of the majority (assuming that assimilation indeed takes place over

4. In another fairly common dynamic playing out in the UK, national party leaderships have had to rebuke and at times suspend Muslim MPs and councilors for promoting anti-Israel conspiracy theories on Facebook (such as claiming that Israel orchestrated the 9/11 attacks or is behind ISIS) or for sending anti-Semitic tweets. These events are often widely publicized in national and even international news outlets and cause internal divisions within parties, so far primarily within Labour. For a few recent examples of this trend, see Marshall (2015), McSmith (2016), and Stewart (2016).

time); or (2) if party elites have the ability to impose candidates on local parties and are concerned that vote-based enclave politicians will cause majority voters in other districts to abandon the party.

EXCLUSION AND MAJORITY PERCEPTIONS OF THE MINORITY

Another option is exclusion. Is exclusion preferable to vote-based inclusion if the goal were to bring about favorable majority perceptions of the minority? If the absence of minority officeholders signals to the majority that minorities lack the "ability to rule,"[5] exclusion would have qualitatively different but nevertheless pernicious consequences. Malicious arguments about a minority group's inferior status or even intellect would be more easily defended.

Additionally, political exclusion could give rise to the impression that minorities are simply not interested in running for office and, by implication, in engaging with majority society more generally. In the debate about European Muslims, talk of "parallel societies" and of Muslims intentionally cutting themselves off from mainstream institutions is common fare. Political exclusion therefore solidifies the idea that Muslims are unassimilable. This notion would be further reinforced if systematic political marginalization spawned antigovernment protests on the part of the minority.[6] Exclusion from elected office is, then, not a prescription for social integration. On top of the alienation felt by the minority group itself, excluding minorities from elected office likely worsens majority perceptions of the group.

Inclusion Types and Minority Integration: The Perspective of the Minority

Not only do different inclusion strategies have the potential to shape majority views about the minority; they also affect minority groups. Party behaviors can leave their mark on a minority's impression of the electoral process, and the political system more broadly, and can benefit or harm different segments within the group.

VOTE-BASED INCLUSION AND MINORITY INTEGRATION

In the cases discussed in this book, vote-based nominations generate the maximum number of minority votes because vote-based candidates are figures of high standing in their communities. They have the authority and capacity to induce fellow group members to go to the polls; this is what makes them vote-

5. Mansbridge (1999).
6. On this point, see Dancygier (2010).

based nominees. Whether or not such politicians benefit individuals within the group depends in part on whether or not interests are aligned. As is the case with most politicians and persons of power, presumably vote-based minority politicians are invested in making sure that the social structures that help them sustain prominence and authority remain intact. As such, group members who benefit from the current order and who chiefly have their own interests in mind will have favorable views of vote-based inclusion. As Chapters 5 and 6 have illustrated, among European Muslims this pertains mostly to men who are deeply enmeshed in the religious life or kinship structures of the enclave. Aspiring female politicians lose out from this arrangement.

This exact claim was made by the "Muslim Women's Network" in the UK, when it sent a letter to Labour leader Jeremy Corbyn in February 2016, calling for an inquiry into "systematic misogyny displayed by significant numbers of Muslim male councillors" in candidate selections. The letter described how these councilors sabotaged campaigns by Muslim women hoping to become elected officials. Allegations included male councilors smearing a woman's reputation by accusing her of an extramarital affair, or pressuring a woman candidate to step down because her father refused to support her.[7]

One can further speculate that vote-based inclusion puts a wider set of Muslim women, not just those who want to enter politics, at a disadvantage. Chapter 3 outlined how the migration process led to the replication of the patriarchal social structures that govern life in the villages of the sending regions. Indeed, other research suggests that similar processes are at work among a range of immigrant groups.[8] The maintenance of inegalitarian gender roles among Muslims has in turn been a major lightning rod in Europe, where gender norms have slowly liberalized over the decades. Inasmuch as Muslims' conservative gender roles act as an impediment to integration, vote-based inclusion can be detrimental. It can slow down integration directly in cases where vote-based politicians stand accused of hindering the emancipation of Muslim women in their constituencies. For instance, some of the male Muslim (vote-based) councilors who stand in the way of women's political careers have actively blocked any type of collective organization by women, especially if it addresses issues like forced marriage or honor-based violence. Non-Muslim politicians and law enforcement are in turn complicit when they fail to intervene.[9]

In these ways, the persistent selection of vote-based male candidates can be detrimental to some women residing in the enclave. Moreover, the systematic privileging of male over female candidates—which Chapter 6 has shown

7. Mortimer (2016).
8. See, e.g., Pedraza (1991).
9. Brandon and Hafez (2008).

proceeds very much in complicity with existing non-Muslim party elites—deprives Muslim women of an important access point to influence, authority, and independence.

Vote-based inclusion also tends to sideline the younger generation. Accounts of "disaffected youth" highlight not only alienation from mainstream institutions, but also disappointment with co-ethnic representatives. Vote-based candidates are often blamed for neglecting the interests of young people, in particular when it comes to addressing the difficulties and discrimination they experience in the labor market. It is therefore no accident that challenges to vote-based enclave politicians have been mounted by coalitions of women and youth.[10] Yet, these challenges tend to be difficult to sustain. After all, vote-based candidates obtain their political positions because they enjoy support (whether it be genuine or more coerced) from a large number of constituents and from mainstream party elites.

In brief, in electoral systems where spatial concentration matters, vote-based inclusion will reinforce the social structures that operate in the enclave. The effect on the integration of minorities overall as well as on segments within these groups thus depends on the nature of these social structures and how they compare to those of the majority. Among European Muslims, vote-based recruitment tends to shut out women and young people. It is important to note that this state of affairs—that is, the marginalization of women and youth—also commonly applies to the political process outside of the enclave, among members of the majority. The difference may be in degree, rather than in kind.

SYMBOLIC INCLUSION AND MINORITY INTEGRATION

Whereas vote-based inclusion raises the number of minority politicians but has potentially deleterious effects on minority integration, symbolic inclusion is associated with different trade-offs. One irony that this book has pointed to is that the forces that push parties towards symbolic candidates make it unlikely that large sections of the minority population will, in fact, accept these candidates as legitimate representatives of the group. Because these candidates have to please the majority electorate, they often fall short in representing the minority.

Political theorists who extol the virtues of symbolic representation posit that it could erode negative stereotypes. Yet, we must also consider the electoral calculus that leads parties to opt for this strategy in the first place. If parties' primary goal is not to seek out candidates who are easily compatible with the preferences of the minority but to maximize votes by also wooing majority voters, it is unclear and probably unlikely that they will settle on

10. Peace and Akhtar (2015) and Zibouh and (2010).

candidates that minority voters accept as symbolic representatives. The symbolization may very well work for some majority voters, but less so for minority electorates. In fact, minority communities have come up with terms that indicate their dissatisfaction with parties engaging in symbolic inclusion. In Belgium, minority candidates whose main purpose is to give a party an image of openness and diversity without being tasked to actually work on pro-minority policies are designated "Alibi Alis." In France, they are labeled "Arabes de service." In Germany, "Vorzeigetürke."

It is unclear what the consequences are of such candidates on how minorities perceive the political system, though it is probably safe to say that symbolic inclusion cannot be the key to minority integration. If it helps the socio-political integration of minorities, it is only via the more indirect channel of improved majority opinion of the group.

EXCLUSION AND MINORITY INTEGRATION

Exclusion is possibly the least desirable outcome, and not only from a normative perspective. Systematic exclusion sustains the view that the minority is unable or unwilling to participate in democratic governance, and it can also cause minorities to distrust and ultimately turn against government institutions. The persistent political marginalization of immigrant-origin minorities has fostered antistate riots in countries like France, the UK, Sweden, and Belgium. The deliberate exclusion of African Americans from positions of political authority has also been cited as contributing to violent disturbances in U.S. cities.[11] Once such protests proliferate, the negative repercussions of political exclusion multiply. They weaken minority neighborhoods through property damage and hasten the departure of residents with sufficient means to leave, and they can create the image, broadcast by the media, that minorities are prone to crime and violence.[12]

It is difficult to see, then, how exclusion from elected office can benefit minority integration in other realms or to think of circumstances in which exclusion would be preferable to vote-based or symbolic inclusion. Nonetheless, as this discussion has brought to light, the latter two incorporation types, while better for minority social integration than exclusion, involve trade-offs as well.

If a benevolent social planner were to devise the optimal inclusion strategy, she would first have to decide which aspects to prioritize: majority perceptions of the minority; minority perceptions of the political system; or interests of subgroups within the minority population, to name but a few.

---

11. On Europe, see Dancygier (2010); on the relationship between local government responsiveness and black protest in the United States, see, e.g., Kerner Commssion (1968) and Spilerman (1970).

12. Dancygier and Laitin (2014) and Wasow (2016).

Given that political parties are most definitely not benevolent social planners, understanding these trade-offs may suggest both issues to consider and strategies for success to those seeking to pursue integration along multiple dimensions.

THE ROLE OF PREFERENCE DIVERGENCE

Many of the trade-offs and dilemmas this book has explored arise because minority group preferences and practices clash with those of the majority, and it is important to keep this divergence in mind when generalizing this book's arguments. Chapter 3 has illustrated some of the major fault lines between Muslims and non-Muslims in Europe and how these are magnified where Muslims concentrate and have electoral power. The remaining chapters have illuminated the inclusion dilemmas that ensue as a result. However, it is not always the case that values and behaviors diverge; often minority groups embrace principles and practices that resemble those of the majority. Where this is the case, vote-based inclusion should not produce the same type of negative majority perceptions. To be sure, political entrepreneurs who benefit from intergroup discord will still try to convince majority voters that minority electorates and their representatives are in some ways incompatible with majority interests or norms. Parties bent on winning ethnocentrist support frequently portray minorities as prone to crime, welfare abuse, or other immoral behavior. But it is less likely that majority voters who are broadly supportive of diversity will take the bait. It should therefore be easier to construct coalitions consisting of liberal cosmopolitans and minorities in situations where these two groups have roughly similar views on salient issues. In such a setting, vote-based inclusion will pose fewer dilemmas for centrist parties because vote-based candidates do not collide with party principles.

One may wonder, then, why minorities frequently remain so underrepresented in elected office even when preference gaps are small. Naturally, ethnocentrism and the ability of politicians to stir up ethnic hatreds play a role. Additionally, internal party battles over who is allowed a slot contribute to the exclusion of any new group. But one somewhat paradoxical dynamic may have to do with the relationship between assimilation and turnout. If a minority group has assimilated to majority preferences (or never had distinct preferences to begin with) and exhibits social structures and value systems that are easily compatible with majority mainstream society, the group may no longer feature the tightly connected networks, community leaders, and intraethnic loyalties that can characterize minority groups, especially those of relatively recent immigrant-origin. These traits are, however, what make these groups attractive to party strategists looking for mobilization shortcuts. Though, all else equal, parties are more likely to welcome minorities whose views and values mesh well with those of existing voters than those who clash in significant ways, their enthusiasm will decline precipitously if these new constituencies can't deliver on Election Day. By contrast, as the previous chapters have shown, parties are willing to turn a blind eye on seemingly irreconcilable differences if they can be assured that minority recruitment leads to electoral victory.

Future research can assess whether, under what circumstances, and for what groups this inverse relationship between assimilation and turnout might hold. In addressing this question, it can also examine how mobilization structures of the majority society influence minority turnout, a topic I address in the next section.

Traditional Mobilization Structures and Minority Inclusion

Political incorporation of minorities has (at least) two components: the selection of candidates and the mobilization of voters. In the previous sections, I considered the consequences of varying candidate selection strategies for minorities' social integration. In this section, I investigate the consequences of different voter mobilization strategies. The foregoing chapters have made plain that the ability of ethnic leaders, village elders, or religious elites to rally votes effectively and efficiently is prized by party strategists intent on winning elections. But this book has also demonstrated that this mobilization tactic can come with a hefty price tag: When parties tap into ethnoreligious bloc votes they risk compromising core party values, an ensuing hollowing out of the party brand, and ultimately usher in a change in the salient political cleavages that govern elections.

So why do parties make this Faustian bargain? To answer this question, it is useful to take into account the economic and social contexts of the present age and place them in comparative perspective. When doing so, it becomes apparent that parties appreciate ethnoreligious bloc votes in part because other organizational conduits for generating reliable and predictable turnout are less readily available. This section spells out two implications that follow: first, the comparatively weaker organizational networks among the majority electorate can make a mobilization strategy that targets the minority more attractive; second, the waning of these networks over time has made it more difficult to fold minority voters into politics without upsetting existing cleavages.

CLASS-BASED ORGANIZATIONS AND TURNOUT

Consider the organizational landscape that parties confront when they thrash out campaign tactics. Historically and presently, ethnoreligious minority voters, particularly those with recent immigrant origins, frequently live in economically disadvantaged areas (see Chapters 3 and 5 on this point). Their low-income native neighbors tend to have low levels of electoral participation, and parties struggle to get out the vote in economically deprived neighbor-hoods.[13] The problem of turning out the low-skilled also dogged parties in the past. Studies of working-class mobilization in late nineteenth- and early twentieth-century Western Europe routinely refer to the problems of recruit-ing the "slum vote."[14] Faced with a working class that can be hard to reach, local parties in Europe and the US have often turned to ethnoreligious minor-ity populations, such as Irish Catholic immigrants or Orthodox Jews, who are more residentially rooted, embedded in social structures that facilitate elec-toral mobilization, and who have community representatives that can both articulate their interests and produce bloc votes (see Chapter 2). In other words, it is not just the mobilizational capacity of ethnic minorities but also the comparative organizational weakness of their neighbors that can prompt parties to privilege minority over majority votes.

But ethnoreligious organizations are not the only mobilizing institutions. Labor unions have served this role for left parties over the course of the twen-tieth century. Yet, labor unions differ in a key way from ethnoreligious orga-nizations as a mobilizing force. They delivered votes *and* ideological fit. While the closeness between center-left parties and trade unions has varied across industrialized democracies, on the whole contact with and membership in unions tends to raise turnout and leftist votes among lower-income elector-ates.[15] Even though the labor movement and its associated unions are no uni-tary actor, strong and encompassing unions make it nonetheless possible for left parties to hook into a class-based machinery that generates votes on Elec-tion Day.

A well-organized working class can make recruiting ethnic minority voters less necessary. Moreover, when parties do feel electoral pressures to bring minority electorates on board, inclusion involves fewer dilemmas. The avail-ability of trade unions allows parties on the Left to fold in ethnic outsiders via ostensibly class-based channels—provided existing union members do not protest such entry, which they have often done.[16]

---

13. For a meta-analysis of individual-level research on voter turnout, see Smets and van Ham (2013).

14. In the past, transient housing and work arrangements made registration and effective canvassing difficult. Lacking leisure time also prevented many among the poor from developing political interest and from engaging in political activities (Lawrence 1997). See, for instance, Thompson (1967, 239) on political apathy among the poor in early twentieth-century London.

15. Lamare (2010), Leighley and Nagler (2007), and Przeworski (1985).

16. For a comparative study of union approaches to immigrant workers, see Schmitter-Heisler (2006). See Frymer (2007) on African Americans' incorporation into unions.

To be sure, underneath the union label, ethnic identities can still run strong; union bloc votes may not be easily distinguishable from ethnic bloc votes where these two categories coincide. In fact, in American and British cities, local union branches were often associated with certain immigrant groups such as the Irish.[17] Yet, where unions are important players, left parties are much less dependent on nonclass actors with distinct interests, such as clerics. And, over time, unions can integrate new groups into the broader economic and sociopolitical fabric in ways that minority-based ethnic or religious organizations most likely cannot. For example, in the United States, some have considered unions to be among the "greatest 'Americanization agents'" of Mexican Americans.[18]

In short, the existence of a strong labor movement mitigates the dilemmas outlined in this book. When the native working class is electorally mobilized, which often occurs through trade unions, left parties may not look to recruit minority votes to boost turnout in low-income districts. If the Left does seek to be inclusive, unions can give ethnic minorities an entry into electoral politics that makes it easier to pursue these new voters without having to rely on explicitly ethnic appeals or on ethnoreligious actors, alliances which, as this book has clarified, can dilute a party's image and mar its reputation.[19]

By implication, the collapse of the manufacturing sector, the rise of irregular types of employment, and the associated decline of labor unions across advanced democracies has deprived the Left of its traditional turnout structures and instead elevated the attractiveness of and need for other types of mobilization mechanisms.[20] As deindustrialization gained momentum across Europe and North America, so has the growth of immigrant-origin populations. The severity of inclusion dilemmas that left parties face will likely depend in part on the ability of the working class to retain or rebuild robust and politically active labor movements.

RELIGIOUS ORGANIZATIONS AND TURNOUT

Because immigrant-origin minorities are often members of the working class and commonly settle in areas where the Left has strong roots, left parties tend to be the first to confront questions of inclusion. But I have also made evident that electoral calculations can compel center-right parties to eventually grapple with minority incorporation. Whereas the Left risks watering down its

17. See, e.g., Erie (1988) and McDermott (1979).
18. Sanchez (1993, 249), cited in Schmitter-Heisler (2006, 204).
19. Others have argued that the existence of local political machines has an effect on parties' approach to minority voters; see, e.g., Trounstine (2008) and Wong (2006).
20. On the relationships between unions, left parties and falling turnout, see Gray and Caul (2000).

class credentials by shifting towards ethnoreligious recruitment, the Right risks being faulted for betraying the nation's religious and cultural heritage when doing so.

At the same time, just like the Left, the contemporary Right has had to contend with a decline in its traditional mobilization structures. Church organizations were historically a repository of votes for conservative politicians. The emergence of confessional parties further solidified the role of religion as "primarily an electoral and organizational asset" on the Right.[21] In the absence of such parties, as in the United States and Britain, church attendance has also been linked to political participation.[22] But across Western Europe and beyond (though not necessarily in the United States), religiosity and church membership have been dwindling. For instance, in France, Britain, Belgium, and the Netherlands, about half of all residents state that they never attend religious services.[23]

Conservative parties may therefore look towards more religious immigrant and ethnic minority groups to get out the vote. The recruitment of more pious electorates on the basis of religious attachment (or social conservatism, which often accompanies religiosity) can be an opportunity for center-right parties, especially where such groups do not necessarily benefit from the Right's economic policies. As Chapter 5 has made clear, economically deprived districts that are typically out of reach for fiscally conservative parties can become viable for the Right if ethnoreligious ties take precedence over class. In the United States, for example, the Republican Party has tried to make inroads among religious Hispanics by emphasizing its commitments to religion and family values.[24]

More comfortable with mixing religion and politics, center-right parties nevertheless have to walk a fine line: Where new minorities do not belong to the dominant religion or ethnicity, the ethnocentrist backlash looms large. Convincing core voters that religiosity and attendant social values unite minority and majority voters irrespective of denominational or ethnic differences will be a key challenge for center-right parties that want to expand their electoral coalitions.

In Western Europe, then, traditional mobilization structures of both the Left and the Right have been eroding just as electorates have become more ethnically diverse. These concurrent trends, which are both brought on by,

21. Kalyvas and van Kersbergen (2010, 186). See Kalyvas (1996) for a detailed account of the emergence of Christian Democracy.

22. Rosenstone and Hansen (1993) and Verba et al. (1995).

23. These data are taken from the 2008 European Social Survey; see The Economist Online (2010).

24. However, religious Hispanics do not necessarily share preferences with core Republican voters when it comes to social issues; see Valenzuela (2014).

and part of, larger globalization processes, make it more likely that party systems that bring in immigrant-origin minorities—and especially those whose preferences do not map onto existing coalitions—will experience transformative change.

Voter and Party Realignments

This book has made the case that political parties and salient electoral cleavages can change when new groups enter the political system, even—and, in fact, especially—when parties are simply pursuing short-run electoral gains. The argument that I have developed emphasizes the importance of minority preferences, their social organization, and mobilizational deftness. I have further provided evidence that parties' recruitment decisions are chiefly motivated by the desire to win votes, not by ideological commitments. When vote-maximizing parties encounter electorally pivotal minority groups, their accommodation of minority preferences and adoption of group-based campaign styles can then alter the identities of parties and electoral cleavages.

Notably, much of the transformation described in the previous chapters originates from minorities and parties seeking minority votes, rather than from within the majority electorate. By taking a close look at this type of change, the book complements existing studies that investigate the political impact of diversity through the eyes of majority voters. A large body of research documents how racial, ethnic, and religious diversity shakes up party systems by prompting white native voters to leave diversifying parties. According to this account, majority voters abandon parties that appear to do more for newly included minorities than for long-established core partisans. If these departures are sizable and sustained, the inclusion of minorities can reorder the party system.[25]

The most prominent example of such realignment is found in the United States. During the 1960s, the two parties' national platforms began to diverge on racial issues and helped turn a once solidly Democratic South into a stronghold of the Republican Party. Today, views about African Americans, civil rights, and, increasingly, immigration, still critically influence party choice. The growing presence of blacks and other minorities in the Democratic Party has further cemented this partisan realignment.[26]

25. See, e.g., Carmines and Stimson (1989), Edsall and Edsall (1992), Kriesi et al. (2008), and Roemer et al. (2007).

26. Carmines and Stimson (1989) offer the now-conventional account, in which national party repositioning on civil rights in the 1960s caused this realignment, while Schickler (2016) argues that opinion shifts in the electorate originating in earlier decades were the driving force. See also Huckfeldt and Kohfeld (1989) for subnational examples of realignment. Abrajano and Hajnal (2015) maintain that immigration is further polarizing the U.S. electorate along partisan lines.

Are we witnessing similar shifts in Europe? The persistence and continued rise of far-right, anti-immigrant parties certainly suggests that comparable processes are at play. Unsurprisingly, ethnocentrism is a good predictor for far-right voting. Moreover, parties that are perceived as too immigrant-friendly or too accommodating of Islam run the risk of losing majority support. For instance, nearly one in four German citizens (24 percent) who think that "more is being done for refugees than for native Germans" state they will vote for the anti-immigrant *Alternative für Deutschland* (AfD), but this share drops to only 2 percent among Germans who disagree with the idea that refugees receive preferential treatment.[27]

Similar sentiments are felt across Europe. Additionally, the increased presence of liberal cosmopolitans in left-of-center coalitions further generates a sense that commitments to multicultural policies and minority constituents have supplanted obligations to indigenous voter groups. Feeling economically and culturally deserted by mainstream parties, a substantial slice of European voters has therefore turned to movements of the Far-Right that promise to safeguard native interests and wrest control from the political establishment.[28] The referendum on Brexit is a dramatic manifestation of this general trend.

These developments resemble the American experience to a degree. One important difference is that the prevalence of proportional electoral rules in much of Europe makes it more likely that smaller parties can benefit from and instigate antiminority sentiments. Even in areas where centrist parties hold clear majorities, proportional representation allows nativist parties to enter parliaments. Unlike in the United States, European electorates can thus shift allegiances across parties, even if major parties do not differ in their stances towards immigrants and other minority groups. In fact, when voters view the Center-Right and the Center-Left as interchangeable they may opt for a far-right party that offers alternatives.[29] In the United States, such upheavals are more likely to occur *within* parties, as the rise of Donald Trump indicates.

In today's Europe, a significant portion of majority voters sorts themselves into parties based on positions about ethnocultural diversity. This realignment, scholars have noted, has helped transform the political space and can effect seismic shifts in party systems.[30] Yet, when we don't confine ourselves to

27. These figures are based on a survey fielded in Germany by the author (with Naoki Egami and Amaney Jamal) in the fall of 2016. Respondents were asked what party they would vote for if the general elections were held "this Sunday."

28. See, e.g., Hewitt (2005), Kitschelt (1996), Mudde (2007), Rhodes (2009), and Roemer et al. (2007). For a recent review of the Far-Right in Europe, see Golder (2016).

29. Golder (2016) briefly reviews how mainstream party positioning may or may not impact the fortunes of the Far-Right.

30. For recent accounts of these phenomena, see Häusermann and Kriesi (2015) and Kitschelt and Rehm (2015).

studying realigning majority voters but also examine how the preferences and behaviors of minority electorates influence party strategy, this transformation could be even more momentous than is commonly assumed. Not only are parties becoming more diverse, this book has demonstrated that in doing so, they frequently abandon their stated principles. As a result, the pursuit of one of Europe's largest and fastest-growing minority groups is changing parties from within. Where vote-based inclusion has taken place, parties have become more diverse, male, religious, and socially conservative. Even socially liberal cosmopolitans may therefore no longer appreciate ethnically diverse parties. Paradoxically, far-right, anti-immigrant parties across the Continent exploit this development by presenting themselves as champions of liberalism, progressivism, and feminism. Whereas the embrace of multiculturalism holds together coalitions between minorities and social liberals in the United States, it threatens to pull them apart in Europe.

The type of realignment that Europe will confront is thus quite variegated. In the United States, majoritarian elections and the associated two-party system can deprive a minority group of leverage: If one party decides to forego the minority's vote, the group's ability to extract concessions is substantially reduced.[31] In European elections, by contrast, I have shown that both the Left and the Right end up recruiting the minority vote where this vote is sizable. Applied to Muslims, this lack of capture—when accompanied by an ability to turn out in significant numbers—permits the group to alter the character of parties. Muslim electorates and the parties that recruit them thus can and have played an active role in reshaping partisan identities and in challenging electoral coalitions from the ground up.

As Muslim immigration and citizenship acquisitions continue to rise, one critical question is how the subnational developments that the previous pages have laid out will aggregate to the national scene. In many contexts, they already have. Relatively small parliamentary districts in the UK have allowed Muslims to be critical voters across the country, even during majoritarian national elections.[32] Depending on the electoral context, parties vacillate as to whether they should nominate vote-based or symbolic candidates, but sometimes regret when they opt for the latter in heavily Muslim areas. Even when they do not nominate Muslim candidates to stand for general election contests, Chapter 5 has indicated that parties pay close attention to Muslim preferences in constituencies with a sizable Muslim presence. In many other European countries electoral districts contain a greater number of voters, but here proportional representation permits minority voters to

31. See Frymer (2010) on the capture of African Americans by the Democratic Party.
32. In the 2015 UK election, the average constituency comprised approximately 70,000 voters.

potentially play a pivotal role. In Belgium, the ethnoreligious and kinship dynamics that permeate local elections (see Chapter 6) also increasingly influence regional and federal campaigns.[33] In Germany, the combination of large electoral districts and a Muslim population with comparatively low (but rising) numbers of citizenship acquisitions still tends to push parties towards nominating symbolic candidates. But even here, non-Muslim candidates tailor their campaign promises to enclave preferences when campaigning in Muslim neighborhoods.

In many cases, these subnational recruitment strategies will scale upwards to the national stage, if they haven't already done so. But even where this doesn't occur, local selection decisions are not made in a vacuum. As mentioned above, the ways in which local parties approach minorities can be broadcast nationally, thereby destabilizing the collective party brand and helping to set off electoral realignments.

Because of the dilemmas that accompany Muslim inclusion, those disenchanted with the new diversity are likely not restricted to ethnocentrists who dislike ethnic diversity no matter what. Rather, the electoral incorporation of Muslims can make it difficult for cosmopolitans who, by definition, value the mix of cultures, to square their openness for diversity with their socially liberal inclinations. For instance, only 3 percent of German citizens who consider themselves to be cosmopolitans would vote for the AfD if they disagree with the idea that most German Muslims believe in the subordination of women. But this number rises to nearly 11 percent when cosmopolitans do believe that Muslims in Germany adhere to patriarchal gender roles.[34] In France, members of another socially liberal voter group are also susceptible to the anti-Muslim appeals of the Far-Right. In the 2015 French regional elections, a third of gay married voters supposedly cast ballots for the *Front National*. By making Muslims' alleged homophobia a campaign issue, the party has made inroads among voters who used to be out-of-reach for rightwing movements.[35]

This strategy is making waves across Europe. Though it is improbable that liberal cosmopolitans will flock to far-right parties in droves, these shifts reveal a tension that may prompt new parties to enter the fray. The political inclusion of Muslims could consequently very well splinter party systems. In addition to reallocating different voter groups to existing parties, as has happened in

33. Zibouh (2010).

34. These figures are drawn from the above-mentioned survey that I carried out in Germany (with Naoki Egami and Amaney Jamal) in September 2016. Respondents are considered cosmopolitan if they "feel more like a citizen of the world than of any country." Overall, 79 percent of respondents agree with the statement that "the majority of Muslims in Germany think that women are subordinate to men." Among cosmopolitans, this number is 72 percent.

35. Polakow-Suransky (2016).

the American case, in Europe, new sets of parties may emerge in which ethnocentrists, cosmopolitans, and minorities can each feel at home.

This fragmentation scenario could unfold if parties carry on as they have, and if the preferences and social structures of electorally pivotal Muslims remain unchanged. It would become especially likely if parties implement policies that mirror the socially conservative preferences of enclave electorates. The wearing of headscarves in public institutions; sex-segregated physical education in schools; the involvement of foreign countries in the training of imams and financing of mosques; the accommodation of sharia-based family law and the operation of sharia councils; placing limits on freedom of speech to protect religious sensibilities; or opposition to granting adoption and marriage rights to gay couples are just some of the stances that divide existing electoral coalitions.

Understanding how Muslim politicians approach these and other policy issues once elected will be a crucial area for future study. On the one hand, candidates who are elected on the basis of their social standing within their communities enjoy some "policy slack."[36] Voters may simply be pleased to have a representative from within their own community and make few legislative demands. The election of minority representatives would consequently not trigger significant policy effects. On the other hand, the evidence in this book indicates that there is no shortage of Muslims aspiring to elected office. As a result, candidates will have to distinguish themselves on traits other than their religion. This has of course already occurred, as smaller-scale identities such as tribe and kinship have gained remarkable salience. But competition over Muslim votes may also enable Muslim electorates to vote for candidates who are best able to translate their preferences into policies. By implication, if parties want to maximize vote shares in enclaves and if enclave preferences influence policy outputs, Muslim political inclusion will have wide-ranging repercussions that go even beyond the ones I have explored here.

———

In light of what we have learned in this book, it is unlikely that parties that are in the business of winning elections will depart from their goal of vote maximization. They may, however, refrain from vote-based inclusion if the ethnocentrist potential rises. Balancing the gains that inclusion generates among the minority against the losses it produces among the majority, the vote that can be garnered in Muslim enclaves may no longer be sizable enough if anti-Muslim sentiment continues to grow and spread to groups that are typically tolerant of diversity.

36. On the notion of policy slack in ethnic politics, see Dickson and Scheve (2006).

A far more attractive scenario is one in which the preference gap between residents in vote-rich minority enclaves and their majority-group neighbors shrinks over time. The integration of Muslims into the social fabrics of European democracies is a worthwhile goal in and of itself, quite aside from its effects on the party system. It would have the added advantage of softening the dilemmas that pervade the politics of Muslim electoral inclusion. Though Muslim integration will ultimately benefit centrist parties by allowing them to broaden their coalitions, this book has made clear that the task of integration is best not left to party strategists.

Electoral and Population Data

The Samples

The election data in Chapters 4, 5, and 6 are based on municipal elections across and within countries. For each country, I gathered information on the composition of city councils in approximately 70 municipalities. In addition, for Belgium and Britain I collected data on each competing candidate. For Austria, Germany, and Belgium I selected the 50 most populous municipalities. Capital cities or city states—Vienna, Berlin, Hamburg, and Brussels—are further subdivided into municipalities (or districts), yielding a total of 72 localities in Austria, and 69 municipalities in Germany and Belgium, respectively. For Britain, I proceeded in a slightly different manner. Because nearly all of Britain's Muslims (98 percent) live in England and because party politics and electoral laws are quite distinct in Scotland and Wales, I limit the sample to England. Here, I sampled the 32 municipalities that make up Greater London and 36 "metropolitan districts" that are populous municipalities located throughout the country (more specifically, in the Northeast, the Northwest, the West Midlands, and in Yorkshire and the Humber). Tables A1 through A4 list the municipalities.

The idea behind sampling the most populous areas is twofold. First, I wanted the sample to comprise a large share of each country's population, Muslim and non-Muslim. For instance, 70 percent of England's Muslims lived in the sampled municipalities in 2001. Second, because Muslims are not evenly spread out across populous municipalities there is still a great deal of variation in the size of the Muslim population across the sampled municipalities.

Identifying Muslim Candidates

One of the biggest data challenges lies in the identification of Muslim candidates and elected politicians. To the best of my knowledge, no existing dataset has information on the religious (or ethnic) background of local, regional, or national politicians, let alone of candidates that do not obtain seats. As a result, I rely on an onomastic approach, coding the religious background of candidates by their first and last names. Most of the names are coded "by hand" by myself and by several research assistants. The intercoder reliability is high, with correlations above .90. For the English sample I also use a software program (Onomap) that has been developed for the UK population to code religion and ethnicity by name.[1] Given the relatively recent migration background of Europe's present-day Muslim population, the names of this population are quite distinct from those of the majority population.

The name-based approach has drawbacks, of course. We might be especially concerned that assimilated Muslim candidates do not have Muslim-sounding names. To help validate the results, I therefore conducted several reliability checks. For the English sample, I was able to obtain data on London councilors whose religious background was verified by contacting local authorities directly.[2] The correlation between these data and my own coding is .90 (p = .000). Types of coding errors are almost evenly split: in 48.9 (51.1) percent of errors, I classify candidates as Muslim (non-Muslim) even though they are non-Muslim (Muslim). Additionally, for England and all other countries I consulted secondary sources, newspaper articles, and candidate websites. The latter will often mention the religious background or country of origin.

Though some error will be unavoidable, the great advantage of this approach is that it allows me to assemble datasets that cover winners and losers for any type of election and for many cities, countries, and years, so long as municipalities or other sources provide electoral data. By contrast, sending questionnaires about the composition of councils to municipalities has several disadvantages: It restricts the analysis to a particular point in time; it is unlikely to include results about losing candidates; not all municipalities will respond; and response rates may vary in ways that could be correlated with patterns of minority representation.

Parity Ratios

Another challenge pertains to the calculation of religious parity ratios. The parity ratio—the proportion of a group in the legislature divided by its proportion in the population—requires the collection of population data. However, most European countries do not enumerate religion in their censuses. Below I detail my methodology for obtaining estimates of the Muslim population at the municipal level.

1. For a detailed explanation of Onomap's methodology, see Lakha et al. (2011) and Mateos (2013). I am aware of two other programs developed for the UK that identify religion on the basis of names (SANGRA and Nam Pehchan). However, these rely on dictionaries of South Asian names only, and the sample used here also includes Muslims who are not of South Asian origin.

2. Eren Tatari generously provided me with this list of Muslim councilors representing London's 32 authorities between 2002 and 2010.

AUSTRIA

The Austrian census last enumerated religion in 2001. Since then, however, the Muslim population has increased considerably in size. I therefore rely on recent population estimates for the year 2012 carried out by Statistik Austria (see Aslan et al. 2014). In 2001, 4.2 percent of Austria's population was Muslim, and this share is estimated to have grown to 6.8 percent by 2012. I collected 2001 census data at the level of the municipality and apply the same growth rate to the municipalities in my sample.

BELGIUM

For Belgian municipalities, I draw on data by sociologist Jan Hertogen who, to the best of my knowledge, is the only source to provide estimates at the municipality level.[3] Hertogen's figures are based on the nationality of non-Belgian citizens and on the previous nationality of naturalized Belgian citizens. They are said to overestimate the size of the Muslim population (Fadil 2013). To adjust for this upward bias, I took the average of the national Muslim population as calculated by Hertogen (2013) and as estimated by the sources cited in Fadil (2013). This average is 15 percent lower than the figure calculated by Hertogen. I therefore decrease Hertogen's estimates by 15 percent when determining parity ratios.

GERMANY

Estimating the size of Germany's Muslim population at the municipality level presented the greatest challenge. There is no official data collection on religion aside from members of the Catholic and Protestant Church for taxation issues. Even large-scale surveys such as the 2011 census only included an optional question on religion, but nearly one in five did not answer this item. The share of non-Christians, including of Muslims, is assumed to be disproportionately high among these nonrespondents, leading the Federal Statistical Office to conclude that the religion figures are unreliable (Statistisches Bundesamt 2013).

The most widely used estimates of the national Muslim population are those generated by the *Deutsche Islam Konferenz* (German Islam Conference) and the *Bundesamt für Migration und Flüchtlinge* (Federal Office for Migration and Refugees). The methodology is based on the nationalities of foreign citi-

---

3. Hertogen uses data on national origins of migrants, their children and the naturalized, and bases his estimates on the size of the Muslim population in the country of origin. For more detailed information, see Hertogen (2013).

zens and the prior nationalities of naturalized German citizens as well as on a large-scale survey that includes questions about religious identification among a sample of respondents with origins in 49 countries with sizable Muslim population shares. The survey produced estimates of how many migrants coming from majority-Muslim countries actually identified as Muslim, and it used these estimates to determine the overall Muslim population living in Germany. It concluded that between 3.8 and 4.3 million Muslims, or between 4.6 and 5.2 percent of the population (95 percent confidence interval), lived in Germany in 2008 (Bundesamt für Migration und Flüchtlinge 2009). Critics of this method are mostly skeptical of the fact that this approach is based on country of origin, though they agree that there is currently no better method available (e.g., Spielhaus 2013).

Since virtually no statistics exist at the municipal level, I employed two procedures that are based on the above-cited 2009 study. The first procedure makes use of the fact that municipalities collect information on the nationality of foreign citizens, and the second procedure relies on municipal-level estimates of residents with a "migration background;" an official classification that includes (1) all those who immigrated to Germany (in its present borders) after 1949; (2) foreigners (noncitizens) born in Germany; (3) all German citizens born in Germany with at least one parent born abroad; and (4) all German citizens born in Germany with at least one parent who was also born in Germany but without German citizenship.

The first procedure is based on the number of residents with Turkish origins, who constitute the largest Muslim-nationality group. According to the Federal Office for Migration and Refugees (Bundesamt für Migration und Flüchtlinge 2014; see Table 7.2), 2,998,000 residents with Turkish roots lived in Germany in 2012. Among those, slightly over half (52.56 percent) were Turkish citizens with the rest having German citizenship. I collected data on the size of the Turkish-citizen population across municipalities in 2012 (no data are available on naturalized former Turkish citizens), and divided this population by .5256 to obtain an estimate of the Turkish-origin population (i.e., those with and without German citizenship). In the 69 municipalities in my sample, the estimated Turkish-origin population is 1,353,381 or 6.16 percent of the overall population. I next divided this figure by .631555, since the 2009 study estimates that approximately 63.1555 percent of Muslims living in Germany are of Turkish origin. The overall estimate of the Muslim population for my sample is 2,142,935, or 9.75 percent. This procedure likely overestimates the Muslim population share, however, since Turks predominantly settle in large cities and therefore potentially constitute a bigger percentage of Muslims in my sample than they do in the country as a whole.

In the second procedure, I first calculate the percentage of residents with a migration background who are Muslim. I use the mean estimate of the national Muslim population in 2008 (4,055,129; note that this estimate assumes that all Muslims have a migration background), and divide this figure by the size of the entire population with a migration background (15,566,000). According to this calculation, the percentage of residents with a migration background who are Muslim is 26.05. I next collected 2011 municipal-level census figures on residents with a migration background. In my sample of 69 municipalities, 5,807,060 residents have a migration background, representing 26.84 percent of the overall population in these cities. To obtain the share of Muslims among this population, I multiply this figure by .2605, resulting in an estimated Muslim population of 1,512,809, or 6.99 percent of the population. Note that this methodology probably underestimates the Muslim population because among those with a migration background Muslims are more likely to settle in cities.

At the municipal level, the two measures correlate at .71 ($p = .000$). Since the first measure is most likely an overestimate whereas the second measure is most likely an underestimate, I take the average, yielding a Muslim population of 8.31 percent. The parity ratios are calculated using this percentage.

UNITED KINGDOM

The UK is the only country sampled here whose census currently enumerates religion in a reliable manner. The parity ratios I present are based on data from the 2001 and 2011 censuses (with missing years interpolated linearly). The ward-level analyses in Chapter 5 (covering elections between 2002 and 2010) are based on 2001 census data.

TABLE A.1. Austrian Municipalities

Amstetten	Linz	3. Wien, Landstraße
Bad-Ischl	Lustenau	4. Wien, Wieden
Baden	Mödling	5. Wien, Margareten
Bludenz	Perchtoldsdorf	6. Wien, Mariahilf
Braunau	Saalfelden	7. Wien, Neubau
Bregenz	Salzburg	8. Wien, Josefstadt
Bruck an der Mur	Sankt Veit	9. Wien, Alsergrund
Dornbirn	Schwaz	10. Wien, Favoriten
Feldkirch	Schwechat	11. Wien, Simmering
Feldkirchen	Spittal-Drau	12. Wien, Meidling
Gmunden	St. Polten	13. Wien, Hietzing
Graz	Steyr	14. Wien, Penzing
Hallein	Stockerau	15. Wien, Rudolfsheim- Fünfhaus
Hohenems	Telfs	16. Wien, Ottakring
Innsbruck	Ternitz	17. Wien, Hernals
Kapfenberg	Traiskirchen	18. Wien, Währing
Klagenfurt	Traun	19. Wien, Döbling
Klosterneuburg	Tulln	20. Wien, Brigittenau
Knittelfeld	Villach	21. Wien, Floridsdorf
Krems	Voecklabruck	22. Wien, Donaustadt
Kufstein	Waidhofen	23. Wien, Liesing
Leoben	Wels	Wiener Neustadt
Leonding	1. Wien, Innere Stadt	Wolfsberg
Lienz	2. Wien, Leopoldstadt	Zwettl

TABLE A.2. Belgian Municipalities

Brussels	Flanders	Wallonia
Anderlecht	Aalst	Binche
Auderghem	Antwerpen	Braine l'Alleud
Berchem-Sainte-Agathe	Beringen	Charleroi
Bruxelles	Beveren	Chatelet
Etterbeek	Brasschaat	Herstal
Evere	Brugge	La Louviere
Forest	Dendermonde	Liege
Ganshoren	Dilbeek	Mons
Ixelles	Evergem	Mouscron
Jette	Geel	Namur
Koekelberg	Genk	Seraing
Molenbeek	Gent	Tournai
Saint-Gilles	Grimbergen	Verviers
Saint-Josse	Halle	Wavre
Schaerbeek	Hasselt	
Uccle	Heist-op-den-Berg	
Watermael-Boitsfort	Ieper	
Woluwe-Saint-Lambert	Knokke-Heist	
Woluwe-Saint-Pierre	Kortrijk	
	Leuven	
	Lier	
	Lokeren	
	Lommel	
	Maasmechelen	
	Mechelen	
	Mol	
	Ninove	
	Oostende	
	Roeselare	
	Schoten	
	Sint-Niklaas	
	Sint-Truiden	
	Tienen	
	Turnhout	
	Vilvoorde	
	Waregem	

TABLE A.3. German Municipalities

Aachen	Duisburg	Leipzig
Augsburg	Erfurt	Leverkusen
Berlin Charlottenburg	Essen	Ludwigshafen
Berlin Friedrichshain	Frankfurt/Main	Lübeck
Berlin Lichtenberg	Freiburg	Magdeburg
Berlin Marzahn	Gelsenkirchen	Mainz
Berlin Mitte	Hagen	Mannheim
Berlin Neukölln	Halle	Mönchengladbach
Berlin Pankow	Hamburg Altona	Mülheim
Berlin Reinickendorf	Hamburg Bergedorf	München
Berlin Spandau	Hamburg Eimsbüttel	Münster
Berlin Steglitz	Hamburg Harburg	Neuss
Berlin Tempelhof	Hamburg Mitte	Nürnberg
Berlin Treptow	Hamburg Nord	Oberhausen
Bielefeld	Hamburg Wandsbek	Oldenburg
Bochum	Hamm	Osnabrück
Bonn	Hannover	Potsdam
Braunschweig	Herne	Rostock
Bremen	Karlsruhe	Saarbrücken
Chemnitz	Kassel	Solingen
Dortmund	Kiel	Stuttgart
Dresden	Köln	Wiesbaden
Düsseldorf	Krefeld	Wuppertal

TABLE A.4. English Municipalities

London	Outside London
Barking and Dagenham	Barnsley
Barnet	Birmingham
Bexley	Bolton
Brent	Bradford
Bromley	Bury
Camden	Calderdale
Croydon	Coventry
Ealing	Doncaster
Enfield	Dudley
Greenwich	Gateshead
Hackney	Kirklees
Hammersmith and Fulham	Knowsley
Haringey	Leeds
Harrow	Liverpool
Havering	Manchester
Hillingdon	Newcastle-upon-Tyne
Hounslow	North Tyneside
Islington	Oldham
Kensington and Chelsea	Rochdale
Kingston-upon-Thames	Rotherham
Lambeth	Salford
Lewisham	Sandwell
Merton	Sefton
Newham	Sheffield
Redbridge	Solihull
Richmond-upon-Thames	South Tyneside
Southwark	St Helens
Sutton	Stockport
Tower Hamlets	Sunderland
Waltham Forest	Tameside
Wandsworth	Trafford
Westminster, City of	Wakefield
	Walsall
	Wigan
	Wirral
	Wolverhampton

Statistical Analyses and Descriptive Statistics

Chapter 3 Analyses

TABLE B.1. Religiosity and Views on Social Issues and Redistribution, by Religion and Place of Residence (EU-15, Norway, and Switzerland)

			Not supportive of:					
	Religiosity		Gender Equality		Gay Rights		Redistribution	
	All	Citizens	All	Citizens	All	Citizens	All	Citizens
Muslim	2.332***	2.591***	.431***	.348***	.837***	.794***	−.183*	−0.148
	(0.329)	(0.319)	(0.0674)	(0.0560)	(0.0853)	(0.110)	(0.0780)	(0.0781)
Living in City	−.420***	−.426***	−.164***	−.164***	−.166***	−.175***	.0339	.0374
	(0.0555)	(0.0567)	(0.0169)	(0.0170)	(0.0338)	(0.0349)	(0.0362)	(0.0372)
Muslim X Living in City	.674**	.656**	.463***	.617***	.204**	.275*	−.0324	.00876
	(0.189)	(0.218)	(0.0688)	(0.0837)	(0.0685)	(0.111)	(0.0654)	(0.0704)
Constant	5.185***	5.180***	−.054***	−.054***	−1.09***	−1.09***	−1.07***	−1.07***
	(0.0122)	(0.0108)	(0.00365)	(0.00322)	(0.00680)	(0.00588)	(0.00703)	(0.00698)
N	134,372	132,375	78,087	76,909	131,951	130,048	132,522	130,616
R^2	0.121	0.120						
Pseudo-R^2			0.073	0.072	0.055	0.053	0.067	0.067

Note: Parenthesized standard errors are clustered on country. All models include country fixed effects and are probit models, except for the two models with "Religiosity" as the dependent variable, which use OLS.
$*p < .05, **p < .01, ***p < .001$
Source: European Social Survey, waves 1–5. (The Gender Equality item was only asked in waves 2, 4, and 5.)

Dependent Variables

Religiosity: How religious are you?
0: not at all religious; 10: very religious
Gender Equality: A woman should be prepared to cut down on her paid work for the sake of her family.
0: Neither agree nor disagree, disagree or disagree strongly; 1: Agree or agree strongly
Gay rights: Gay men and lesbians should be free to live their own life as they wish.
0: Neither agree nor disagree, agree, or agree strongly; 1: Disagree or disagree strongly
Redistribution: The government should take measures to reduce differences in income levels.
0: Neither agree nor disagree, agree, or agree strongly; 1: Disagree or disagree strongly

Independent Variables

Muslim: Religion or denomination belonging to at present.
1: Muslim, 0: non-Muslim native
Living in City: Which phrase on this card best describes where you live in?
1: A big city; 0: the suburbs or outskirts of a big city; a town or a small village; a farm or home in the countryside.
Note that results are similar when including "suburbs or outskirts of a big city" in the measure of urban residence.

TABLE B.2. Support for Gender Equality among Non-Muslims (England and Wales, 1991–2008)

	1	2
% Muslim (Municipality)	.00802*	.00915*
	(.00367)	(.00370)
Tertiary Education	.148*	.145*
	(.0692)	(.0694)
Secondary Education	.192**	.190**
	(.0699)	(.0701)
Age	−.0109***	−.0149***
	(.000955)	(.00260)
Employed	.0566**	.0562**
	(.0178)	(.0178)
Income (Log)	.00554	.00556
	(.00498)	(.00498)
Married	−.0452**	−.0446**
	(.0169)	(.0169)
Number of Children in Household	−.0171*	−.0169*
	(.00851)	(.00853)
% Females Economically Inactive (Municipality)		−.00521
		(.00311)
% Population Density (Municipality)		.000592
		(.000672)
Individual Fixed Effects	Yes	Yes
Constant	3.809***	4.214***
	(.0731)	(.258)
N	55,862	55,862
Number of Municipalities	346	346
R^2	.722	.722

The dependent variable is agreement with the statement "A husband's job is to earn money; a wife's job is to look after the home and family." Answers include: (1) Strongly agree; (2) agree; (3) neither agree nor disagree; (4) disagree; (5) strongly disagree. The sample is restricted to native Britons who are not Muslim. OLS coefficients with standard errors, in parentheses, clustered on the local authority. * $p < 0.05$, ** $p < 0.01$, *** $p < 0.001$
Source: University of Essex (2010) (weighted data).

Chapter 5 Analyses

TABLE B.3. Summary Statistics for Analyses with Dependent Variable Muslim or Hindu Candidate Selected (Ward-level, England)

Variable	Obs.	Mean	Stnd. Dev.	Minimum	Maximum
Muslim Candidate Selected	19,110	0.10	0.30	0	1
Hindu Candidate Selected	19,110	0.03	0.16	0	1
Muslim Population (%)	19,110	5.32	9.20	0	66.94
Hindu Population (%)	19,110	1.64	3.57	0	42.64
Economic Deprivation	19,110	28.95	14.16	3.67	79.65
Muslim Population (%) × Economic of Deprivation	19,110	200.21	460.69	0	4274.86
Hindu Population (%) × Economic of Deprivation	19,110	42.77	90.35	0	1202.60
Number of Seats	19,110	1.81	0.97	1	3
Non-Muslim Incumbent in Previous Election	12,767	0.31	0.46	0	1
Non-Hindu Incumbent in Previous Election	12,767	0.33	0.47	0	1
Labour Party	19,110	0.35	0.48	0	1
Liberal Democrats	19,110	0.31	0.46	0	1
Conservatives	19,110	0.34	0.47	0	1
London	19,110	0.28	0.45	0	1
North West	19,110	0.28	0.45	0	1
North East	19,110	0.10	0.29	0	1
West Midlands	19,110	0.15	0.35	0	1
Yorkshire and the Humber	19,110	0.19	0.39	0	1
Year	19,110	2005.29	2.57	2002	2010

TABLE B.4. Summary Statistics for Analyses with Dependent Variable Proportion Labour Winners (Ward-level, England; Years Aggregated)

Variable	Obs.	Mean	Stnd. Dev.	Minimum	Maximum
Labour Party Volatility	2,265	0.06	0.05	0	0.46
Proportion Labour Winner	2,265	0.50	0.45	0	1
Muslim Population<5%	2,265	0.72	0.45	0	1
Muslim Population between 5–20%	2,265	0.22	0.42	0	1
Muslim Population between 20–35%	2,265	0.03	0.18	0	1
Muslim Population > 35%	2,265	0.02	0.16	0	1
Economic Deprivation	2,265	30.02	15.94	1.59	83.08
Maximum BNP Vote	2,265	0.05	0.09	0	0.52
Respect Party Runs	2,265	0.04	0.19	0	1
Proportion Liberal Democrat Winner	2,265	0.20	0.37	0	1
London	2,265	0.28	0.45	0	1
North West	2,265	0.10	0.30	0	1
North East	2,265	0.29	0.45	0	1
West Midlands	2,265	0.14	0.35	0	1
Yorkshire and the Humber	2,265	0.19	0.39	0	1

TABLE B.5. Variables used in Ward-Level Analyses in Chapter 5

Election Variables	Rallings et al. (2006)
	Local Government Chronicles Elections Centre (personal communication) Local Elections Archives Project, available at http://www.andrewteale.me.uk/leap/
	London DataStore, available at http://data.london.gov.uk/datastore/package/borough-council-election-results-2010
Economic Deprivation	English Indices of Deprivation, available at: http://webarchive.nationalarchives.gov.uk/20100410180038/; http://communities.gov.uk/ communities/neighbourhoodrenewal /deprivation/deprivation07/ (accessed February 28, 2011)
	and at: http://webarchive.nationalarchives.gov.uk/; http://www.communities.gov.uk/archived/general-content/communities/indicesofdeprivation/216309/ (accessed April 19, 2011)
	and at: http://www.communities.gov.uk/publications/corporate/statistics/indices2010 (accessed November 11, 2011)
	The index is composed of the following domains (with weights given in parentheses): Income (22.5%), Employment (22.5%), Health Deprivation and Disability (13.5%), Education, Skills and Training (13.5%), Barriers to Housing and Services (9.3%), Crime (9.3%), and Living Environment (9.3%).
	Indices are published at the Super Output Area (SOA) level, an area smaller than the ward. The statistical analyses aggregate SOA level scores up to the ward level.
All other variables	UK Office of National Statistics, 2001 census (available at www.nomisweb.co.uk)

TABLE B.6. Selection of Hindu Candidates across Wards in English Municipalities

Hindu Population (%)	.0887***	.0826***
	(.0152)	(.0175)
Economic Deprivation	.00479	.00549
	(.00259)	(.00319)
Hindu Population (%) × Economic Deprivation	−.000315	−.000172
	(.000577)	(.000676)
Number of Seats		.801***
		(0.209)
Non-Hindu Incumbent in Previous Election		−.281***
		(.0714)
Conservatives	−.118	−.150*
	(.0647)	(.0729)
Liberal Democrats	−.304***	−.413***
	(.0744)	(.0944)
Constant	−3.221***	−3.874***
	(.234)	(.372)
Region Fixed Effects	Yes	Yes
Year Fixed Effects	Yes	Yes
Pseudo-R^2	.323	.346
N	19,110	12,767

Note: The dependent variable is whether a party selects (1) or does not select (0) a Hindu candidate. The unit of analysis is the ward party during a given election.

Coefficients are from a probit model. Robust standard errors (clustered on the ward) are in parentheses.

$*p < 0.05; **p < 0.01; ***p < .001$

TABLE B.7. Proportion Labour Winners across Elections within Wards (English Municipalities)

Muslim Population between 5–20%	.0191	.0266	.0248	.0409	.00568
	(.0444)	(.0454)	(.0458)	(.0344)	(.0146)
Muslim Population between 20–35%	−.00884	−.00102	−.0137	.00499	.0338**
	(.0700)	(.0729)	(.0701)	(.0537)	(.0121)
Muslim Population > 35%	−.264**	−.250**	−.270**	−.171**	−.0333
	(.0880)	(0.0908)	(.0867)	(.0625)	(.0233)
Index of Deprivation	.0189***	.0188***	.0187***	.0163***	.00204**
	(.00178)	(.00181)	(.00182)	(.00174)	(.000765)
Maximum BNP Vote		.205	.206	.0510	−.103*
		(.147)	(.147)	(.120)	(.0495)
Respect Party Runs			.0512	.0355	−.0173
			(.0687)	(.0532)	(.0134)
Proportion Liberal Democrat Winners				−.554***	−.908***
				(.0380)	(.0215)
Proportion Conservative Winners					−.894***
					(.0267)
Constant	−.0440	−.0496	−.0500	.0907	.870***
	(.0463)	(.0446)	(.0444)	(.0503)	(.0407)
Region Fixed Effects	Yes	Yes	Yes	Yes	Yes
R^2	.352	.354	.354	.547	.894
N	2,265	2,265	2,265	2,265	2,265

Note: The dependent variable is the proportion of Labour winners across elections (2002–2010) in a given ward. The unit of analysis is the ward. The variables capturing Muslim population sizes are dummies. The *Maximum BNP Vote* is the highest vote attained by the BNP across elections (similar results obtain when using the average BNP vote). *Respect Party Runs* is a dummy variable indicating whether the Respect Party competed in the ward. *Proportion Liberal Democrat/Conservative Winners* measures the proportion of Liberal Democrat/Conservative winners across elections.

Coefficients are from OLS models. Robust standard errors, clustered on the ward, are in parentheses.

$*p < 0.05$; $**p < 0.01$; $***p < .001$

Note that in the last model (column 5), *Muslim Population > 35%* is significantly different from *Muslim Population between 5–20%* / *Muslim Population between 20–35%* at $p = .141$ / $.003$.

Chapter 6 Analyses

TABLE B.8. Variables Used in Municipality-Level Analyses in Chapter 6

Election Variables:

Brussels 2012	http://bruxelleselections2012.irisnet.be/
Flanders 2012	http://www.vlaanderenkiest.be/verkiezingen2012/index.html
Wallonia 2012	http://elections2012.wallonie.be/results/fr/com/preferred /preferred_CGM52011_43.html
Brussels 2006	http://www.bruxelleselections2006.irisnet.be/results/fr/local _brussels/home.html
Flanders 2006	http://www.vlaanderenkiest.be/verkiezingen2006/index.html
Wallonia 2006	http://elections2006.wallonie.be/Site_Internet_RW/fr/local _wallonia/home.html
	Additional election data were provided by Tom Doesselaere (manager of elections, Flemish government).

Population Variables:

Population	http://statbel.fgov.be/
Population Density	http://statbel.fgov.be/
Muslim Population	http://www.npdata.be/

Party Manifesto
Coding Methodology

This project was carried out with Yotam Margalit. For each major center-right and center-left party general election manifesto across 12 Western European countries (as well as for a selection of far-right parties), coders were instructed to identify statements dedicated to the issue of immigration and of ethnic diversity that has resulted from immigration. The sentences touching on these issues were further coded as falling into the issue categories listed below. A statement can pertain to more than one category. Moreover, coders were instructed to indicate the tone of the statement (positive, neutral, or negative). Positive statements refer to 1) increasing immigration; 2) immigrants' having a positive impact on a given issue/area; or 3) enacting policies that favor immigrants. Negative statements refer to the opposite. Neutral statements either include no indication of a policy preference or evaluation, or they balance negative with positive assessments. Coders were also asked to evaluate a given statement in context, examining the preceding or following sentence to gauge the tone and intent.

The manifesto texts are taken from the Comparative Manifesto Project, the Political Documents Archive, or downloaded directly from party websites.[1]

The categories are listed below along with examples (the examples are not exhaustive). The instructions to the coders were mode detailed and are available from the author upon request.

List of categories:

ECONOMIC ISSUES: LABOR MARKET

1. Labor market: Impact on job availability of natives; facilitating the recruitment of high-skill or low-skill labor; this includes references to labor shortages in certain sectors (e.g., statements referring to immigration filling labor shortages).
2. Labor market: Impact on wages of natives.

---

1. See Volkens et al. (2014) and Benoit et al. (2009).

ECONOMIC ISSUES: IMPACT ON
PUBLIC RESOURCES

3. Welfare system: Abuse of public services; service/welfare provision for immigrants (for example, in health, income support, etc.).
4. Education system: Migrants being a burden on education resources/schools; larger class sizes due to immigration; challenge of educating immigrant school children.
5. Housing: Competition over public housing; finding accommodation for refugees; housing conditions for immigrants.

OTHER ECONOMIC ISSUES

6. Immigrants' economic integration: Immigrants being unemployed; immigrants receiving labor market training; immigrants receiving special consideration for job placements.
7. Other economic issues not classified.

INTEGRATION-RELATED ISSUES

8. Integration: This is a broad category, and sentences may fall into several categories, e.g., integration and language; peaceful co-existence; participation in civil society.
9. Language: Lacking language acquisition of immigrants, providing language courses; reducing language barriers; imposing language requirements.

IMPACT ON RIGHTS OF VULNERABLE
OR MINORITY GROUPS

10. Women's issues: Women's rights; concerns related to women; for example, making it easier for women to enter the labor market/learn the language; forced marriage; honor killings, etc.
11. Gay rights

ADDITIONAL ISSUES

12. Tolerance and racism: Statements condemning racism/racist acts; establishment of hate crime laws; Islamophobia; statements challenging the seriousness of racism/racist acts.
13. Law and order/public safety: Immigrant-on-native crime, crime rates, incarceration rates; immigrants disregarding domestic laws;

immigrants being law-abiding; establishing hate crime laws; immigrants joining the local police force. Note: references to illegal immigration do not fall under this category.

14. National culture/national identity/national values: References to the impact of immigration on national culture, identity, values; immigrants following national code of conduct/basic values/rule of law; references to multiculturalism; references to shared values/ assimilation.

15. Citizenship: Requirements for citizenship; value of citizenship.

16. Religion: Accommodating the religious needs of immigrant groups; need to protect religious freedom; references to Christian/Judeo-Christian values.

17. Islam/Muslims: Wearing of religious symbols (even if the headscarf/ burka is not explicitly stated); Islamic education; girls participating in physical education at school; Islamophobia; issues related to the integration of Muslims/Islam; "Islamization."

18. Deportation: Conditions for deportation; this category also includes repatriation.

19. Immigration policy: References to restrictions on immigration; quotas/point systems; relaxation of restrictions; residence status of immigrants; rules for letting in certain types of immigrants (e.g., by skill level, sector, family status/spouses).

20. Spatial clustering of immigrants/spatial segregation: References to residential clustering, physical segregation.

21. Slaughtering of animals: References to ritual slaughtering performed by immigrant-origin Muslim populations.

22. Equal Treatment and nondiscrimination: Statements referring to the treatment of immigrants as equals or not (whether in support or in opposition). These can be general statements (e.g., "everyone is equal regardless of gender, heritage, or skin color"), as well as specific statements. For example, the sentence "Full social benefits for citizens only" should be coded under this category, "negative" (as well as under the "welfare system" category). References to the issue of immigrant discrimination and "affirmative action" should also be coded under this category.

23. Border protection: Providing resources to protect the border; status of border security. Note: broad statements about opening/not opening borders to immigrants should fall under "immigration policy", unless they clearly reference border security.

24. National Security (incl. terrorism): Risk of terrorism due to immigration; immigration undermining national security.

25. Overpopulation/overcrowding: References to congestion due to immigration; overcrowded housing conditions.
26. Civil liberties/freedom of expression: This category refers to the *impact* of immigrants on civil liberties or the freedom of expression in the country. This category is not about the freedom and liberty or equal treatment of immigrants themselves.
27. Asylum/refugees: Inflow of refugees; asylum system.
28. Illegal immigration: Inflow of/combating illegal immigrants.
29. Voting rights of immigrants: References relating to immigrants having the right to vote (generally in local elections) should be coded under this category, not under the "equal treatment" category.
30. Other (if a sentence cannot be classified in any of the above categories)

BIBLIOGRAPHY

Abrajano, Marisa, and Zoltan Hajnal. 2015. *White Backlash: Immigration, Race, and American Politics*. Princeton: Princeton University Press.

Adida, Claire. 2014. *Immigrant Exclusion and Insecurity in Africa*. New York: Cambridge University Press.

Adida, Claire, David Laitin, and Marie-Anne Valfort. 2010. "Identifying Barriers to Muslim Integration in France." *Proceedings of the National Academy of Sciences* 107 (52): 22384–90.

Adida, Claire, David Laitin, and Marie-Anne Valfort. 2014. "Muslims in France: Identifying a Discriminatory Equilibrium." *Journal of Population Economics* 27 (4): 1039–86.

Adida, Claire L., David D. Laitin, and Marie-Anne Valfort. 2015. *Why Muslim Integration Fails in Christian-Heritage Societies*. Cambridge: Harvard University Press.

Afshar, Haleh. 1989. "Gender Roles and the 'Moral Economy of Kin' among Pakistani Women in West Yorkshire." *New Community* 15 (2): 211–25.

Ahmed, Ali M., Lina Andersson, and Mats Hammarstedt. 2010. "Can Discrimination in the Housing Market Be Reduced by Increasing the Information about Applicants?" *Land Economics* 86 (1): 79–90.

Ajala, Imène. 2010. "The Muslim Vote and Muslim Lobby in France: Myths and Realities."

Ahmed, Ali M., and Mats Hammarstedt. 2008. "Discrimination in the Rental Housing Market: A Field Experiment on the Internet." *Journal of Urban Economics* 64 (2): 362–72.

Akgündüz, Ahmet. 2008. *Labour Migration from Turkey to Western Europe, 1960–1974: A Multidisciplinary Analysis*. Aldershot: Ashgate.

Akhtar, Navid. 2003. *Pakistan Clans 'Abusing' British Politics* Available from http: //news.bbc .co.uk/2/hi/uk_news/magazine/3181851.stm. Accessed June 4, 2015.

Akhtar, Parveen. 2013. *British Muslim Politics: Examining Pakistani Biraderi Networks*. New York: Palgrave Macmillan.

Akkerman, Tjitske. 2015. "Immigration Policy and Electoral Competition in Western Europe: A Fine-Grained Analysis of Party Positions over the Past Two Decades." *Party Politics* 21 (1): 54–67.

Aktürk, Şener. 2010. "The Turkish Minority in German Politics: Trends, Diversification of Representation, and Policy Implications." *Insight Turkey* 12 (1): 65–80.

Alesina, Alberto, and Edward L. Glaeser. 2004. *Fighting Poverty in the US and Europe: A World of Difference*. Oxford: Oxford University Press.

Algan, Yann, Camille Hémet, and David Laitin. 2016. "The Social Effects of Ethnic Diversity at the Local Level: A Natural Experiment with Exogenous Residential Allocation." *Journal of Political Economy* 124 (3): 696–733.

Ali, Rushanara, and Colm O'Cinneide. 2002. *Our House? Race and Representation in British Politics*. London: Institute for Public Policy Research.

Allen, Chris. 2005. "From Race to Religion: The New Face of Discrimination." In *Muslim Britain: Communities Under Pressure*, ed. T. Abbas, 49–65. New York: Palgrave Macmillan.

Amjahad, Anissa, and Giulia Sandri. 2012. "The Voting Behaviour of Muslim Citizens in Belgium." Presented at the 22nd World Congress of Political Science, Madrid, Spain, July 8–12.

André, Audrey, Bram Wauters, and Jean-Benoit Pilet. 2012. "It's Not Only About Lists: Explaining Preference Voting in Belgium." *Journal of Elections, Public Opinion, and Parties* 22 (3): 293–313.

Anwar, Muhammad. 1998. *Between Cultures: Community and Change in the Lives of Young Asians.* London: Routledge.

Aslan, Ednan, Erol Yildiz, Jonas Kolb, and Birgit Mattausch-Yildiz. 2014. "Muslimische Alltagspraxis in Österreich: Ein Kompass zur religiösen Diversität—Zwischenbericht für das Projektjahr 2013." Vienna: Universität Wien Institut für Islamische Studien.

Balakan, David. 1905. *Die Sozialdemokratie und das jüdische Proletariat.* Czernowitz: Engel & Suchanka.

Bale, Tim. 2008. "Turning Round the Telescope: Centre-Right Parties and Immigration and Integration Policy in Europe." *European Journal of Public Policy* 15 (3): 315–30.

Ballard, Roger. 1994. "Introduction: The Emergence of Desh Pardesh." In *Desh Pardesh: The South Asian Presence in Britain*, ed. R. Ballard, 1–34. London: Hurst & Company.

Banducci, Susan A., Todd Donovan, and Jeffrey A. Karp. 2004. "Minority Representation, Empowerment, and Participation." *Journal of Politics* 66 (2): 534–56.

Barnett, Adam. 2014. "Mayor Accused at High Court of Using 'Spiritual Influence' for Re-Election." *East London Advertiser*, August 21, 2014.

Barreto, Matt A. 2007. "*Sí Se Puede!* Latino Candidates and the Mobilization of Latino Voters." *American Political Science Review* 101 (3): 425–41.

Barreto, Matt A., Gary M. Segura, and Nathan D. Woods. 2004. "The Mobilizing Effect of Majority-Minority Districts on Latino Turnout." *American Political Science Review* 98 (1): 65–75.

Barry, Brian. 2001. *Culture and Equality: An Egalitarian Critique of Multiculturalism.* Cambridge: Harvard University Press.

Baston, Lewis. 2013. "The Bradford Earthquake." Liverpool: Democratic Audit.

Bebel, August. 1910. *Woman and Socialism.* New York: Socialist Literature Co.

Bechtel, Michael M., Jens Hainmueller, and Yotam Margalit. 2014. "Preferences for International Redistribution: The Divide over the Eurozone Bailouts." *American Journal of Political Science* 58 (4): 835–56.

Beer, Max. 1893–94. "Die russischen und polnischen Juden in London." *Die Neue Zeit* 12 (49): 730–34.

Beig, Stefan. 2010. "Der Islam—Spielball der Parteien." *Wiener Zeitung*, October 4.

Bengtsson, Ragnar, Ellis Iverman, and Björn Tyrefors Hinnerich. 2012. "Gender and Ethnic Discrimination in the Rental Housing Market." *Applied Economic Letters* 10 (1): 1–5.

Benhabib, Seyla. 2002. *The Claims of Culture: Equality and Diversity in the Global Era.* Princeton: Princeton University Press.

Benoit, Kenneth, Thomas Bräuninger, and Marc Debus. 2009. "Challenges for Estimating Policy Preferences: Announcing an Open Access Archive of Political Documents." *German Politics* 18 (3): 440–53.

Benoit, Kenneth, and Michael Laver. 2006. *Party Policy in Modern Democracies.* New York: Routledge.

Beramendi, Pablo, Silja Häusermann, Herbert Kitschelt, and Hanspeter Kriesi, eds. 2015. *The Politics of Advanced Capitalism*: New York: Cambridge University Press.

Berger, Peter. 2009. "Interview mit Peter Kurth: 'Die CDU hat ein Akzeptanzproblem.'" *Kölner Stadtanzeiger*, August 31.

Berger, Joseph. 2013. "Out of Enclaves, a Pressure to Accommodate Traditions." *New York Times*, August 21.

Berger, Joseph. 2014. "Are Liberal Jewish Voters a Thing of the Past?" *New York Times*, September 13.

Bhavnani, Rikhil. 2013. "A Primer on Discrimination Against India's Lower Caste Politicians: Evidence from Natural and Survey Experiments." Working Paper.

Bird, Karen. 2005. "The Political Representation of Visible Minorities in Electoral Democracies: A Comparison of France, Denmark, and Canada." *Nationalism and Ethnic Politics* 11 (4): 425–65.

Bird, Karen, Thomas Saalfeld, and Andreas Wüst. 2011a. "Ethnic Diversity, Political Participation and Representation: A Theoretical Framework." In *The Political Representation of Immigrants and Minorities: Voters, Parties, and Parliaments in Liberal Democracies*, ed. K. Bird, T. Saalfeld and A. Wüst, 1–21. New York: Routledge.

Bird, Karen, Thomas Saalfeld, and Andreas Wüst, eds. 2011b. *The Political Representation of Immigrants and Minorities: Voters, Parties and Parliaments in Liberal Democracies*. New York: Routledge.

Blalock, Hubert. 1967. *Toward a Theory of Minority-Group Relations*. New York: John Wiley and Sons.

Blaydes, Lisa, and Drew A. Linzer. 2008. "The Political Economy of Women's Support for Fundamentalist Islam." *World Politics* 60 (4): 576–609.

Bleich, Erik. 2009. "Where Do Muslims Stand on Ethno-racial Hierarchies in Britain and France? Evidence from Public Opinion Surveys, 1988–2008." *Patterns of Prejudice* 43 (3–4): 379–400.

Bloemraad, Irene. 2006. *Becoming a Citizen: Incorporating Immigrants and Refugees in the United States and Canada*. Berkeley: University of California Press.

Bloemraad, Irene. 2013. "Accessing the Corridors of Power: Puzzles and Pathways to Understanding Minority Representation." *West European Politics* 36 (3): 652–70.

Bloemraad, Irene, and Karen Schönwälder. 2013. "Immigrant and Ethnic Minority Representation in Europe: Conceptual Challenges and Theoretical Approaches." *West European Politics* 36 (3): 564–79.

Blomqvist, Paula. 2005. Närvarons politik och det mångetniska Sverige. Om att ta plats i demokratin. Ph.D. Dissertation, University of Gothenburg.

Bloodworth, James. 2015. "Lutfur Rahman turned East London into a Banana Republic." *The Daily Beast*. Available from http: //www.thedailybeast.com/articles/2015/05/01/lutfur-rahman-turned-east-london-into-a-banana-republic.html. Accessed June 3, 2015.

Böcker, Anita. 1994. "Chain Migration over Legally Closed Borders: Settled Immigrants as Bridgeheads and Gatekeepers." *Netherlands' Journal of Social Sciences* 30 (2): 87–106.

Bostanci, Safa A. 1982. *Zum Leben und zu den Rückkehr- bzw. Verbleibeabsichten der türkischen Gastarbeiter in Nürnberg: Eine empirische Regionaluntersuchung*. Berlin: Express Edition.

Bousetta, Hassan, Sonia Gsir, and Dirk Jacobs. 2005. "Active Civic Participation of Immigrants in Belgium: Country Report prepared for the European research project POLITIS." Oldenburg: POLITIS.

Bowen, John. 2007. *Why the French Don't Like Headscarves*. Princeton: Princeton University Press.

Boyd, Monica. 1989. "Family and Personal Networks in International Migration: Recent Developments and New Agendas." *International Migration Review* 23 (3): 638–70.

Bradford Congress. 1996. *The Bradford Commission Report*. London: The Stationary Office.

Bramadat, Paul. 2009. "Religious Diversity and International Migration: National and Global

Dimensions." In *International Migration and the Governance of Religious Diversity*, ed. P. Bramadat and M. Koenig, 1–26. Kingston, ON: School of Policy Studies, Queen's University.

Brandon, James, and Salam Hafez. 2008. "Crimes of the Community: Honour-Based Violence in the UK." London: Centre for Social Cohesion.

Bratton, Kathleen A., and Leonard P. Ray. 2002. "Descriptive Representation, Policy Outcomes, and Municipal Day-Care Coverage in Norway." *American Journal of Political Science* 46 (2): 428–37.

Broockman, David E. 2013. "Black Politicians Are More Intrinsically Motivated to Advance Blacks' Interests: A Field Experiment Manipulating Political Incentives." *American Journal of Political Science* 57 (3): 521–36.

Brouard, Sylvain, and Vincent Tiberj. 2005. *Français comme les autres? Enquête sur les citoyens d'origine maghrébine, africaine et turque*. Paris: Presses de la fondation nationale des sciences politiques.

Brouard, Sylvain, and Vincent Tiberj. 2011. "Yes They Can: An Experimental Approach to the Eligibility of Ethnic Minority Candidates in France." In *The Political Representation of Immigrants and Minorities: Voters, Parties, and Parliaments in Liberal Democracies*, ed. K. Bird, T. Saalfeld and A. Wüst, 164–180. New York: Routledge.

Browning, Rufus P., Dale R. Marshall, and David H. Tabb. 1984. *Protest Is Not Enough: The Struggle of Blacks and Hispanics for Equality in Urban Politics*. Berkeley: University of California Press.

Brubaker, Rogers. 1992. *Citizenship and Nationhood in France and Germany*. Cambridge: Harvard University Press.

Brubaker, Rogers. 2013. "Categories of Analysis and Categories of Practice: A Note on the Study of Muslims in European Countries of Immigration." *Ethnic and Racial Studies* 36 (1): 1–8.

Budge, Ian, David Robertson, and Derek Hearl, eds. 1987. *Ideology, Strategy, and Party Change: Spatial Analyses of Post-War Election Programmes in 19 Democracies*. Cambridge: Cambridge University Press.

Bundesamt für Migration und Flüchtlinge. 2009. "Muslimisches Leben in Deutschland." Nuremberg: Bundesamt für Migration und Flüchtlinge.

Bundesamt für Migration und Flüchtlinge. 2014. "Migrationsbericht." Berlin: Bundesministerium des Innern.

Butler, Daniel M., and David E. Broockman. 2011. "Do Politicians Racially Discriminate Against Constituents? A Field Experiment on State Legislators." *American Journal of Political Science* 55 (3): 463–77.

Cağlar, Ayse S. 1995. "German Turks in Berlin: Social Exclusion and Strategies for Social Mobility." *New Community* 21 (3): 309–23.

Canon, David T. 1999. *Race, Redistricting, and Representation: The Unintended Consequences of Black Majority Districts*. Chicago: University of Chicago Press.

Carmines, Edward G., and James A. Stimson. 1989. *Issue Evolution: Race and the Transformation of American Politics*. Princeton: Princeton University Press.

Casanova, José. 2007. "Immigration and the New Religious Pluralism." In *Democracy and the New Religious Pluralism*, ed. T. Banchoff, 59–84. Oxford: Oxford University Press.

Celis, Karen, Sarah Childs, Johanna Kantola, and Mona Lena Krook. 2008. "Rethinking Women's Substantive Representation." *Representation* 44 (2): 99–110.

Celis, Karen, Silvia Erzeel, Liza Mügge, and Alyt Damstra. 2014. "Quotas and Intersectionality: Ethnicity and Gender in Candidate Selection." *International Political Science Review* 35 (1): 41–54.

Centraal Bureau voor de Statistiek (CBS). 2009. "Religie aan het begin van de 21ste eeuw." The Hague: Centraal Bureau voor de Statistiek.

Cesari, Jocelyne. 2013. *Why the West Fears Islam: An Exploration of Muslims in Liberal Democracies*. New York: Palgrave Macmillan.

Chandra, Kanchan. 2004. *Why Ethnic Parties Succeed: Patronage and Ethnic Headcounts in India*. Cambridge: Cambridge University Press.

Chandra, Kanchan, ed. 2012. *Constructivist Theories of Ethnic Politics*. Oxford: Oxford University Press.

Chattopadhyay, Raghabendra, and Esther Duflo. 2004. "Women as Policy Makers: Evidence from a Randomized Policy Experiment in India." *Econometrica* 72 (5): 1409–43.

Constant, Amelie, and Klaus F. Zimmermann. 2005. "Immigrant Performance and Selective Immigration Policy: A European Perspective." *National Institute Economic Review* 194 (1): 94–105.

Copus, Colin. 2004. *Party Politics and Local Government*. Manchester: Manchester University Press.

Corluy, Vincent, Ive Marx, and Gerlinde Verbist. 2011. "Employment Chances of Immigrants in Belgium: The Impact of Citizenship." *International Journal of Comparative Sociology* 52 (4): 350–68.

Cronin, James E., George W. Ross, and James Shoch, eds. 2011. *What's Left of the Left: Democrats and Social Democrats in Challenging Times*. Durham, NC: Duke University Press.

Curtice, John, Stephen Fisher, and Robert Ford. 2010. "Appendix 2: An Analysis of the Results." In *The British General Election of 2010*, ed. D. Kavanagh and P. Cowley, 385–426. New York: Palgrave Macmillan.

Dahl, Robert. 1964. *Who Governs? Democracy and Power in an American City*. New Haven, CT: Yale University Press.

Dale, Angela. 2002. "Social Exclusion of Pakistani and Bangladeshi Women." *Sociological Research Online* 7 (3).

Dancygier, Rafaela. 2010. *Immigration and Conflict in Europe*. New York: Cambridge University Press.

Dancygier, Rafaela. 2013. "The Left and Minority Representation: The Labour Party, Muslim Candidates, and Inclusion Tradeoffs." *Comparative Politics* 46 (1): 1–21.

Dancygier, Rafaela. 2014. "Electoral Rules or Electoral Leverage? Explaining Muslim Representation in England." *World Politics* 66 (2): 229–63.

Dancygier, Rafaela, and David Laitin. 2014. "Immigration into Europe: Economic Discrimination, Violence and Public Policy." *Annual Review of Political Science* 17: 43–64.

Dancygier, Rafaela, Karl-Oskar Lindgren, Sven Oskarsson, and Kåre Vernby. 2015. "Why Are Immigrants Underrepresented in Politics? Evidence from Sweden." *American Political Science Review* 109 (4): 703–24.

Dancygier, Rafaela, and Yotam Margalit. 2014. "The Changing Politics of the Immigration Debate: New Evidence on an Evolving Divide." Paper presented at the Annual Meeting of the American Political Science Association. Washington, D.C.

Dancygier, Rafaela, and Elizabeth Saunders. 2006. "A New Electorate? Comparing Preferences and Partisanship Between Immigrants and Natives." *American Journal of Political Science* 50 (4): 962–81.

Dasetto, Felice. 1996. *La construction de l'islam européen* Paris: L'Harmattan.

Dasetto, Felice. 2011. *L'Iris et le Croissant: Bruxelles et l'Islam au défi de la co-inclusion*. Louvain: Presses Universitaires de Louvain.

Dawson, Michael. 1994. *Behind the Mule: Race and Class in African-American Politics*. Princeton: Princeton University Press.

De La O, Ana L., and Jonathan A. Rodden. 2008. "Does Religion Distract the Poor?: Income and Issue Voting Around the World." *Comparative Political Studies* 41 (4/5): 437–76.

De Vries, Michiel S. 2000. "Left and Right Among Local Elites: Comparative Figures from Switzerland, Spain, Germany and the Netherlands." *Local Government Studies* 26 (3): 91–118.

De Winter, Lieven, Silvia Erzeel, Sylvia Vandeleene, and Bram Wauters. 2013. "Nationale bemoeienis of lokale autonomie? Het Lijstvormingsproces bij gemeenteraadsverkiezingen." In *Op Zoek Naar De Kiezers*, ed. K. Deschouwer, T. Verthé and B. Rihoux, 93–122. Brussels: Academic & Scientific Publishers.

Dickson, Eric S., and Kenneth Scheve. 2006. "Social Identity, Political Speech, and Electoral Competition." *Journal of Theoretical Politics* 18 (1): 5–39.

Diehl, Claudia, Matthias Koenig, and Kerstin Ruckdeschel. 2009. "Religiosity and Gender Equality: Comparing Natives and Muslim Migrants in Germany." *Ethnic and Racial Studies* 32 (2): 278–301.

Donavan, Barbara. 2012. "Intersectionality and the Substantive Representation of Migrant Interests in Germany." *German Politics and Society* 30 (4): 23–44.

Dovi, Suzanne. 2002. "Preferable Descriptive Representatives: Will Just Any Woman, Black, or Latino Do?" *American Political Science Review* 96 (4): 729–43.

Downs, Anthony. 1957. *An Economic Theory of Democracy*. New York: Harper and Row.

Dunning, Thad, and Janhavi Nilekani. 2013. "Ethnic Quotas and Political Mobilization: Caste, Parties, and Distribution in Indian Village Councils." *American Political Science Review* 107 (1): 35–56.

Eade, John. 1989. *The Politics of Community*. Aldershot: Avebury.

Eaton, George. 2010. "A Bad Night for Labour in Tower Hamlets." New Statesman's Rolling Politics Blog. Available from http://www.newstatesman.com/blogs/the-staggers/2010/10/labour-rahman-respect-beaten. Accessed June 3, 2015.

Edsall, Thomas. 2015. "The Gentrification Effect." *New York Times*, February 25.

Edsall, Thomas, and Mary Edsall. 1992. *Chain Reaction: The Impact of Race, Rights, and Taxes on American Politics*. New York: Norton.

Eelbode, Floor. 2013. Yes We Can? Parties' Impact on the Political Representation of Ethnic Minorities: A Comparative Case Study Research At the Local Level in Belgium and the United Kingdom. Doctoral Dissertation, Political and Social Science, Ghent University, Ghent.

Eelbode, Floor, Bram Wauters, Karen Celis, and Carl Devos. 2013. "Left, Right, Left. The Influence of Party Ideology on the Political Representation of Ethnic Minorities in Belgium." *Politics, Groups, and Identities* 1 (3): 451–67.

The Economist. 2009. "Antwerp's Muslim Headscarf Row, the Story on the Ground." September 17.

The Economist Online. 2010. "Europe's Irreligious." August 9.

EMBES (Ethnic Minority British Election Study). 2010. University of Essex.

Engelbrektsson, Ulla-Brit. 1978. *The Force of Tradition: Turkish Migrants at Home and Abroad*. Göteborg: Acta Universitatis Gothoburgensis.

Erie, Steven P. 1988. *Rainbow's End: Irish-Americans and the Dilemmas of Urban Machine Politics, 1840–1985*. Berkeley: University of California Press.

Ernst, Dagobert. 2009. "Eine Null vor dem Komma und trotzdem im Rat." *Der Westen*, August 30, 2009. Available from http://www.derwesten.de/politik/eine-null-vor-dem-komma-und-trotzdem-im-rat-id153939.html. Accessed June 17, 2015.

Escobar-Lemmon, Maria C., and Michelle M. Taylor-Robinson, eds. 2014. *Representation: The Case of Women*. Oxford: Oxford University Press.

European Monitoring Centre on Racism and Xenophobia (EUMC). 2006. "Muslims in the European Union: Discrimination and Islamophobia." Austria: European Monitoring Centre on Racism and Xenophobia.

European Social Survey (ESS). 2013. Rounds 1–5, Cumulative Data File. Norwegian Social Science Data Services, Norway—Data Archive and distributor of ESS data.

Fadil, Nadia. 2013. "Belgium." In *Yearbook of Muslims in Europe*, ed. J. Nielsen, S. Akgönül, A. Alibašić and E. Racius, 99–122. Leiden: Brill.

Fearon, James D. 1999. "Why Ethnic Politics and 'Pork' Tend to Go Together." Working Paper, Department of Political Science, Stanford University.

Ferree, Karen. 2006. "Explaining South Africa's Racial Census." *Journal of Politics* 68 (4): 803–15.

Fetzer, Joel S., and J. Christopher Soper. 2005. *Muslims and the State in Britain, France, and Germany*. New York: Cambridge University Press.

Field, Clive D. 2012. "Revisiting Islamophobia in Contemporary Britain, 2007–10." In *Islamophobia in the West: Measuring and Explaining Individual Attitudes*, ed. M. Helbling, 147–161. London: Routledge.

Fieldhouse, Edward, and David Cutts. 2008. "Mobilisation or Marginalisation? Neighbourhood Effects on Muslim Electoral Registration in Britain in 2001." *Political Studies* 56 (2): 333–54.

Fielding, Steven. 1993. *Class and Ethnicity: Irish Catholics in England, 1880–1939*. Buckingham: Open University Press.

Fielding, Steven, and Andrew Geddes. 1998. "The British Labour Party and 'Ethnic Entryism': Participation, Integration and the Party Context." *Journal of Ethnic and Migration Studies* 24 (1): 57–72.

Fisher, Stephen, Anthony F. Heath, David Sanders, and Maria Sobolewska. 2015. "Candidate Ethnicity and Vote Choice in Britain." *British Journal of Political Science* 45 (4): 883–905.

Fiske, Susan. 2010. *Social Beings: Core Motives in Social Psychology*. Hoboken, NJ: Wiley.

Fleischmann, Fenella, and Karen Phalet. 2012. "Integration and Religiosity among the Turkish Second Generation in Europe: A Comparative Analysis across Four Capital Cities." *Ethnic and Racial Studies* 35 (2): 320–241.

Flinn, Andrew. 2005. "Labour's Family: Local Labour Parties, Trade Unions and Trades Councils in Cotton Lancashire, 1931–39." In *Labour's Grass Roots: Essays on the Activities of Local Labour Parties and Members, 1918–45*, ed. M. Worley, 102–123. Aldershot: Ashgate.

Foblets, Marie-Claire, and Sander Loones. 2006. "Belgium." In *Acquisition and Loss of Nationality, Volume 2*, ed. R. Bauböck, E. Ersbøll, K. Groenendijk, and H. Waldrauch, 63–104. Amsterdam: Amsterdam University Press.

Ford, Robert. 2011. "Acceptable and Unacceptable Immigrants: How Opposition to Immigration in Britain Is Affected by Migrants' Region of Origin." *Journal of Ethnic and Migration Studies* 37 (7): 1017–37.

Ford, Robert. 2016. "Who Should We Help? An Experimental Test of Discrimination in the British Welfare State." *Political Studies* 64 (3): 630–50.

Franck, Raphaël, and Ilia Rainer. 2012. "Does the Leader's Ethnicity Matter? Ethnic Favoritism, Education, and Health in Sub-Saharan Africa." *American Political Science Review* 106 (2): 294–325.

Fraser, Giles. 2015. "The Lutfur Rahman Verdict and the Spectre of 'Undue Spiritual Influence.'" *The Guardian*, April 29.

Frymer, Paul. 2007. *Black and Blue: African Americans, the Labor Movement, and the Decline of the Democratic Party*. Princeton: Princeton University Press.

Frymer, Paul. 2010. *Uneasy Alliances: Race and Party Competition in America*. Princeton: Princeton University Press.

Frymer, Paul, and John David Skrentny. 1998. "Coalition-Building and the Politics of Electoral

Capture During the Nixon Administration: African Americans, Labor, Latinos." *Studies in American Political Development* 12 (1): 131–61.

Gale, Richard. 2005. "Representing the City: Mosques and the Planning Process in Birmingham." *Journal of Ethnic and Migration Studies* 31 (6): 1161–79.

Gallagher, Michael. 1988. "Introduction." In *Candidate Selection in Comparative Perspective: The Secret Garden of Politics*, ed. M. Gallagher and M. Marsh, 1–19. London: Sage.

Gallagher, Michael, and Michael Marsh, eds. 1988. *Candidate Selection in Comparative Perspective: The Secret Garden of Politics*. London: Sage.

Garbaye, Romain. 2005. *Getting into Local Power: The Politics of Ethnic Minorities in British and French Cities*. Oxford: Blackwell Publishing.

Gay, Claudine. 2001. "The Effect of Black Congressional Representation on Political Participation." *American Political Science Review* 95 (3): 589–602.

Geisser, Vincent. 1997. *Ethnicité Républicaine*. Paris: Presses de Sciences Po.

Geisser, Vincent, and El Yamine Soum. 2012. "The Legacies of Colonialism: Migrant-Origin Minorities in French Politics." In *Immigrant Politics: Race and Representation in Western Europe*, ed. T. Givens and R. Maxwell. Boulder, CO: Lynne Rienner.

German Marshall Fund of the United States (GMF). 2014. "Transatlantic Trends: Mobility, Migration and Integration." German Marshall Fund.

Gest, Justin. 2011. "Alienation in Modernity: The Case of European Muslims " In *Politics of Religion in Western Europe: Modernities in Conflict?*, ed. F. Foret and X. Itçaina, 53–65. Milton Park, Abingdon, Oxon.: Routledge.

Giffinger, Rudolf, and Ursula Reeger. 1997. "Turks in Austria: Background, Geographical Distribution and Housing Conditions." In *Turks in European Cities: Housing and Urban Segregation*, ed. Ş. Özüekren and R. van Kempen, 41–66. Utrecht, Netherlands: ERCOMER.

Gijsberts, Mérove, and Jaco Dagevos. 2010. "At Home in the Netherlands? Trends in Integration of non-Western Migrants." The Hague: The Netherlands Institute for Social Research.

Gilligan, Andrew. 2012. "A Runaway Victory for George Galloway—and All Praise to Allah." *The Telegraph*, March 30.

Gitmez, Ali S. 1991. "Migration Without Development: The Case of Turkey." In *The Unsettled Relationship: Labor Migration and Economic Development*, ed. D. G. Papademetriou and P. L. Martin, 115–134. New York: Greenwood Press.

Gitmez, Ali, and Czarina Wilpert. 1987. "A Micro-Society or an Ethnic Community? Social Organization and Ethnicity amongst Turkish Migrants in Berlin." In *Immigrant Associations in Europe*, ed. J. Rex, D. Joly and C. Wilpert, 86–125. Aldershot: Gower.

Gledhill, Ruth. 2006. "Muslim Veils Suck, Rushdie Says." *Times of London*, October 11.

Glynn, Sarah. 2008. "East End Bengalis and the Labour Party—the End of a Long Relationship?" In *New Geographies of Race and Racism*, ed. C. Dwyer and C. Bressey, 67–82. Aldershot: Ashgate.

Golder, Matt. 2016. "Far Right Parties in Europe." *Annual Review of Political Science* 19: 477–97.

Goodhart, David. 2012. "Making Sense of Bradford West." *Prospect Magazine*, April 12.

Goodman, Sara Wallace. 2014. *Immigration and Membership Politics in Western Europe*. Cambridge: Cambridge University Press.

Gray, Mark, and Miki Caul. 2000. "Declining Voter Turnout in Advanced Industrial Democracies, 1950 to 1997: The Effects of Declining Group Mobilization." *Comparative Political Studies* 33 (9): 1091–122.

Gressgård, Randi, and Christine M. Jacobsen. 2003. "Questions of Gender in a Multicultural Society." *Nordic Journal of Feminist and Gender Research* 11 (2): 69–77.

Grose, Christian R. 2011. *Congress in Black and White: Race and Representation in Washington and at Home*. Cambridge: Cambridge University Press.

Grzymala-Busse, Anna. 2013. "Good Clubs and Community Support: Explaining the Growth of Strict Religions." *Journal of Church and State* 56 (2): 269–99.

Guinier, Lani. 1991. "The Triumph of Tokenism: The Voting Rights Act and the Theory of Black Electoral Success." *Michigan Law Review* 89 (5): 1077–154.

Hagan, Jacqueline M. 1998. "Social Networks, Gender, and Immigrant Incorporation: Resources and Constraints." *American Sociological Review* 63 (1): 55–67.

Hainmueller, Jens, and Dominik Hangartner. 2013. "Who Gets a Swiss Passport? A Natural Experiment in Immigrant Discrimination." *American Political Science Review* 107 (1): 259–187.

Hajnal, Zoltan, and Taeku Lee. 2011. *Why Americans Don't Join the Party: Race Immigration, and the Failure (of Political Parties) to Engage the Electorate.* Princeton: Princeton University Press.

Hattersley, Roy. 2005. "I took the Muslim vote for granted—but that has all changed." *The Guardian*, April 7.

Häusermann, Silja, and Hanspeter Kriesi. 2015. "What Do Voters Want? Dimensions and Configurations in Individual-Level Preferences and Party Choice." In *The Politics of Advanced Capitalism*, ed. P. Beramendi, S. Häusermann, H. Kitschelt and H. Kriesi, 202–230. New York: Cambridge University Press.

Hazan, Reuven, and Gideon Rahat. 2006. "Candidate Selection: Methods and Consequences." In *Handbook of Party Politics*, ed. R. S. Katz and W. Crotty, 109–122. London: Sage.

Heath, Anthony, and Sin Yi Cheung, eds. 2007. *Unequal Chances: Ethnic Minorities in Western Labour Markets.* Oxford: Oxford University Press.

Heath, Anthony, and Neil Demireva. 2014. "Has Multiculturalism Failed in Britain?" *Ethnic and Racial Studies* 37 (1): 161–80.

Heath, Anthony, Stephen D. Fisher, David Sanders, and Maria Sobolewska. 2011. "Ethnic Heterogeneity in the Social Bases of Voting in the 2010 General Election." *Journal of Elections, Public Opinion, and Parties* 21 (2): 255–77.

Heilman, Samuel C. 2000. "Orthodox Jews, the City and the Suburb." *Studies in Contemporary Jewry* 15: 19–34.

Heimann, Siegfried, and Franz Walter. 1993. *Religiöse Sozialisten und Freidenker in der Weimarer Republik.* Bonn: J. H. W. Dietz.

Helbling, Marc. 2011. "Which Indicators Are Most Useful for Comparing Citizenship Policies?" In *Which Indicators are Most Useful for Comparing Citizenship Policies?*, ed. R. Bauböck and M. Helbling, 1–6. San Domenico di Fiesole, Italy: European University Institute.

Helbling, Marc, ed. 2012. *Islamophobia in the West: Measuring and Explaining Individual Attitudes.* Abingdon, Oxon.: Routledge.

Hellwig, Timothy. 2014. *Globalization and Mass Politics: Retaining the Room to Maneuver.* New York: Cambridge University Press.

Hertogen, Jan. 2014. *Aantal en % moslims per nationaliteit in Belgische gemeenten (BuG 186)* 2013. Available from http: //www.npdata.be/. Accessed January 1, 2014.

Hewitt, Roger L. 2005. *White Backlash and the Politics of Multiculturalism.* Cambridge: Cambridge University Press.

Hewstone, Miles, Mark Rubin, and Hazel Willis. 2002. "Intergroup Bias." *Annual Review of Psychology* 53: 575–604.

Hill, Dave. 2010. "Labour Well Beaten in Tower Hamlets." *The Guardian*, October 21.

Hills, John, Mike Brewer, Stephen Jenkins, Ruth Lister, Ruth Lupton, Stephen Machin, Colin Mills, Tariq Modood, Teresa Rees, and Sheila Riddell. 2010. "An Anatomy of Economic Inequality in the UK: Report of the National Equality Panel." London: Government Equalities Office.

Hobsbawm, E. J. 1984. *Worlds of Labour: Further Studies in the History of Labour*. London: Weidenfeld and Nicolson.

Hochschild, Jennifer, Jacqueline Chattopadhyay, Claudine Gay, and Michael Jones-Correa, eds. 2013. *Outsiders No More? Models of Immigrant Political Incorporation*. New York: Oxford University Press.

Holtbrügge, Heiner. 1975. *Türkische Familien in der Bundesrepublik: Erziehungsvorstellungen und familiale Rollen- und Autoritätsstruktur*. Duisburg: Sozialwissenschaftliche Kooperative.

Holtkamp, Lars. 2006. "Parteien und Bürgermeister in der repräsentativen Demokratie: Kommunale Konkordanz- und Konkurrenzdemokratie im Vergleich." *Politische Vierteljahresschrift* 47 (4): 641–61.

Holtkamp, Lars, Elke Wiechmann, and Caroline Friedhoff. 2013. "Intersektionale Analyse der Parlamente—Repräsentation von Migrantinnen in bundesdeutschen Parlamenten." Polis Nr. 72/2013.

Hopkins, Daniel J. 2010. "Politicized Places: Explaining Where and When Immigrants Provoke Local Opposition." *American Political Science Review* 104 (1): 40–60.

Howard, Marc Morjé. 2009. *The Politics of Citizenship in Europe*. New York: Cambridge University Press.

Howard, Marc Morjé. 2012. "Germany's Citizenship Policy in Comparative Perspective." *German Politics and Society* 30 (1): 39–51.

Htun, Mala. 2014. "Political Inclusion and Representation of Afrodescendant Women in Latin America." In *Representation: The Case of Women*, ed. M. C. Escobar-Lemmon and M. M. Taylor-Robinson, 118–134. Oxford: Oxford University Press.

Huckfeldt, Robert, and Carol Weitzel Kohfeld. 1989. *Race and the Decline of Class in American Politics*. Urbana and Chicago: University of Illinois Press.

Hughes, Melanie. 2011. "Intersectionality, Quotas, and Minority Women's Political Representation." *American Political Science Review* 105 (3): 604–20.

Huschek, Doreen, Helga A. G. de Valk, and Aart C. Liefbroer. 2012. "Partner Choice Patterns Among the Descendants of Turkish Immigrants in Europe." *European Journal of Population* 28 (3): 241–68.

Inglehart, Ronald. 1990. *Culture Shift in Advanced Industrial Society*. Princeton: Princeton University Press.

Jamal, Amaney. 2005. "The Political Participation and Engagement of Muslim Americans: Mosque Involvement and Group Consciousness." *American Politics Research* 33 (4): 521–44.

Janoski, Thomas. 2010. *The Ironies of Citizenship*. New York: Cambridge University Press.

Joppke, Christian. 2004. "The Retreat of Multiculturalism in the Liberal State: Theory and Practice." *British Journal of Sociology* 55 (2): 237–57.

Just, Aida, Maria Elena Sandovic, and Ola Listhaug. 2014. "Islam, Religiosity, and Immigrant Political Action in Western Europe." *Social Science Research* 43: 127–44.

Kabeer, Naila. 2000. *The Power to Choose: Bangladeshi Garment Workers in London and Dhaka*. London: Verso.

Kalyvas, Stathis. 1996. *The Rise of Christian Democracy in Europe*. Ithaca, NY: Cornell University Press.

Kalyvas, Stathis, and Kees van Kersbergen. 2010. "Christian Democracy." *Annual Review of Political Science* 13: 183–209.

Karakoyun, Ercan. 2014. *Nur Türken kandidieren in Kreuzberg*, August 17, 2011. Available from http://www.deutsch-tuerkische-nachrichten.de/2011/08/169943/nur-tuerken-kandidieren-in-kreuzberg/. Accessed June 17, 2014.

Katz, Richard. 2001. "The Problem of Candidate Selection and Models of Party Democracy." *Party Politics* 7 (3): 277–96.

Kerner Commssion. 1968. "Kerner Report on Civil Disorders: Supplemental Studies for the National Advisory Commission on Civil Disorders." New York: Praeger.

Kesteloot, Christian, Pascal de Decker, and Altay Manço. 1997. "Turks and Housing in Belgium, with Special Reference to Brussels, Ghent and Visé." In *Turks in European Cities: Housing and Urban Segregation*, ed. A. S. Özüekren and R. Van Kempen, 67–97. Utrecht, Netherlands: European Research Centre on Migration and Ethnic Relations.

Key, V. O. 1949. *Southern Politics in State and Nation*. New York: A. A. Knopf.

Khan, Saira. 2006. "Why Muslim women should thank Straw." *The Times of London*, October 9.

Kitschelt, Herbert. 1994. *The Transformation of European Social Democracy*. New York: Cambridge University Press.

Kitschelt, Herbert. 1996. *The Radical Right in Western Europe: A Comparative Analysis*. Ann Arbor: University of Michigan Press.

Kitschelt, Herbert. 2000. "Linkages between Citizens and Politicians in Democratic Polities." *Comparative Political Studies* 33 (6–7): 845–79.

Kitschelt, Herbert, and Philipp Rehm. 2015. "Party Alignments: Change and Continuity." In *The Politics of Advanced Capitalism*, ed. P. Beramendi, S. Häusermann, H. Kitschelt and H. Kriesi, 179–201. New York: Cambridge University Press.

Klausen, Jytte. 2005. *The Islamic Challenge: Politics and Religion in Europe*. Oxford: Oxford University Press.

Klingemann, Hans-Dieter, Richard Hofferbert, and Ian Budge. 1994. *Parties, Policies, and Democracy*. Boulder, CO: Westview Press.

Knott, Mélanie, and Altay Manço. 2010. "Policy Interactions in Belgium." In *Naturalisation: A Passport for the Better Integration of Immigrants?*, ed. OECD, 278–299. Paris: OECD.

Knox, W. W. 1988. "Religion and the Scottish Labour Movement." *Journal of Contemporary History* 23 (4): 609–30.

Koksal, Mehmet. 2007. "La mosquée au milieu du village politique." *La Revue Nouvelle* (9): 12–19.

Koopmans, Ruud. 2010. "Trade-Offs between Equality and Difference: Immigrant Integration, Multiculturalism, and the Welfare State in Cross-National Perspective." *Journal of Ethnic and Migration Studies* 36 (1): 1–26.

Koopmans, Ruud. 2015. "Religious Fundamentalism and Hostility against Out-Groups: A Comparison of Muslims and Christians in Western Europe." *Journal of Ethnic and Migration Studies* 41 (1): 33–57.

Koopmans, Ruud, Ines Michalowksi, and Stine Waibel. 2012. "Citizenship Rights for Immigrants: National Political Processes and Cross-National Convergence in Western Europe." *American Journal of Sociology* 117 (4): 1202–45.

Kriesi, Hanspeter, Edgar Grande, Romain Lachat, Martin Dolezat, Simon Bornschier, and Timotheos Frey. 2008. *West European Politics in the Age of Globalization*. Cambridge: Cambridge University Press.

Krook, Mona Lena. 2013. "Electoral Gender Quotas: A Conceptual Analysis." *Comparative Political Studies* 20 (10): 1–27.

Kuenssberg, Laura. 2016. *Is Labour Making a Mess of Bradford West?* 2015. Available from http://www.bbc.com/news/uk-31749227. Accessed January 14, 2016.

Kymlicka, Will. 1995. *Multicultural Citizenship: A Liberal Theory of Minority Rights*. Oxford: Clarendon Press.

Kymlicka, Will. 2012. "Multiculturalism: Success, Failure, and the Future." Washington, DC: Migration Policy Institute.

La Dernière Heure. 2013. *Le mur (de cuisine) de la honte*, February 16 Available from http: //www .dhnet.be/actu/faits/le-mur-de-cuisine-de-la-honte-51b740b0e4b0de6db9770901. Accessed April 26, 2015.

Labour Party. 2008. *The Labour Party Rule Book 2008*. London: The Labour Party.

Lakha, F, Dermot Gorman, and Pablo Mateos. 2011. "Name Analysis to Classify Population by Ethnicity in Public Health: Validation of Onomap in Scotland." *Public Health* 125 (10): 688–96.

LaLibre.be. 2012. *De Permentier: "les mosquées ont aidé le PS à Forest et à Molenbeek"*, October 16 2012 Available from http: //www.lalibre.be/actu/politique-belge/de-permentier-les-mosquees -ont-aide-le-ps-a-forest-et-a-molenbeek-51b8f29ae4b0de6db9c8423d. Accessed April 28, 2015].

Lamare, J. Ryan. 2010. "Union Influence on Voter Turnout: Results from Three Los Angeles County Elections." *Industrial and Labor Relations Review* 63 (3): 454–70.

Lange, Anders. 2000. "Diskriminering, integration och etniska relationer." Norrköping: Integrationsverket.

Langvasbråten, Trude. 2008. "A Scandinavian Model? Gender Equality Discourses on Multiculturalism." *Social Politics* 15 (1): 32–52.

Laurence, Jonathan. 2012. *The Emancipation of Europe's Muslims: The State's Role in Minority Integration*. Princeton: Princeton University Press.

Laurence, Jonathan. 2013. "Islam and Social Democrats: Integrating Europe's Muslim Minorities." *Dissent* 60 (4): 18–23.

Laurence, Jonathan, and Justin Vaisse. 2006. *Integrating Islam: Political and Religious Challenges in Contemporary France*. Washington D.C.: Brookings Institution Press.

Laver, Michael, and Kenneth A. Shepsle. 1996. *Making and Breaking Governments*. New York: Cambridge University Press.

Lawless, Jennifer, and Richard Fox. 2010. *It Still Takes a Candidate: Why Women Don't Run for Office*. New York: Cambridge University Press.

Lawrence, Jon. 1997. "Dynamics of Urban Politics, 1867–1914." In *Party, State, and Society: Electoral Behavior in Britain since 1820*, ed. J. Lawrence and M. Taylor, 79–105. Aldershot: Scolar Press.

Le Lohé, M. J. 1975. "Participation in elections by Asians in Bradford." In *The Politics of Race*, ed. I. Crewe, 84–122. New York: John Wiley and Sons.

Leach, Steve. 2004. "Political Parties at the Local Level." In *British Local Government into the 21st Century*, ed. G. Stoker and D. Wilson, 76–90. Houndmills: Palgrave Macmillan.

Leach, Steve. 2006. *The Changing Role of Local Politics in Britain*. Bristol: The Policy Press.

Leighley, Jan, and Jonathan Nagler. 2007. "Unions, Voter Turnout, and Class Bias in the U.S. Electorate, 1964–2004." *Journal of Politics* 69 (2): 430–41.

Leß, Daniela. 2012. "Kommunales Wahlrecht in Deutschland." In *Grundwissen Kommunalpolitik*, ed. Friedrich-Ebert-Stiftung. Bonn: FES.

Lesthaeghe, Ron, and Johan Surkyn. 1995. "Heterogeneity in Social Change: Turkish and Moroccan Women in Belgium." *European Journal of Population* 11 (1): 1–29.

Levitt, Peggy, and Nadya B. Jaworsky. 2007. "Transnational Migration Studies: Past Developments and Future Trends." *Annual Review of Sociology* 33: 129–56.

Lewis, Philip. 1994. *Islamic Britain: Religion, Politics, and Identity among British Muslims: Bradford in the 1990s*. London; New York: I. B. Tauris.

Lewis, Philip. 2002. "Between Lord Ahmed and Ali G: Which Future for British Muslims." In *Religious Freedom and the Neutrality of the State: The Position of Islam in the European Union*, ed. W. A. R. Shalid and P. S. van Konigsveld, 129–144. Leuven: Peeters.

Lieberman, Evan, and Gwyneth McClendon. 2012. "The Ethnicity-Policy Link in Sub-Saharan Africa." *Comparative Political Studies* 46 (5): 574–602.

Lindekilde, Lasse. 2013. "How Politically Integrated Are Danish Muslims? Evidence from the Muhammad Cartoons Controversy." In *Muslim Political Participation in Europe*, ed. J. Nielsen, 140–162. Edinburgh: Edinburgh University Press.

Linden, Franz. 1932. *Sozialismus und Religion*. Leipzig: Bernhard Tauchnitz.

Lipset, Seymour M., and Stein Rokkan, eds. 1967. *Party Systems and Voter Alignments: Cross-National Perspectives*. New York: Free Press.

Macey, Marie. 2009. *Multiculturalism, Religion, and Women: Doing Harm by Doing Good?* Basingstoke, UK: Palgrave Macmillan.

Maliepaard, Mieke, Marcel Lubbers, and Mérove Gijsberts. 2010. "Generational Differences in Ethnic and Religious Attachment and Their Interrelation. A Study among Muslim Minorities in the Netherlands." *Ethnic and Racial Studies* 33 (3): 451–72.

Mansbridge, Jane. 1999. "Should Blacks Represent Blacks and Women Represent Women? A Contingent 'Yes.'" *Journal of Politics* 61 (3): 628–57.

Mansbridge, Jane. 2003. "Rethinking Representation." *American Political Science Review* 97 (4): 515–28.

Marchant, Rob. 2012. "Time for Labour to Root Out the Rotten Politics of Race in the Tower Hamlets Party." Available at http://labour-uncut.co.uk/2012/07/25/time-for-labour-to-root-out-the-rotten-politics-of-race-in-the-tower-hamlets-party/. Accessed February 2, 2017.

Marshall, Tom. 2015. "Beinazir Lasharie: Ex-Big Brother Contestant Suspended from Labour Party over 'Anti-Israel' Facebook Posts." *Evening Standard*, October 19.

Martin, Daniel, and Martin Robinson. 2015. "Fury at Labour's Segregated Rally: Sexism Row after Senior Party Figures Attend Birmingham Election Meeting where Muslim Men and Women Are Seated Separately." *Daily Mail*, May 5.

Massey, Douglas S. 1985. "Ethnic and Residential Segregation: A Theoretical Synthesis and Empirical Review." *Sociology and Social Research* 69 (3): 315–50.

Massey, Douglas S., Rafael Alarcón, Jorge Durand, and Humberto González. 1987. *Return to Aztlan: The Social Process of International Migration from Western Mexico*. Berkeley: University of California Press.

Mateos, Pablo. 2013. *Names, Ethnicity and Populations*. Heidelberg, Germany: Springer.

Maxwell, Rahsaan. 2012. *Ethnic Minority Migrants in Britain and France: Integration Trade-Offs*. New York: Cambridge University Press.

Maxwell, Rahsaan. 2013. "The Geographic Context of Political Attitudes among Migrant-Origin Individuals in Europe." *World Politics* 65 (1): 116–55.

McAndrew, Siobhan, and David Voas. 2014. "Immigrant Generation, Religiosity and Civic Engagement in Britain." *Ethnic and Racial Studies* 37 (1): 99–119.

McCarty, Nolan, Keith T. Poole, and Howard Rosenthal. 2006. *Polarized America: The Dance of Ideology and Unequal Riches*. Cambridge: MIT Press.

McDermott, M. 1979. Irish Catholics and the British Labour Movement; A Study with Particular Reference to London 1918 to 1970, University of Kent, Kent.

McDermott, Monika. 1998. "Race and Gender Cues in Low-Information Elections." *Political Research Quarterly* 51 (4): 895–918

McHugh, Declan. 2006. *Labour in the City: The Development of the Labour Party in Manchester, 1918–31*. Manchester: Manchester University Press.

McLaren, Lauren M. 2001. "Immigration and the New Politics of Inclusion and Exclusion in the European Union: The Effect of Elites and the EU on Individual-level Opinions Regarding

European and non-European Immigrants." *European Journal of Political Research* 39 (1): 81–108.

McLaren, Lauren M. 2003. "Anti-Immigrant Prejudice in Europe: Contact, Threat Perception, and Preferences for the Exclusion of Migrants." *Social Forces* 81 (3): 909–36.

McSmith, Andy. 2016. "Khadim Hussain: Former Lord Mayor of Bradford Suspended by Labour Party over anti-Semitism." *The Independent*, March 23.

Meetoo, Veena, and Haidi Safia Mirza. 2011. "There is Nothing 'Honourable' about Honour Killings": Gender, Violence, and the Limits of Multiculturalism." In *Honour, Violence, Women and Islam*, ed. M. M. Idriss and T. Abbas, 42–66. Abingdon, Oxon.: Routledge

Meier, Petra. 2004. "The Mutual Contagion Effect of Legal and Party Quotas: A Belgian Perspective." *Party Politics* 10 (5): 583–600.

Messina, Anthony M. 1989. *Race and Party Competition in Britain*. Oxford: Oxford University Press.

Michon, Laure, and Floris Vermeulen. 2013. "Explaining Different Trajectories in Immigrant Political Integration: Moroccans and Turks in Amsterdam." *West European Politics* 36 (3): 597–614.

Mickey, Robert. 2015. *Paths out of Dixie: The Democratization of Authoritarian Enclaves in America's Deep South, 1944–1972*. Princeton: Princeton University Press.

Migration in Germany. 2009. *Fastenbrechen, Wahlkampf, Optionsmodell*, August 25, 2009. Available from http://www.migazin.de/2009/08/25/turkische-presse-europa-vom-25-08-2009-fastenbrechen-wahlkampf-optionsmodell/. Accessed June 17, 2015.

Minkenberg, Michael. 2002. "Religion and Public Policy: Institutional, Cultural, and Political Impact on the Shaping of Abortion Policies in Western Democracies." *Comparative Political Studies* 35 (2): 221–47.

Mirbach, Ferdinand. 2008. *Die deutschen Parteien und der Islam: Politische Konzepte zur Integration von Muslimen*. Marburg: Tectum Verlag.

Modood, Tariq. 2009. "Muslims and the Politics of Difference." In *Muslims in Britain: Race, Place and Identities*, ed. P. Hopkins and R. Gale, 193–209. Edinburgh: Edinburgh University Press.

Mortimer, Caroline. 2016. "Women's rights organisation says Muslims women 'blocked from seeking office by male Labour councillors.' " *The Independent*, February 5.

Mudde, Cas. 2007. *Populist Radical Right Parties in Europe*. Cambridge: Cambridge University Press.

Murray, Rainbow. 2008. "The Power of Sex and Incumbency: A Longitudinal Study of Electoral Performance in France." *Party Politics* 14 (5): 539–54.

Musterd, Sako. 2005. "Social and Ethnic Segregation in Europe: Levels, Causes, and Effects." *Journal of Urban Affairs* 27 (3): 331–48.

Musterd, Sako. 2012. "Ethnic Residential Segregation: Reflections on Concepts, Levels and Effects." In *The SAGE Handbook of Housing Studies*, ed. D. F. Clapham, W. A. V. Clark and K. Gibb, 419–438. Los Angeles: Sage.

Muttarak, Raya, and Anthony Heath. 2010. "Who Intermarries in Britain? Explaining Diversity in Intermarriage Patterns." *British Journal of Sociology* 61 (2): 277–305.

Myrberg, Gunnar. 2007. Medlemmar och medborgare: Föreningsdeltagande och politiskt engagemang i det etnifierade samhället, Ph.D. Dissertation, Uppsala University.

Nathan-Kazis, Josh. 2010. "New York Candidates Court Hasidic Vote." *The Forward*, October 22.

National Centre for Social Research (NatCen). 2010. "British Social Attitudes Survey, 2008 (SN: 6390)." Colchester: UK Data Archive.

Nielsen, Jørgen S. 1999. *Towards a European Islam*. New York: St. Martin's Press.

Nooruddin, Irfan, and Pradeep Chhibber. 2008. "Unstable Politics: Fiscal Space and Electoral Volatility in the Indian States." *Comparative Political Studies* 41 (8): 1069–91.

Norris, Pippa, ed. 1997. *Passages to Power: Legislative Recruitment in Advanced Democracies*. New York: Cambridge University Press.

Norris, Pippa, and Ronald Inglehart. 2004. *Sacred and Secular: Politics and Religion Worldwide*. Cambridge: Cambridge University Press.

Norris, Pippa, and Joni Lovenduski. 1995. *Political Recruitment: Gender, Race and Class in the British Parliament*. Cambridge: Cambridge University Press.

Norton, Anne. 2013. *On the Muslim Question*. Princeton: Princeton University Press.

OECD. 2013. *International Migration Outlook*. Paris: OECD.

Okin, Susan Moller. 1999. "Is Multiculturalism Bad for Women?" In *Is Multiculturalism Bad for Women? Susan Moller Okin with Respondents*, ed. J. Cohen, M. Howard and M. C. Nussbaum, 7–24. Princeton: Princeton Univesity Press.

O'Loughlin, John, Brigitte Waldorf, and Günther Glebe. 1987. "The Location of Foreigners in an Urban Housing Market: A Micro-Level Study of Düsseldorf-Oberbilk." *Geographische Zeitschrift* 75 (1): 22–41.

O'Loughlin, John. 1980. "Distribution and Migration of Foreigners in German Cities." *Geographical Review* 70 (3): 253–75.

Open Society Foundation. 2011a. "Muslims in Antwerp." New York: Open Society Foundations.

Open Society Foundation. 2011b. "Muslims in Marseille." New York: Open Society Foundations.

Open Society Foundation. 2012. "Muslims in Paris." New York: Open Society Foundation.

Open Society Institute (OSI). 2010. "Muslims in Europe: A Report on 11 EU Cities." New York: Open Society Institute.

Ouseley, Herman. 2001. "Community Pride Not Prejudice: Making Diversity Work in Bradford." Bradford: Bradford Vision.

Özüekren, Şule, and Ronald van Kempen, eds. 1997. *Turks in European Cities: Housing and Urban Segregation*. Utrecht, Netherlands: ERCOMER.

Palloni, Alberto, Douglas S. Massey, Miguel Ceballos, Kristin Espinosa, and Michael Spittel. 2001. "Social Capital and International Migration: A Test Using Information on Family Networks." *American Journal of Sociology* 106 (5): 1262–98.

Parekh, Bhikhu. 2008. "Europe, Liberalism, and the 'Muslim Question.'" In *Multiculturalism, Muslims and Citizenship: A European Approach*, ed. T. Modood, A. Triandafyllidou and R. Zapata-Barrero, 179–203. London: Routledge.

Patel, David S. 2012. "Concealing to Reveal: The Informational Role of Islamic Dress." *Rationality and Society* 24 (3): 295–323.

Paxton, Pamela, Sheri Kunovich, and Melanie Hughes. 2007. "Gender in Politics." *Annual Review of Sociology* 33: 263–84.

Peace, Timothy. 2013. "Muslims and Electoral Politics in Britain: The Case of the Respect Party." In *Muslim Political Participation in Europe*, ed. J. Nielsen, 299–321. Edinburgh: Edinburgh University Press.

Peace, Timothy, and Parveen Akhtar. 2015. "Biradei, Bloc Votes and Bradford: Investigating the Respect Party's Campaign Strategy." *British Journal of Politics and International Relations* 17 (2): 224–43.

Peach, Ceri. 2006. "Muslims in the 2001 Census of England and Wales: Gender and Economic Disadvantage." *Ethnic and Racial Studies* 29 (4): 629–55.

Peach, Ceri, and Richard Gale. 2003. "Muslims, Hindus, and Sikhs in the New Religious Landscape of England." *The Geographical Review* 93 (4): 469–90.

Pedraza, Silvia. 1991. "Women and Migration: The Social Consequences of Gender." *Annual Review of Sociology* 17: 303–25.

Pędziwiatr, Konrad. 2010. *The New Muslim Elites in European Cities: Religion and Active Social*

Citizenship Amongst Young Organized Muslims in Brussels and London. Saarbrücken, Germany: VDM Verlag Dr. Müller.

Pelling, Henry. 1967. *Social Geography of British Elections, 1885–1910*. London: Macmillan.

Pew Global Attitudes Project. 2006. "Muslims in Europe: Economic Worries Top Concerns about Religious and Cultural Identity." Washington DC: Pew Research Center.

Phillips, Anne. 1995. *The Politics of Presence*. Oxford: Oxford University Press.

Phillips, Anne, and Sawitri Saharso. 2008. "Guest Editorial: The Rights of Women and the Crisis of Multiculturalism." *Ethnicities* 8 (3): 291–301.

Pink, Oliver. 2013. "SPÖ: Wahlkarten in Moscheen ausgefüllt?" *Die Presse*, October 17.

Pitcher, Ben. 2009. *The Politics of Multiculturalism: Race and Racism in Contemporary Britain*. Basingstoke: Palgrave Macmillan.

Pitkin, Hanna. 1967. *The Concept of Representation*. Berkeley: University of California Press.

Polakow-Suransky, Sasha. 2016. "The Ruthlessly Effective Rebranding of Europe's New Far Right." *The Guardian*, November 1.

Popkin, Samuel L. 1991. *The Reasoning Voter: Communication and Persuasion in Presidential Campaigns*. Chicago: University of Chicago Press.

Popp, Maximilian, and Markus Sehl. 2011. "Migrantenpartei BIG: Erdogans Berliner Lobby Truppe." *Spiegel Online*, September 16. Available at http://www.spiegel.de/politik/deutsch land/migrantenpartei-big-erdogans-berliner-lobby-truppe-a-786207.html. Accessed February 20, 2017.

Portes, Alejandro, and Julia Sensenbrenner. 1993. "Embeddedness and Immigration: Notes on the Social Determinants of Economic Action." *American Journal of Sociology* 98 (6): 1320–50.

Posner, Daniel P. 2004. "The Political Salience of Cultural Difference: Why Chewas and Tumbukas Are Allies in Zambia and Adversaries in Malawi." *American Political Science Review* 98 (4): 529–45.

Posner, Daniel P. 2005. *Institutions and Ethnic Politics in Africa*. Cambridge: Cambridge University Press.

Preuhs, Robert. 2006. "The Conditional Effect of Minority Descriptive Representation: Black Legislators and Policy Influence in the American States." *Journal of Politics* 68 (3): 585–99.

Profil Online. 2013. *Resul Ekrem Gönültas: "Der Sieg gehört mir."* October 29. Available from http://www.profil.at/articles/1344/560/368626/nationalratswahlen-resul-ekrem -goenueltas-der-sieg. Accessed March 26, 2014.

Przeworski, Adam. 1985. *Capitalism and Democracy*. Cambridge: Cambridge University Press.

Przeworski, Adam, and John Sprague. 1986. *Paper Stones: A History of Electoral Socialism*. Chicago: University of Chicago Press.

Pugh, Martin. 2002. "The Rise of Labour and the Political Culture of Conservatism." *History* 87 (288): 514–37.

Purdam, Kingsley. 1998. The Impact of Democracy on Identity: Muslim Councillors and their Experiences of Local Politics in Britain, Doctoral thesis, Department of Government, University of Manchester, Manchester.

Purdam, Kingsley. 2001. "Democracy in Practice: Muslims and the Labour Party at the Local Level." *Politics* 21 (3): 147–57.

Rallings, Colin, and Michael Thrasher. 1997. *Local Elections in Britain*. London: Routledge.

Rallings, Colin, Michael Thrasher, Galina Borisyuk, and Mary Shears. 2010. "Parties, Recruitment and Modernisation: Evidence from Local Election Candidates." *Local Government Studies* 36 (3): 361–79.

Rallings, C.S., M.A.M. Thrasher, and L. Ware. 2006. "SN: 5319: British Local Election Database, 1889–2003 [computer file]." Colchester, Essex: UK Data Archive [distributor].

Ramakrishnan, S. Karthick. 2005. *Democracy in Immigrant America*. Stanford: Stanford University Press.

Rath, Jan. 1981. "The Big Men are Rising! The Case of Migrants Participation in District Council Elections in the Netherlands." *European Demographic Bulletin* 22 (4): 137–47.

Rath, Jan, Rinus Penninx, Kees Groenendijk, and Astrid Meyer. 2001. *Western Europe and Its Islam*. Leiden: Brill.

Reimann, Anna. 2010. *Türkischstämmige CDU-Ministerin; Demontage einer Vorzeige-Migrantin*, April 26 Available from http: //www.spiegel.de/politik/deutschland/tuerkischstaemmige -cdu-ministerin-demontage-einer-vorzeige-migrantin-a-691190.html. Accessed November 2, 2015.

Reitz, Rüdiger. 1983. *Christen und Sozialdemokratie: Konsequenzen aus einem Erbe*. Stuttgart: Radus Verlag.

Rhodes, James. 2009. "The Political Breakthrough of the BNP: The Case of Burnley." *British Politics* 4 (1): 22–46.

Rivera, Ray, and Sharon Otterman. 2012. "For Ultra-Orthodox in Abuse Cases, Prosecutor Has Different Rules." *New York Times*, May 10.

Rockmann, Ulrike. 2011. "Wer sind und wo leben die Zuwanderer in Berlin?" Berlin: Amt für Statistik Berlin-Brandenburg.

Rodden, Jonathan A. 2010. "The Geographic Distribution of Political Preferences." *Annual Review of Political Science* 13: 297–340.

Rodden, Jonathan A. 2011. *The Long Shadow of the Industrial Revolution: Political Geography and the Representation of the Left*. Unpublished Book Manuscript.

Roemer, John E., Woojin Lee, and Karine Van der Straeten. 2007. *Racism, Xenophobia and Redistribution: A Study of Four Democracies*. Cambridge: Harvard University Press.

Roggeband, Conny, and Mieke Verloo. 2007. "Dutch Women Are Liberated, Migrant Women Are a Problem: The Evolution of Policy Frames on Gender and Migration in the Netherlands." *Social Policy and Administration* 41 (3): 271–88.

Rohrschneider, Robert, and Stephen Whitefield. 2012. *The Strain of Representation: How Parties Represent Diverse Voters in Western and Eastern Europe*. Oxford: Oxford University Press.

Rosenstone, Steven J., and John M. Hansen. 1993. *Mobilization, Participation, and Democracy in America*. New York: Macmillan.

Ruedin, Didier. 2013. *Why Aren't They There? The Political Representation of Women, Ethnic Groups and Issue Positions in Legislatures*. Colchester: ECPR Press.

Saggar, Shamit. 2000. *Race and Representation: Electoral Politics and Ethnic Pluralism in Britain*. Manchester: Manchester University Press.

Saggar, Shamit. 2009. *Pariah Politics: Understanding Western Radical Islamism and What Should be Done*. Oxford: Oxford University Press.

Saifullah Khan, Verity. 1976. "Pakistanis in Britain." *New Community* 5 (3): 222–29.

Samad, Yunas. 1996. "The Politics of Islamic Identity among Bangladeshis and Pakistanis in Britain." In *Culture, Identity and Politics*, ed. T. Ranger, Y. Samad and O. Stuart, 90–98. Avebury: Aldershot.

Sanchez, George. 1993. *Becoming Mexican American: Ethnicity, Culture and Identity in Chicano Los Angeles 1900–1945*. New York: Oxford University Press.

Sauer, Martina, and Dirk Halm. 2009. *Erfolge und Defizite der Integration türkeistämmiger Einwanderer*. Wiesbaden: VS Verlag.

Schattschneider, E. E. 1942. *Party Government*. New York: Holt, Rinehart & Winston.

Schickler, Eric. 2016. *Racial Realignment: The Transformation of American Liberalism, 1932–1965*. Princeton: Princeton University Press.

Schmitter-Heisler, Barbara. 2006. "Trade Unions and Immigrant Incorporation: The US and Europe Compared." In *Paths of Integration*, ed. L. Lucassen, D. Feldman and J. Oltmer, 201–221. Amsterdam: Amsterdam University Press.

Schönwälder, Karen. 2013. "Immigrant Representation in Germany's Regional States: The Puzzle of Uneven Dynamics." *West European Politics* 36 (3): 634–51.

Schwaiger, Rosemarie. 2013. *SPÖ-Kandidat Resul Ekrem Gönültas bekam erstaunlich viele Vorzugsstimmen*, October 29. Available from http://www.profil.at/articles/1344/560/368624/nationalratswahlen-spoe-kandidat-resul-ekrem-goenueltas-vorzugsstimmen. Accessed March 26, 2014.

Scott, Duncan. 1972/73. "West Pakistanis in Huddersfield: Aspects of Race Relations in Local Politics." *New Community* 2 (1): 38–43.

Segura, Gary M. 2013. "Behavioral and Attitudinal Components of Immigrant Political Incorporation." In *Outsiders No More? Models of Immigrant Political Incorporation*, ed. J. Hochschild, J. Chattopadhyay, C. Gay, and M. Jones-Correa, 254–269. Oxford: Oxford University Press.

Shachar, Ayelet. 2001. *Multicultural Jurisdictions: Cultural Differences and Women's Rights*. Cambridge: Cambridge University Press.

Shaw, Alison. 1994. "The Pakistani Community in Oxford." In *Desh Pardesh: The South Asian Presence in Britain*, ed. R. Ballard, 88–116. London: Hurst & Company.

Shaw, Alison. 2000. *Kinship and Continuity: Pakistani Families in Britain*. Amsterdam: Harwood Academic.

Shaw, Alison. 2001. "Kinship, Cultural Preference and Immigration: Consanguineous Marriage among British Pakistanis." *Journal of the Royal Anthropological Institute* 7 (2): 315–34.

Shefter, Martin. 1994. *Political Parties and the State: The American Historical Experience*. Princeton: Princeton University Press.

Shugart, Matthew S., Melody E. Valdini, and Kati Suominen. 2005. "Looking for Locals: Voter Information Demands and Personal Vote-Earning Attributes of Legislators under Proportional Representation." *American Journal of Political Science* 49 (2): 437–49.

Sides, John, and Jack Citrin. 2007. "European Opinion about Immigration: The Role of Identities, Interests and Information." *British Journal of Political Science* 37 (3): 477–504.

Siim, Birte, and Hege Skjeie. 2008. "Tracks, Intersections, and Dead Ends: Multicultural Challenges to State Feminism in Denmark and Norway." *Ethnicities* 8 (3): 322–44.

Sinno, Abdulkader. 2009. "An Institutional Approach to the Politics of Western Muslim Minorities." In *Muslims in Western Politics*, ed. A. Sinno, 1–10. Bloomington: Indiana University Press.

Smets, Kaat, and Carolien van Ham. 2013. "The Embarrassment of Riches? A Meta-analysis of Individual-Level Research on Voter Turnout." *Electoral Studies* 32 (2): 344–59.

Smith, Leonard. 1993. *Religion and the Rise of Labour: Nonconformity and the Independent Labour Movement*. Keele, Staffordshire: Keele University Press.

Sniderman, Paul M., and Louk Hagendoorn. 2007. *When Ways of Life Collide*. Princeton: Princeton University Press.

Sniderman, Paul M., Michael Bang Petersen, Rune Slothuus, and Rune Stubager. 2014. *Paradoxes of Liberal Democracy: Islam, Western Europe, and the Danish Cartoon Controversy*. Princeton: Princeton University Press.

Sobolewska, Maria, Stuart Wilks-Heeg, Eleanor Hill, and Magda Borkowska. 2015. "Understanding Electoral Fraud Vulnerability in Pakistani and Bangladeshi Origin Communities in England." Manchester: University of Manchester.

Solomos, John, and Les Back. 1995. *Race, Politics, and Social Change*. London: Routledge.

Song, Sarah. 2007. *Justice, Gender, and the Politics of Multiculturalism*. Cambridge: Cambridge University Press.

Spielhaus, Riem. 2013. *Muslime in der Statistik: Wer ist Muslim und wenn ja wie viele?* Berlin: Mediendienst Integration.

Spilerman, Seymour. 1970. "The Causes of Racial Disturbances: A Comparison of Alternative Explanations." *American Sociological Review* 35 (4): 627–49.

Statistisches Bundesamt. 2013. "Pressekonferenz: "Zensus 2011—Fakten zur Bevölkerung in Deutschland"." Wiesbaden: Statistisches Bundesamt.

Stewart, Heather. 2016. "Naz Shah Suspended by Labour Party amid Antisemitism Row." *The Guardian*, April 27.

Stokes, Susan C., Thad Dunning, Marcelo Nazareno, and Valeria Brusco. 2013. *Brokers, Voters, and Clientelism: The Puzzle of Distributive Politics*. New York: Cambridge University Press.

Straube, Hanne. 1987. *Türkisches Leben in der Bundesrepublik*. Frankfurt: Campus.

Street, Alexander. 2014. "Representation Despite Discrimination: Minority Candidates in Germany." *Political Research Quarterly* 67 (2): 374–85.

Tatari, Eren. 2010. The Contingency Theory of Descriptive Representation: Muslims in British Local Government, Department of Political Science, Indiana University, Bloomington.

Tate, Katherine. 2003. *Black Faces in the Mirror: African Americans and their Representatives in the U.S. Congress*. Princeton: Princeton University Press.

Teney, Celine, Dirk Jacobs, Andrea Rea, and Pascal Delwit. 2010. "Ethnic Voting in Brussels: Voting Patterns among Ethnic Minorities in Brussels (Belgium) during the 2006 Local Elections." *Acta Politica* 45 (3): 273–97.

Thompson, Paul. 1967. *Socialists, Liberals and Labour: The Struggle for London, 1885–1914*. London: Routledge & K. Paul.

Tiefenbach, Paul. 2006. "Kumulieren, Panaschieren, Mehrmandatswahlkreise—Mehr Demokratie beim Wahlrecht?" *Zeitschrift für Parlamentsfragen* 37 (1): 115–25.

Timmerman, Christiane. 2006. "Gender Dynamics in the Context of Turkish Marriage Migration: The Case of Belgium." *Turkish Studies* 7 (1): 125–43.

Togeby, Lise. 2008. "The Political Representation of Ethnic Minorities: Denmark as a Deviant Case." *Party Politics* 14 (3): 325–43.

Torrekens, Corinne. 2012. "Un vote musulman aux élections communales?" *Le Soir*, October 16.

Triandafyllidou, Anna, Tariq Modood, and Nasar Meer, eds. 2012. *European Multiculturalisms: Cultural, Religious and Ethnic Challenges*. Edinburgh: Edinburgh University Press.

Trounstine, Jessica. 2008. *Political Monopolies in American Cities*. Chicago: University of Chicago Press.

Trounstine, Jessica. 2016. "Segregation and Inequality in Public Goods." *American Journal of Political Science* 60 (3): 709–25.

Trounstine, Jessica, and Melody E. Valdini. 2008. "The Context Matters: The Effects of Single-Member versus At-Large Districts on City Council Diversity." *American Journal of Political Science* 52 (3): 554–69.

Ulram, Peter, and Svila Tributsch. 2013. "Muslime in Österreich." Ecoquest.

University of Essex. 2010. "British Household Panel Survey; Waves 1–18, 1991–2009." UK Data Service.

Valenzuela, Ali. 2014. "Tending to the Flock: Latino Religious Commitments and Political Preferences." *Political Research Quarterly* 67 (4): 930–42.

van der Kolk, Henk. 2007. "Local Electoral Systems in Western Europe." *Local Government Studies* 33 (2): 159–80.

van Kempen, Ronald. 2005. "Segregation and Housing Conditions of Immigrants in Western European Cities." In *Cities of Europe: Changing Contexts, Local Arrangements, and the Challenge to Urban Cohesion*, ed. Y. Kazepov, 190–209. Malden, MA: Blackwell Publishing.

Van Robaeys, Bea, and Nathalie Perrin. 2006. *Armoede bij personen van vreemde herkomst becijferd*. OASES and KBS. Available from http://www.kifkif.be/sites/default/files/armoede _bij_personen_van_vreemde.pdf. Accessed February 10, 2017.

Verba, Sidney, Kay Schlozman, and Henry E. Brady. 1995. *Voice and Equality: Civic Voluntarism in American Politics*. Cambridge: Harvard University Press.

Vertovec, Steven, and Susanne Wessendorf. 2010. "Introduction: Assessing the Backlash against Multiculturalism." In *The Multiculturalism Backlash: European Discourses, Policies, and Practices*, ed. S. Vertovec and S. Wessendorf, 1–31. Abingdon, Oxon.: Routledge.

Voas, David, and Fenella Fleischmann. 2012. "Islam Moves West: Religious Change in the First and Second Generations." *Annual Review of Sociology* 38: 525–45.

Volkens, Andrea, Pola Lehman, Nicolas Merz, Sven Regel, Annika Werner, Onawa Promise Lacewell, and Henrike Schultze. 2014. "The Manifesto Data Collection. Manifesto Project (MRG/CMP/MARPOR). Version 2014a." Berlin: Wissenschaftszentrum Berlin für Sozialforschung (WZB).

von Mittelstaedt, Juliane. 2009. "Muslime und Christen in Köln: "Der Islam fordert uns heraus." *Spiegel Online*, December 20. http://www.spiegel.de/panorama/gesellschaft/muslime-und -christen-in-koeln-der-islam-fordert-uns-heraus-a-667692.html. Accessed February 12, 2017.

Voogt, Fabrice, and Hugues Dorzee. 2006. "Le 'stemblok' à la manière CDH." *Le Soir*, October 13.

Walker, Jonathan. 2015. "Labour Defends Election Rally where Men and Women Sat Separately." *Birmingham Mail*, May 4.

Wasow, Omar. 2016. "Do Protest Tactics Matter? Evidence from the 1960s Black Insurgency." Working Paper, Politics Department, Princeton University.

Wauters, Bram, Dries Verlet, and Johan Ackaert. 2012. "Giving More Weight to Preferential Votes: Welcome or Superfluous Reform? The Case of the Local Elections in Flanders (Belgium)." *Local Government Studies* 38 (1): 91–111.

Webster, Philip, and Russell Jenkins. 2006. "Straw Tells Muslims to Lift Their Veils." *Times of London*, October 6.

Wegner, Kai. 2014. "Die großen Städte zurückerobern." Strategiepapier des Großstadtbeauftragten der CDU/CSU-Bundestagsfraktion zur erfolgreichen Arbeit der CDU für urbane Räume.

Werbner, Pnina. 1990. *The Migration Process: Capital, Gifts and Offerings among British Pakistanis*. Oxford: Berg Publishers.

Wikan, Unni. 2002. *Generous Betrayal: Politics of Culture in the New Europe*. Chicago: University of Chicago Press.

Wilkinson, Steven. 2004. *Votes and Violence: Electoral Competition and Ethnic Riots in India*. New York: Cambridge University Press.

Wistrich, Robert S. 1981. "Austrian Social Democracy and the Problem of Galician Jewry 1890–1914." *Leo Baeck Institute Yearbook* 26: 89–124.

Wistrich, Robert S. 1982. *Socialism and the Jews: The Dilemmas of Assimilation in Germany and Austria-Hungary*. Rutherford, NJ: Fairleigh Dickinson University Press.

Wolfinger, Raymond. 1965. "The Development and Persistence of Ethnic Voting." *American Political Science Review* 59 (4): 896–908.

Wong, Janelle. 2006. *Democracy's Promise: Immigrants and American Civic Institutions*. Ann Arbor: University of Michigan Press.

Wright, Matthew, and Irene Bloemraad. 2012. "Is There a Trade-off between Multiculturalism and Socio-Political Integration? Policy Regimes and Immigrant Incorporation in Comparative Perspective." *Perspectives on Politics* 10 (1): 77–95.

Zeegers, Marten. 2014. "Moslimstemmen gelden." *de Volkskrant*, March 15.

Zetterbaum, Max. 1893. "Klassengegensätze bei den Juden." *Die Neue Zeit* 11 (28): 4–12, 36–43.

Zibouh, Fatima. 2010. *La participation politique des élus d'origine maghrébine: Elections régionales bruxelloises et stratégies électorales*. Louvain-la-Neuve: Bruylant-Academia.

Zimmermann, Klaus, Martin Kahanec, Amelie Constant, Don DeVoretz, Liliya Gataullina, and Anzelika Zaiceva. 2008. "Study on the Social and Labour Market Integration of Ethnic Minorities." IZA Research Report No. 16.

Zingher, Joshua N., and Benjamin Farrer. 2016. "The Electoral Effects of the Descriptive Representation of Ethnic Minority Groups in Australia and the UK." *Party Politics* 22 (6): 691–704.

INDEX

Akgün, Lale, 5
"Alibi Alis," 28, 179
anticlericalism, 24–25, 86–88
anti-Muslim prejudice, 2, 4, 14, 18, 24; and appeals to ethnocentrists, 180, 189; as barrier to inclusion, 78, 80; in Britain, 108–9; employment discrimination, 83; inclusion types and changes in majority perceptions, 171, 174–76; isolation in enclaves linked to, 58–59; resistance to integration linked to, 2, 24, 29; the Right and, 79, 88, 99, 188; symbolic inclusion and, 178–79
assimilation. *See* integration, Muslim
at-large elections, 12, 37–38, 46, 91–93, 125
Australia, 2
Austria: appeals to minority voters in, 79, 90; citizenship acquisition in, 1–3, 80, 103–4; citizenship regime and electoral laws in, 12, 80, 91–93, 95; ethnoreligious campaigning in, 103–4; gender parity in, 4, 152–53, 155–57; identity-based campaigning in, 103; ideology and inclusion in, 18; multiculturalism in, 101, 103; Muslim parity ratios in, 4, 19–20, 80, 94–97, 100–101, 103; population data for, 193; proportional representation in, 93; support for antidiscrimination measures in, 83–86; symbolic inclusion in, 19–20; vote-based inclusion in, 19; women as candidates in, 142

backlash, 18, 33–34, 36–37, 40, 65, 106–9
Ballard, Roger, 54
Bangladeshis, 71; as candidates, 47; chain migration and, 53, 55; electoral inclusion of, 89, 119; female employment and, 53; kinship networks and politics in, 4, 135–37
Belgium: appeals to minority voters in, 79; citizenship regime and electoral laws in,

12, 91–93, 95; equality and nondiscrimination in, 94–95; gender parity in, 4–5, 143, 152–53; identity politics in, 101–2; ideology and inclusion in, 18; importance of Muslim vote in, 94–95; multiculturalism in, 101; Muslim parity ratios in, 4, 80, 94–97; Muslim women as candidates in, 142–43; population data, 193; proportional representation in, 93; symbolic inclusion, 20; vote-based inclusion in, 19
Bencheikh, Kébir, 144
Brexit, 186
Britain: appeals to minority voters in, 79; citizenship regime and electoral laws in, 12, 91–93, 95; demographics, Muslim population in, 193–95; gender parity and, 4, 152–53, 155–56; General Election (2015), 1; ideology and inclusion in, 18; Irish Catholic inclusion in, 43–44, 135–36, 182, 193; multiculturalism in, 101; Muslim female representation in, 4–5; Muslim parity ratios in, 4, 80, 94–97; Muslim women as candidates in, 142; religion as identity attribute in, 15; symbolic inclusion in, 20; vote-based inclusion in, 19, 106–8
Bündnis für Innovation und Gerechtigkeit (BIG, Germany), 48

campaign strategies, 16; candidate-centered, 18–19, 107, 122; clan-based, 19, 122–23, 127–28, 132–40; communal, 103, 121–23, 125, 132, 169; identity-based, 102–4, 143–44
Canada, 2
candidate-centered politics, 18–19, 44, 107, 122
candidates: "assimilated" candidates and symbolic inclusion and, 30–32, 142, 147, 170, 174; authenticity of minority candidates, 32; identifying Muslim, 191–92;

A NOTE ON THE TYPE

This book has been composed in Adobe Text and Gotham.
Adobe Text, designed by Robert Slimbach for Adobe,
bridges the gap between fifteenth- and sixteenth-century
calligraphic and eighteenth-century Modern styles.
Gotham, inspired by New York street signs, was designed
by Tobias Frere-Jones for Hoefler & Co.